React and Libraries

Your Complete Guide to the React Ecosystem

Elad Elrom

Apress®

React and Libraries

Elad Elrom
Montvale, NJ, USA

ISBN-13 (pbk): 978-1-4842-6695-3   ISBN-13 (electronic): 978-1-4842-6696-0
https://doi.org/10.1007/978-1-4842-6696-0

Managing Director, Apress Media LLC: Welmoed Spahr
Acquisitions Editor: Louise Corrigan
Development Editor: James Markham
Coordinating Editor: Nancy Chen

Cover designed by eStudioCalamar

Cover image designed by upklyak / Freepik

Distributed to the book trade worldwide by Springer Science+Business Media New York, 1 New York Plaza, New York, NY 10004. Phone 1-800-SPRINGER, fax (201) 348-4505, e-mail orders-ny@springer-sbm.com, or visit www.springeronline.com. Apress Media, LLC is a California LLC and the sole member (owner) is Springer Science + Business Media Finance Inc (SSBM Finance Inc). SSBM Finance Inc is a **Delaware** corporation.

For information on translations, please e-mail booktranslations@springernature.com; for reprint, paperback, or audio rights, please e-mail bookpermissions@springernature.com.

Apress titles may be purchased in bulk for academic, corporate, or promotional use. eBook versions and licenses are also available for most titles. For more information, reference our Print and eBook Bulk Sales web page at www.apress.com/bulk-sales.

Any source code or other supplementary material referenced by the author in this book is available to readers on GitHub via the book's product page, located at www.apress.com/9781484266953. For more detailed information, please visit www.apress.com/source-code.

Printed on acid-free paper

This book is dedicated to the reader who reaches higher, never stops learning, and keeps being inspired.

Table of Contents

About the Author

Elad Elrom is a technical coach. As a writer, he has authored and co-authored several technical books. Elad has consulted for a variety of clients, from large corporations such as AT&T, HBO, Viacom, NBC Universal, and Weight Watchers, to smaller startups. In addition to coding, Elad is a PADI diving instructor and a pilot.

About the Technical Reviewer

Alexander Chinedu Nnakwue has a background in mechanical engineering from the University of Ibadan, Nigeria, and has been a front-end developer for more than three years working on both web and mobile technologies. He also has experience as a technical author, writer, and reviewer. He enjoys programming for the Web, and occasionally, you can also find him playing soccer. He was born in Benin City and is currently based in Lagos, Nigeria.

Introduction

Congratulations on deciding to learn React (also known as ReactJS)! There are plenty of ways to learn, such as training courses, YouTube videos, and blog posts, among many others.

Much of the information out there is good quality. However, developers often get confused because each piece of content is based on a different technology stack, and they need to adjust to a different writing style or piece things together with other information to understand the topic. For these reasons, using a book like this one is a better choice when you want to understand the concepts at a deeper level.

For this book, it makes the most sense to read the chapters in chronological order. I will be building on each topic as we go, and it will be an exciting development journey.

Additionally, there are thousands of React libraries that can help expedite your development effort and make your life easier. It can be confusing to decide what libraries to learn and use. Therefore, in this book, one of my goals is to ease that pain and not only help you pick the best and most popular libraries but also give you a rundown of the other options.

My aim is not just to teach you React. The book will put you on the road to success by learning how to use other tools and libraries. You'll be part of the React community that utilizes the latest and best libraries.

From my experience, the tools that have a steep learning curve are the ones that are usually worth the time and make you more valuable. A good example is choosing TypeScript or JavaScript to write your code. I hear that many professional JavaScript developers want to learn TypeScript one day. However, that day never comes. However, by starting with TypeScript, you set yourself up for not just increasing the quality of your code, but for potentially earning more as a developer because you have mastered the harder language to learn. You also gain the satisfaction of writing quality code.

Although it is good to be comfortable using HTML, JavaScript, and CSS, it is not a requirement that you know these languages in the book.

In terms of the book's organization, we will create a project that includes commonly used components and architecture. I will give you helpful libraries and show you the complete full development cycle. I will describe how to publish your app on a server as well as ensure the quality of the code.

You can download the book's code examples from here:

```
https://github.com/Apress/react-and-libraries
```

You should follow the steps in the book and examples to completion. Not only will you become a full-stack React developer able to complete projects and publish them in the wild, but you will be able to take on any other React-related library that comes your way with confidence.

Lastly, as a bonus to you, the reader, and as a thank-you for purchasing this book, you can sign up to receive a free ebook that includes many typical React interview questions. With these questions, you can increase your knowledge as well as practice for a job interview. You can sign up here:

```
https://elielrom.com/ReactQuestions
```

If you find errors in the book, do not hesitate to point them out. You can also stay in touch at `elad.ny@gmail.com`. Additionally, I would love to hear about your projects and if this book has helped you.

Thanks for purchasing this book. Now it's time to get started on your development journey.

CHAPTER 1

Learn React Basic Concepts

This chapter serves as the ground school before we take off and start flying with React. We will create a minimalistic, stand-alone React application called "Hello World." Then we will review how it works and see what's happening under the hood. We will also learn about TypeScript and the starter template projects we can use to expediate development.

This chapter is the basis for understanding React, and although we are not building a flashy application here, the concepts that are covered are crucial. Feel free to return to the chapter again once you complete the book or even while reading later chapters if you need to reference some of the basic concepts.

Let's get started!

Getting Started with React

In this section, we will create a minimalistic, stand-alone "Hello World" React example. We will be installing an integrated development environment (IDE), and we will cover crucial concepts such as JSX, the DOM, the React virtual DOM, Babel, and ES5/ES6.

First, though, we'll talk about what React is and why to use it. Although it may be more gratifying to jump right in and start writing code, paying attention to the key concepts will help you understand React better. The entire book relies on you understanding the ideas in this section.

What Is React?

React (also known as ReactJS) is a JavaScript library developed by Facebook (`https://github.com/facebook/react`) to create user interfaces for the Web. React was invented by Jordan Walke, who was working at Facebook Ads at the time. It competes with other front-end development frameworks and libraries such as jQuery, Angular, Vue.js, Svelte, etc.

1

© Elad Elrom 2021
E. Elrom, *React and Libraries*, https://doi.org/10.1007/978-1-4842-6696-0_1

In its previous version, React 16.x, which was released in September 2017, the React team added more tools and development support and eliminated bugs. React 17 was released in October 2020.

Note   React 17 is a "stepping-stone" release, and the release is primarily focused on making it easier to upgrade React in future versions as well as improving compatibility with browsers. React team's support shows that the library has great momentum and is not going away anytime soon.

Why React?

Did you know?

- React is a favorite among developers. In fact, according to a StackOverFlow survey (`https://insights.stackoverflow.com/survey/2020`), React.js has been the "most loved" web framework for two consecutive years.

- The need for React developers has ballooned; according to Indeed.com (`https://www.indeed.com/q-React-jobs.html`), there are close to 56,000 open React developer positions.

- The React library itself is lighter than competing Web frameworks such as Ember or Angular, see here: `https://gist.github.com/Restuta/cda69e50a853aa64912d` (around 100KB) and fast.

- React is easy to get started with.

Installing an IDE

When working with code, it's recommended that you use an IDE.

Why Do I Even Need an IDE?

You don't "need" an IDE; you can always write your code with a text editor. However, an IDE helps write people code and increases productivity. This is done by providing common needed functionality for writing code, such as source code editor, build automation tools, and a debugger, as well as many other functionalities.

When it comes to IDEs, there are many to choose from. Some examples are Microsoft Visual Studio, IntelliJ IDEA, WebStorm, NetBeans, Eclipse, and Aptana Studio.

For this book, I selected Visual Studio Code (VS Code) since it's a lightweight, free, cross-platform (Linux, macOS, Windows) editor that can be extended with plugins. You may be working for a company that will provide you with a specific IDE, or you may decide to invest and buy a top-rated IDE license. Most top IDEs mentioned offer similar functionalities, so it boils down to what you are used to using, licenses, etc.

Note   Choosing an IDE depends on many factors that I will not get into. You can install or use whatever IDE you are used to using; VS Code is just a suggestion.

You can also pick the Microsoft Visual Studio Express version instead of VS Code, which has reduced functionality compared to Microsoft Visual Studio.

How to Install VS Code?

To get started, go to the VS Code download page:

https://code.visualstudio.com/download

Choose your platform, and once the download is complete, open VS Code. You should see the Welcome page shown in Figure 1-1.

Figure 1-1. *Visual Studio Code Welcome page*

Creating a Minimalistic Stand-Alone "Hello World" Program

It's time to create our new "Hello World" app and run the project in our browser. To create a new file in VS Code, select New File. Then, paste in the following code and save the file anywhere you want:

```
<html>
  <head>
      <meta charSet="utf-8">
          <title>Hello world</title>
          <script src="https://cdnjs.cloudflare.com/ajax/libs/react/17.0.0/
          umd/react.production.min.js"></script>
          <script src="https://unpkg.com/react-dom@17.0.0/umd/react-dom.
          production.min.js"></script>
          <script src="https://unpkg.com/@babel/standalone/babel.min.js">
          </script>
  </head>
  <body>
  <div id="app"></div>
  <script type="text/babel">
      ReactDOM.render(
      <h1>Hello World</h1>,
      document.getElementById('app')
      );
  </script>
  </body>
</html>
```

You can download this code from the book's GitHub location:

```
https://github.com/Apress/react-and-libraries/tree/master/01/index.html
```

Note   You can download all the code and exercises you see in this book from the book's GitHub location (`https://github.com/Apress/react-and-libraries`). The files are organized by chapter.

Now that we have created the file, rename it to index.html and open it with your favorite browser (see Figure 1-2).

Hello World

Figure 1-2. *React "Hello World" index.html app in the browser*

Congratulations, you just created your first React application!

Now, let's decode this example to understand what's happening here.

Look at the ReactDOM.render function we created. It looks like this:

```
ReactDOM.render(
<h1>Hello World</h1>,
document.getElementById('app')
);
```

Although the code looks like HTML, it is not. It's JavaScript eXtension (JSX) code.

Note   JSX is a React extension that uses JavaScript tags to mimic HTML code, so the code is similar to HTML but not the same.

What Is JSX, and Why Do We Need It?

To understand why React is using JSX instead of just HTML, we first need to talk about the Document Object Model (DOM). The quick answer is that React processes your JSX code in the background before committing these changes to the user's browser to speed up how quickly the user's page loads. Let's dive deeper into that process.

Note   The DOM in HTML stands for Document Object Model. It is an in-memory representation of HTML and is tree-structured.

DOM

The Document Object Model is the API for HTML and even XML documents such as SVG images. The API describes the document by including interfaces that define the functionality of the HTML's elements as well as any interfaces and types they rely on. The HTML document includes support and access to various things such as interacting with users such as event handlers, focus, copy and paste, etc.

The DOM document consists of a hierarchical tree of nodes (`https://developer.mozilla.org/en-US/docs/Web/API/Node`), and the node interface allows access not just to the document but to each element, as shown in Figure 1-3.

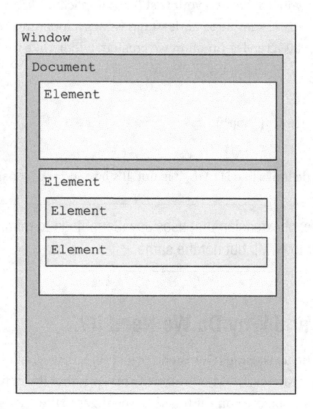

Figure 1-3. *A DOM document consists of a hierarchical tree*

Use Chrome's DevTools Console inspector (right-click a web page and select Inspect ➤ Console) and type this in the console:

```
window.document
```

Figure 1-4 shows the result. You can access the document hierarchical tree structure and the elements that make that tree.

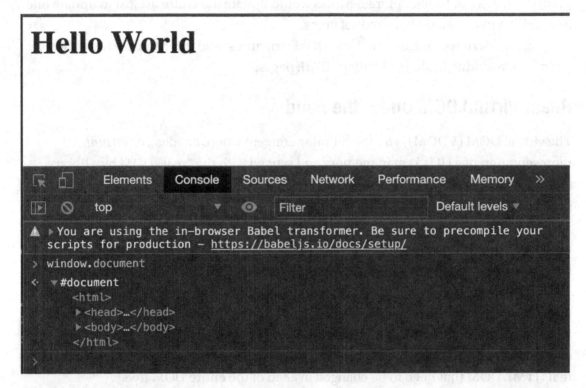

Figure 1-4. *Chrome's DevTools Console inspector showing the DOM document*

DOM manipulation is the core of modern interactive web pages and can dynamically change the content of a web page. Technically speaking, this can be done using JavaScript with methods such as getElementById and getElementsByClassName as well as removeChild and getElementById("myElement").remove();. These APIs are exposed by the HTML DOM and intended to provide the ability to change code during runtime.

React determines what changes to make to the actual DOM based on the React element representation and do the changes in the background inside a virtual DOM. You can think of the React virtual DOM as a simulation.

Then it commits only needed changes to the actual user's DOM (browser). The reason behind this process is to speed up performance.

It's crucial that the actual DOM tree-structured manipulation be as quick as possible. For example, say we have a product page, and we want to update the first item of our product's list. Most JavaScript frameworks would update the entire list just to update one item, which may contain hundreds of items.

Most modern web pages hold large DOM structures, and this behavior taxes the user too much, resulting in slower-loading HTML pages.

React Virtual DOM Under the Hood

The virtual DOM (VDOM) is a programming concept where an ideal, or *virtual*, representation of a UI is kept in memory and synced with the "real" DOM by a library such as ReactDOM. This process is called *reconciliation*. The React VDOM's aim is to speed up this process.

React holds a copy of the HTML DOM (that's the virtual DOM). Once a change is needed, React first makes the change to the virtual DOM, and it then syncs the actual HTML DOM, avoiding the need to update the entire HTML DOM, which speeds up the process.

For example, when we render a JSX element, every single virtual DOM object gets updated. This process of updating the entire virtual DOM instead of the actual HTML DOM is faster. In the reconciliation process, React needs to figure out which objects changed, and this process is called *diffing*. Then React updates only the objects in the real HTML DOM that need to be changed instead of the entire DOM tree.

In our code, the JSX code is wrapped inside a `ReactDOM.render` method. To further dig into the process behind the scenes and understand what's happening under the hood, we also need to understand Babel and ES5/ES6.

Babel and ES5/ES6

The JSX code we write is just a terser way to write the `React.createElement()` function declaration. Every time a component uses the render function, it outputs a tree of React elements or the virtual representation of the HTML DOM elements that the component outputs.

ECMAScript version 5 (ES5) is plain old "regular JavaScript," which was finalized in 2009. It is supported by all major browsers. ES6 is the next version; it was released in 2015, and it added syntactical and functional additions. ES6 is almost fully supported by all major browsers at the time of writing. In fact, the React team in version 17 made many changes to be more consistent and compatible with ES6.

We want to take advantage of ES6 functionality; however, at the same time, we want to be backward compatible with the old ES5 so we can be compatible in all versions of browsers. To do that, we use Babel.

Babel is the library that transpiles ES6 to ES5 (needed for browsers that don't support ES6). The ReactDOM.render() function, as the name suggests, renders the DOM. The render function is expected to return a virtual DOM (representation of browser DOM elements).

Note   Starting from Babel 8, React gets a special function. The render method was changed to jsx.

Note that starting from Babel 8, React gets a special function called jsx to replace the render function. In Babel 8, it also automatically imports react (or other libraries that support the new API) when needed, so you don't have to manually include them anymore if you write to Babel directly.

For example, look at this input:

```
function Foo() {
  return <div />;
}
```

Babel will turn the code into this:

```
import { jsx as _jsx } from "react/jsx-runtime";
function Foo() {
  return _jsx("div", ...);
}
```

Also starting from Babel 8, jsx will automatically be the default runtime. You can read more about these changes in my article on Medium: http://shorturl.at/bxPZ7.

Now that you understand what React is doing under the hood and Babel's role, you can look back at our code example. Notice that we imported three libraries.

- *React version 17*: We use React to define and create our elements, for example to use lifecycle hooks (more about hooks later in the book).

- *ReactDOM version 17*: This is used for web applications (there is React Native for mobile devices). That's why there is a split in the code between React and ReactDOM. ReactDOM is the glue between React and the DOM. It includes features that allow us to access the DOM, such as `ReactDOM.findDOMNode()` to find an element or `ReactDOM.render()` to mount our component.

- *Babel version 8*: As we explained, Babel is the library that transpiles ES6 to ES5.

Now that we have looked at the React "Hello World" code, we understand why we imported these libraries and what's happening under the hood. These key concepts are crucial to understanding React. Feel free to return to this chapter if you need a refresher.

In this section, we created a minimalistic stand-alone React application called "Hello World" and reviewed how to works. We installed the VS Code IDE and learned about crucial concepts such as JSX, DOM, the React virtual DOM, Babel, and ES5/ES6.

Getting Started with TypeScript

When it comes to writing React code, there are two options. You can write your code using JavaScript (JS) or TypeScript (TS). TypeScript is a transpiler, meaning ES6 doesn't understand TS, but TS gets compiled down to standard JS, which can be done with Babel. We will configure our project to accept TS files as well as ES6 JS files in the next chapter.

Why Should You Integrate TypeScript into Your React Project?

Here are a few interesting facts:

- Did you know that TypeScript is an open source programming language developed and maintained by Microsoft?

- According to a 2020 StackFlow survey, the TypeScript programming language is second in popularity, surpassing Python!

- The ReactJS framework is second at 35.9 percent and on its way to bypassing the "king" jQuery.

- At the same time, 32.9 percent of respondents said that they actually dreaded TypeScript.

The question is, why TypeScript is so popular?

TypeScript vs. JavaScript: What's the Big Deal?

JavaScript is a scripting language, while TypeScript (TS) is a full-blown programming language. TS, as the name suggests, is all about having more types. TS is easier to debug and test than JS, and TS prevents potential problems by describing what to expect (you will see this in action when we test our components later in this book). Having a full-blown object-oriented programming (OOP) language and modules brings JS to an enterprise level and increases code quality.

These are the advantages of TypeScript over JavaScript:

- TypeScript is an OOP language; JavaScript is a scripting language.

- TypeScript uses static typing following the ECMAScript specification.

- TypeScript support modules.

Note   A type system associates a type to each value. By examining the flow of these values, it ensures there are no type errors.

Static typing means that types are checked before runtime (allowing you to track bugs before runtime). JS includes only the following eight dynamic (at runtime) types: `BigInt`, `Boolean`, `Integer`, `Null`, `Number`, `String`, `Symbol`, `Object` (objects, functions, and arrays), and `Undefined`.

Note   All these types are called *primitive types*, except for `Object`, which is a nonprimitive type. TS adds static types to JavaScript by setting a compiler to type-checking the source code to turn it into dynamic code.

React and TypeScript work nicely together, and by using TypeScript and describing the types your code quality improves the code quality of your app using OOP best practices, it's worth the learning curve.

In the next chapter, we will create a startup project with TypeScript; however, you can start experimenting with TypeScript right now and learn the basics.

This step gives you a good overview of the types of TS and how you can harness the power of TS in your code.

TS is at version 4. To play around with coding TS, you can run actual TS code in the TS Playground, available at `https://tc39.github.io/ecma262/#sec-ecmascript-language-types`, as shown in Figure 1-5.

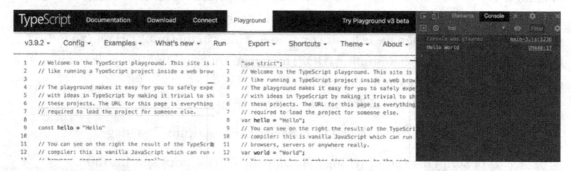

Figure 1-5. *TS Playground*

The left side of the Playground is TS, and the right side is the same code compiled into JS. Next, open the JavaScript Console and hit Run to see the code running.

The Playground site has plenty of examples that can help you better understand TS. I recommend exploring the examples.

Notice the example uses "strict," and in the Config menu item, you can set the compiler options from the Config link. The different compiler options are at `https://www.typescriptlang.org/docs/handbook/compiler-options.html`.

It may be antagonizing writing your code with errors popping up left and right, but it will avoid issues later when the compiler can't figure out the types. I mentioned that TS is OOP and follows the ECMAScript specification; however, the specification is a living thing and changes often, so you can specify the ECMAScript (ES) target. See Figure 1-6.

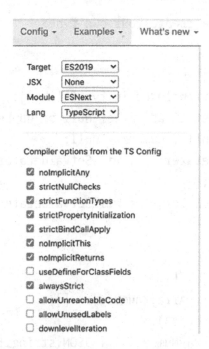

Figure 1-6. *Specifying the ECMAScript (ES) target in TS Playground*

TypeScript Cheat Sheet

A great place to start working with TypeScript is to understand the power of TS by looking at the different types available. My programming style is to follow the function naming conventions of coding like Shakespeare and having the names of the method self-explain themselves.

To try TypeScript, paste the TypeScript cheat sheet code shown here into the TS Playground at `https://www.typescriptlang.org/play/`. Then you can follow along and look at the results of the JS compiler and run the code. As you can see, I split my examples into primitive types and nonprimitive types.

```
// primitive types
// The most basic datatype - true/false switch
const flag1: Boolean = true;
// inferred-type
const flag2 = true;
```

13

```
// Be a programming god - create your own type
type Year = number;
const year: Year = 2020;

// Undefined and null not included in types like js, to
// get a null you will set it as either null or number
let willSetValueLater: null | number = null;
console.log('willSetValueLater: ' + willSetValueLater);
willSetValueLater = 2020;
console.log('willSetValueLater: ' + willSetValueLater);

// none-primitive
// Arrays
let arrayNumber: number[] = [];
let myCastTypeArrayNumber: Array<number> = [];
myCastTypeArrayNumber.push(123);
console.log('myCastTypeArrayNumber: ' + JSON.stringify(myCastTypeArray
Number));

// Tuples (two values)
let longlatSimple: [number, number] = [51.5074, 0.1278];
let longlatInferredType = [51.5074, 0.1278];

// Enums design pattern
enum ChildrenEnum {JOHN = 'John', JANE = 'Jane', MARY = 'Mary'}
let john: ChildrenEnum = ChildrenEnum.JOHN;
console.log('What is JOHN enum? ' + john);

// Maps
// inferred type: Map<string, string>
const myLongLatMapWithInferredType = new Map([
  ['London', '51.5074'],
  ['London', '0.1278'],
]);

// interfaces
```

```
// Typing objects-as-records via interfaces
interface longlat {
  long: number;
  lat: number;
}
function longlatToString(longlat: longlat) {
  return `${longlat.long}, ${longlat.lat}`;
}
// Object literal (anonymous interfaces) inline:
function longlatToStringWithAnonymousInterfaces(longlat: {
  long: number;
  lat: number;
}) {
  return `${longlat.long}, ${longlat.lat}`;
}

// Place optional params (phone) and method in interface
interface Client {
    name: string;
    email: string;
    phone?: string;
    longlatToString(longlat: longlat): string;
}

// Factory design pattern made easy using type cast
interface resultsWithUnkownTypeCast<SomeType> {
  result: SomeType;
}
type numberResult = resultsWithUnkownTypeCast<number>;
type arrayResult = resultsWithUnkownTypeCast<[]>;

// functions

// Simple function
const turnStringToNumber: (str: String) => Number =
    (str: String) => Number(str);
// %inferred-type: (num: number) => string
const turnStringToNumberMinimalist = (str: String) => Number(str);
```

```
console.log('turnStringToNumber: ' + turnStringToNumber('001'));
console.log('turnStringToNumberMinimalist: ' +
turnStringToNumberMinimalist('002'));

function functionWithExplicitReturn(): void { return undefined }
function functionWithImplicitReturn(): void { }

// Simple functions with callbacks
function simpleFunctionWithCallback(callback: (str: string) => void ) {
  return callback('done something successfully');
}
simpleFunctionWithCallback(function (str: string): void {
    console.log(str);
});

// Never callback  - not placing never is inferred as never
function neverCallbackFunction(callback: (str: string) => never ) {
  return callback('fail');
}
// neverCallbackFunction(function(message: string): never {
//     throw new Error(message);
// });

// Complex Callback and specifiy result types
function complexCallbackWithResultType(callback: () => string): string {
  return callback();
}
console.log('doSomethingAndLetMeKnow: ' + (complexCallbackWithResultType
(String), 'Done it!'));

// Function with optional params using '?'
function functionWithOptionalCallbackParams(callback?: (str: String) =>
string) {
  if (callback === undefined) {
    callback = String;
  }
  return callback('sucess');
}
```

```typescript
// Function with setting the type with default values
function createLonglatWithDefaultValues(long:number = 0, lat:number = 0):
[number, number] {
  return [long, lat];
}
console.log('createLonglatWithDefaultValues: ' +
createLonglatWithDefaultValues(51.5074, 0.1278))
console.log('createLonglatWithDefaultValues: ' +
createLonglatWithDefaultValues())

// function with rest parameters
// A rest parameter declared by prefixing an identifier with three dots
(...)
function functionWithRestParams(...names: string[]): string {
  return names.join(', ');
}
console.log(functionWithRestParams('John', 'Jane', 'Mary'));

// Function with potential two params types
function isNumber(numOrStr: number|string): Boolean {
  if (typeof numOrStr === 'string') {
      return false;
  } else if (typeof numOrStr === 'number') {
      return true;
  } else {
    throw new Error('Not sure the type');
  }
}
console.log('isNumber: ' + isNumber('123'));
```

You can download the complete code from here:

https://github.com/Apress/react-and-libraries/tree/master/01/
TS-getting-started.ts

If you need more explanation, see the official TS basic types handbook here:

https://www.typescriptlang.org/docs/handbook/basic-types.html

The JS compiler that turns the code from TS to JS and the console results will help you understand these examples. See Figure 1-7.

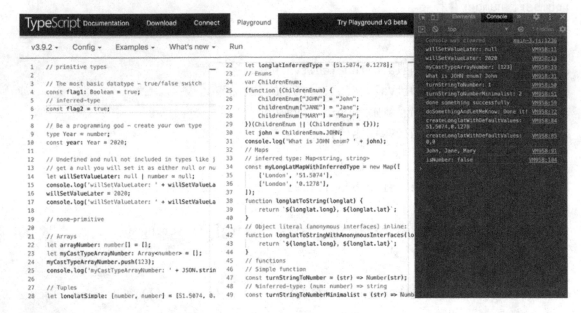

Figure 1-7. TypeScript Playground examples

React Template Starter Project Options

When it comes to writing React applications, you have a few options. You can just write the entire code yourself, as we did for our "Hello World" example, and then add libraries to help you take care of tasks of packaging your code and getting it ready for production. Another option is to use a starter template project that already takes care of the scaffolding and configurations and includes libraries to help you get the job done quickly with just writing your code.

As you have seen, the VDOM process happens behind the scenes, and we don't need to refresh the page when there is a page change.

In fact, the most popular template for creating a React app is the Create-React-App (CRA) project (`https://github.com/facebook/create-react-app`). The project was created by the Facebook team with close to 84,000 stars on GitHub.

CRA is based on a single-page application (SPA), which is great because you don't get a page refresh, and the experience feels like you are inside of a mobile app.

The pages are meant to be rendered on the client side. This is great for small to medium-sized projects.

The other option is server-side rendering (SSR). SSR renders the page on the server so the client (browser) will display the app without doing any work. It's good for certain use cases (usually large apps), where there is much going on and the user experience would be sluggish if the rendering happened on the client side.

CRA doesn't support SSR out of the gate. There are ways to configure and get CRA to work as SSR, but that may be too complex to some developers and involve maintaining configuration on your own, so it may not be worth the effort.

If you're building something bigger that needs SSR, it's better to just work with a different React library that is already configured out of the box with SSR such as the Next. js framework, Razzle, or Gatsby (include a prerender website into HTML at build time).

Note   If you want to do server rendering with React and Node.js, check out Next.js, Razzle, or Gatsby. Create React App is agnostic of the backend and only produces static HTML/JS/CSS bundles. See `https://github.com/facebook/create-react-app`.

With that being said, with CRA we can do a prerender, which is the closest you can get to SSR, as you will see in the last chapter of this book when we optimize our React app.

In this book's examples, we will be using CRA; however, with a solid understanding of this book, you can easily migrate to any template library that uses React.

Summary

In this chapter, we created a minimalistic stand-alone React application called "Hello World" and explored how it worked. We installed the VS Code IDE and learned about crucial concepts such as JSX, DOM, React's virtual DOM, and Babel, as well as ES5/ES, SPA, SSR and TypeScript.

In the next chapter, we will learn more about the CRA project and set up our starter project and development environment with essential libraries.

CHAPTER 2

Starter React Project and Friends

In this chapter, we will be covering lots of libraries, and it might be overwhelming. However, I want to provide you with a great foundation so you can have the best startup project possible. The startup project will serve you well because you can copy and reuse the code for all the projects and examples we will be using in this book. This practice will make you a top-notch React developer who can tackle any size project that comes your way, as well as help you land your dream job. It will also speed up your development.

By the end of this chapter, you will have a starter project that includes many of the libraries we will be covering in this book. Let's get started!

Getting Started with the Create-React-App Starter Project

In the previous chapter, we created a simple "Hello World" application from scratch, and we talked about how it works behind the scenes. We covered topics such as JSX, DOM, the React virtual DOM, Babel, ES5/ES6, and SPAs.

Creating a React app was easy and took just few lines of code. However, to create a real-life application based on one page (an SPA) with multiple views, many user gestures, lists with hundreds or thousands of items, member areas, and other common pieces that are common in today's applications, there is much more we need to learn.

In this book, my goal is to set you up with a large toolbox full of the best libraries and tools so you can build a top-grade React application and get the most out of React. For that, we need to look at several popular libraries and tools in the world of React.

© Elad Elrom 2021
E. Elrom, *React and Libraries*, https://doi.org/10.1007/978-1-4842-6696-0_2

We could start from complete zero, but that's not needed. As I mentioned in the previous chapter, Create-React-App (CRA) is the most popular starter project for a React web-based application. (See `https://github.com/facebook/create-react-app`.) It provides a boilerplate project, and you can be up and running quickly with many of the necessary tools and library that are standards when building a top-grade React application.

It includes vanilla-flavor packages and other more valuable packages. Additionally, CRA has an option to include templates with more sophisticated libraries, or you can create your own template that has certain elements that CRA does not include.

CRA has already made some decisions for us. For example, the build tool is a tool called Webpack over Rollup or Parcel. Task Runners is set up with NPM scripts over other tools such as Gulp. CSS, JS, and Jest are used as the defaults.

After working on and reviewing projects and libraries that help get the job done with React, it's hard to stay neutral and not recommend certain tools, which is why I've chosen to use the tools in this chapter. In addition, since many libraries are not easy to migrate to, you'll want to start on the right foot instead of switching tools later. That's why we are setting up our project with the libraries in this library. These libraries will help you get the job done, and you can use the template for other projects, whether it's a small project or a larger enterprise-level project.

React Developer Road Map

Becoming a true professional React developer is more than just knowing the React library. As we've mentioned, there are tools and libraries that can help expedite development because, remember, React is not a framework. React is a JavaScript library developed by Facebook to handle the user interface and nothing more.

To help figure out the pieces that will turn React into a full-blown framework that is capable of creating quality apps efficiently and that can compete with other JS frameworks, check out the road map in Figure 2-1.

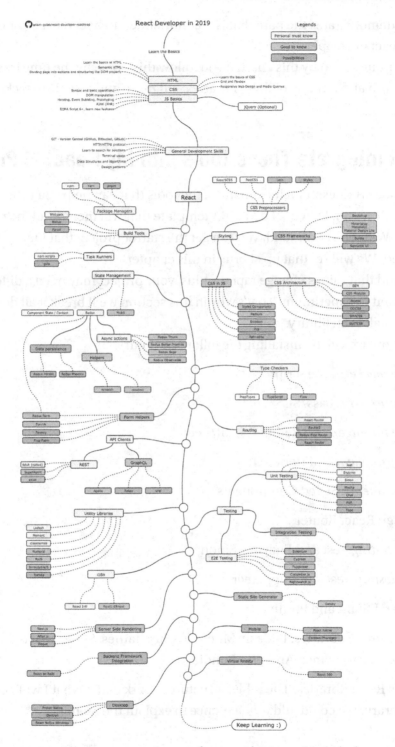

Figure 2-1. *React developer road map (source: https://github.com/adam-golab/react-developer-roadmap)*

This chart demonstrates the path that is recommended to become a top-notch professional React developer.

Do not get intimidated by this chart. If you follow this book, by the time this book is over, you will learn about many of these libraries and more and be able to tackle any size project.

How Can I Integrate These Tools into My ReactJS Project?

As I mentioned, CRA doesn't include many of the tools that can help you tackle real-life React projects. However, I have set up a CRA template that will include all the must-know libraries. With one command, you can get the starter project that includes all the libraries needed. We will set that up shortly in this chapter.

Keep in mind that things change rapidly; plus, your project may need a different tool or you might want to experiment. That's why in this section we'll break it all down and show how to install each library.

In this section, we will be installing the following libraries:

- *Type checker*: TypeScript

- *Preprocessors*: Sass/SCSS

- *State management*: Redux Toolkit/Recoil

- *CSS framework*: Material-UI

- *Components*: Styled Components

- *Router*: React Router

- *Unit testing*: Jest and Enzym + Sinon

- *E2E testing*: Jest and Puppeteer

- *Linter*: ESLint and Prettier

- *Other useful libraries*: Lodash, Moment, Classnames, Serve, react-snap, React-Helmet, Analyzer Bundle

The list was React libraries. The folder structure is park of the what I will be covering but it's not a library. We could add this sentence to explain the readers.

Prerequisites

You can install the libraries using NPM (`https://www.npmjs.com/`). You need Node.js to get NPM.

NPM and Node.js go hand in hand. NPM is the JavaScript package manager and the default package manager for the JavaScript Node.js environment.

Install Node and NPM on a Mac/PC

Node.js needs to be at least version 8.16.0 or 10.16.0. The reason we need that version is that we need to use NPX. NPX is the NPM task runner introduced in 2017, and it is used to set up CRA.

Install it if it's missing by typing the following in the Terminal (Mac) or in Windows Terminal (Windows):

```
$ node -v
```

If it's not installed, you can install it for both Mac and PC from here (see Figure 2-2):

```
https://nodejs.org/en/
```

Figure 2-2. *Nodejs.org*

The installer recognizes your platform, so if you are on a PC, it's the same steps.

Once you download the installer, run it. Once that's complete, run the `node` command in Terminal, as shown here:

```
$ node -v
```

The command will output the Node.js version number.

Download the Libraries: Yarn or NPM

To download packages from the NPM repository, we have two options: Yarn or NPM. NPM is installed when we install Node.js. However, in this book, we will mostly use the Yarn library. We will be using Yarn as much as possible for downloading packages instead of NPM because Yarn is faster than NPM. Yarn caches the installed packages as well as installs packages simultaneously.

Install Yarn on a Mac/PC

To install Yarn on a Mac, use `brew` in the Terminal.

```
$ brew install yarn
```

Just like with Node.js, run `yarn` with the `-v` flag to output the version number.

```
$ yarn -v
```

On a PC, you can download the `.msi` download file from here:

```
https://classic.yarnpkg.com/latest.msi
```

You can find more installation options here:

```
https://classic.yarnpkg.com/en/docs/install/#mac-stable
```

Create-React-App MHL Template Project

Equipped with Node.js as well as NPM and Yarn, we are ready to get started. We can use the CRA Must-Have-Libraries (MHL) template project I created for you, and it will produce the final result of this chapter and include all the libraries we are setting up in this chapter.

You can get it from here:

```
https://github.com/EliEladElrom/cra-template-must-have-libraries
```

It's good to have this template project as your starter library, not just because it is easy and includes all the libraries we need, but also because I will be able to update this starter project long after the book is released in case anything breaks or needs an update, as often happens with NPM libraries.

You can create the final project of this chapter using the CRA template with Yarn with one command, shown here:

```
$ yarn create react-app starter-project --template must-have-libraries
```

Or you can create it with NPX, as shown here:

```
$ npx create-react-app your-project-name --template must-have-libraries
```

To run this project, you can change directory to `starter-project` and run the `start` command in the Terminal, as shown here:

```
$ cd starter-project
$ yarn start
```

This command will install all the dependencies and start the project on a local server. You will learn more about what's happening under the hood in the next section.

In the rest of this chapter, I will explain what this project includes and reverse engineer the project for you, so you can understand fully what is happening under the hood. It is not mandatory to do all the steps in this chapter as you already have the final project ready.

Vanilla-Flavor Create-React-App

Since you were able to install the starter template project, you can get started with development right away. It's good to know each library that is installed so you fully understand what this project includes and can customize your project based on your exact needs. To create CRA without using the CRA MHL template project, you can install each library on our own. Just start a new CRA using the vanilla-flavor template by running the following command in Terminal with `yarn`:

```
$ yarn create react-app hello-cra
```

Keep in mind that the yarn command is equivalent to the following command using the NPM NPX task runner, just as we saw in the MHL template project:

```
$ npx create-react-app hello-cra
```

The first parameter is the library we are downloading. The third parameter's hello-cra is our project name. Next, we need to change directory to our project.

```
$ cd hello-cra
```

Lastly, type the following command to start the project in the Terminal/Windows Terminal:

```
$ yarn start
```

With NPM, it is the same, as shown here:

```
$ npm start
```

We get this message in our Terminal:

```
Happy hacking!
Compiled successfully!
```

You can now view hello-cra in the browser.

```
Local:              http://localhost:3000
On Your Network:    http://192.168.2.101:3000
```

Note that the development build is not optimized. To create a production build, use yarn build.

Our app will open automatically on port 3000 using our default browser. If it doesn't, you can use any browser and use this URL: http://localhost:3000/.

Note   If you want to stop the development server, use Ctrl+C.

What's happening in the background is that the CRA app created a development server for us. See Figure 2-3.

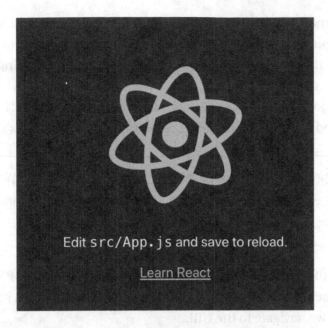

Figure 2-3. *Vanilla CRA on port 3000 in our browser*

Congratulations, you just created and published CRA on the development server! The React project includes all the libraries that come with CRA out of the box.

If you examine the code and files that were created for us (see Figure 2-4), you can see that there are many files that make up our single-page application. Examples include App.js and index.js. We also have style sheet files such as App.css and index.css.

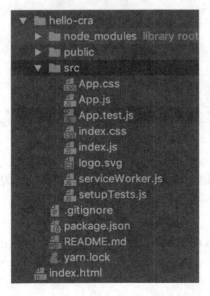

Figure 2-4. *CRA files and folders*

React was originally designed to be a SPA, and normally we would need to write a script to combine our files into one file or a chunk of files that we will need to include in our application for the code to be available. However, since we are using CRA, all of that is done for us automatically.

CRA uses Webpack and Babel to pack our files into a single index.html page and into files called bundle.js and *.chunk.js. It may generate other files as well as needed.

Note   CRA is using the Webpack module bundler out of the box. Webpack is an open source JavaScript bundler that uses loaders to bundle files and create static assets.

When we type the command yarn start, the script initiates an NPM script that creates a development environment for us. The script caches our files in memory and serves them when we navigate to the URL.

Take a look at Figure 2-5, which illustrates this process.

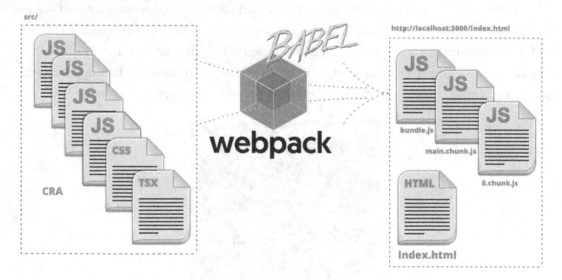

Figure 2-5. *10,000-foot view to illustrate CRA using Webpack and Babel to pack our files into a single index.html page*

To view the application's source code and check the files created for us, go to this URL on Chrome: http://localhost:3000/.

Or we can also inspect the HTML DOM elements with Chrome DevTools. On Chrome right-click and select Inspect to view the DOM tree.

You can see the following files in the body HTML tag:

```
<script src="/static/js/bundle.js"></script>
<script src="/static/js/0.chunk.js"></script>
<script src="/static/js/main.chunk.js"></script>
```

The bundle.js file, as the name suggests, bundles our JavaScript source code files into one file, and the *.chunk.js files bundle our styles into chunks of files. You can go to the URLs of these files to view the content.

The heavy lifting is done inside our project in a folder called node_modules that includes many libraries that are dependencies that our project is using. Take a look at Figure 2-6.

Figure 2-6. *node_modules folder with dependencies*

You can find the list of the dependencies in the node_modules folder in a file called package.json, which is used by Node.js. The file contains information about our project such as the version, the libraries are using, and even the scripts Node.js will be running.

Open the package.json file. Notice that the list of library dependencies our project is using is short if you compare it to the long list in the node_modules folder (keep in mind the library versions are likely to change often after the book is released).

```
"dependencies": {
  "@testing-library/jest-dom": "^4.2.4",
  "@testing-library/react": "^9.3.2",
  "@testing-library/user-event": "^7.1.2",
  "react": "^16.13.1",
  "react-dom": "^16.13.1",
  "react-scripts": "3.4.3"
```

Each dependency holds the name of the library and a version number.

If we check our node_modules folder, it is full of other developers' libraries. In fact, there are more than 1,000, and when we downloaded our CRA, it took a while (depending on your Internet speed, of course) to download the project.

That is because of all these dependencies. Where are all these dependencies coming from then?

Each library includes other dependencies or subdependencies, so although we don't have these libraries listed in our project's package.json file, they are listed in other libraries or sublibraries.

Also notice that there is a section in our package.json file that specify scripts.

```
"scripts": {
  "start": "react-scripts start",
  "build": "react-scripts build",
  "test": "react-scripts test",
  "eject": "react-scripts eject"
}
```

In fact, when we were running yarn start, the process of creating our local server was happening. Where is that script coming from? To answer that, open the following library and look at the following code that builds our development server:

```
hello-cra/node_modules/react-scripts/scripts/start.js
```

react-scripts

These scripts are using a library called `react-scripts`. If you go to the `hello-cra/node_modules/react-scripts/package.json` file, you will see a long list of dependencies that the code is using to package files with Babel and Webpack and build our server. Each of these sublibraries will have other dependencies and so on.

That's how six libraries end up as more than 1,000 in our `node_modules` folder.

Gitignore

It is common practice to create a `.gitignore` file in each project. That file can include files we want to exclude.

For instance, CRA already included a `.gitignore` file, and `node_modules` already listed it to be excluded. Then we ran the `yarn` command and checked the `package.json` file, which installed all these dependencies for us instead of including all these libraries with our project, which will make our project very large.

Public Folder

We also have a folder in our app called `public` that includes our application icon. Specifically, it contains the following:

- `public/favicon.ico`, `logo192.png`, `logo512.png`: Icons used inside the `manifest.json` file

- `public/index.html`: Our index page

- `public/manifest.json`: Information about our application and styles

- `public/robots.txt`: Instructions to search engines

If we check our `index.html` page, we see tokens that were set in the `manifest.json` file, but if we open the `public/index.html` file inside the HTML body tag, we don't see any of the JS bundle chunks such as the `*.chunk.js` and `bundle.js` files that we saw when we inspected the code in the browser. Take a look:

```
public/index.html;
<body>
  <noscript>You need to enable JavaScript to run this app.</noscript>
  <div id="root"></div>
</body>
```

The reason is that the NPM scripts are generating our index file based on this file as well as the files it generates. If we wanted to publish our app to production, for example, we would run a different command (`build` instead of `start`), and different files would be generated. You will learn more about publishing to production as well as how to optimize the JS bundle chunks later in this book.

You can download the code from here:

```
https://github.com/Apress/react-and-libraries/tree/master/01/hello-cra
```

To have Yarn use the `package.json` file and download all the dependencies, run the following:

```
$ yarn start
```

Create-React-App with TypeScript

CRA comes in two flavors: vanilla (JS) and TypeScript. Notice that our application files `src/public/App.js` and `src/public/index.js` have `.js` file extensions, which means they are JavaScript files. CRA sets our project out of the box to JavaScript as the default setting.

However, when it comes to writing React code, there are two main options. We can write our code with JavaScript (JS) or with TypeScript (TS). The vanilla-flavor CRA you downloaded is set to JavaScript. However, we will be writing our code in this book using TypeScript, as we mentioned in the previous chapter.

CRA Template with TypeScript

To set up our project with TS using Yarn, the command is similar to how we set up CRA. The only difference is that we add the TS template for TypeScript created by the React community.

```
$ yarn create react-app starter-project --template TypeScript
```

We are using the `--template` flag with TS, and we name our project `starter-project`.

Now, change the directory to your project and start the project to ensure all went well, just as we did before.

```
$ cd starter-project
```

> **Tip** I recommend testing your project after each install to ensure it's still running. Libraries and dependencies change often, and ensuring the project doesn't break should be your first priority.

```
$ yarn start
```

The app should open on port 3000 just as we did it before: `http://localhost:3000/`. See Figure 2-7.

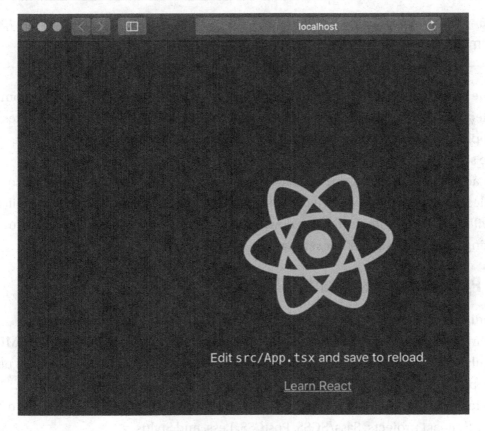

Figure 2-7. *CRA TS app running on port 3000*

Notice that the copy changes on the app to `src/App.tsx` (from Figure 2-3), as well as that the files changed from `.js` to `.tsx` in our app.

Next, we need to add the following types for TS so that Webpack knows how to handle .tsx file types and bundle them and so they can be included as static assets in our project.

```
$ yarn add -D typescript @types/node @types/react @types/react-dom @types/
jest @typescript-eslint/scope-manager
```

When using Yarn, we use the -D flag (which stands for developer "dependencies") when we want to update our project's package.json to include a library under devDependencies. The package.json file holds the project's libraries.

Note   The types installed for TypeScript are used to provide TypeScript with type information about APIs that are written in JavaScript.

The types we just installed include TypeScript for Jest tests and ESLint. CRA comes bundled with Jest and Jest-dom to test our application. We will be learning about testing our application with Jest and ESlint later in this book, but I wanted you to be aware that we are setting up these types already.

In addition to changing our code files from .js to .ts, the template project also includes a file called tsconfig.json. This file holds a specific setting for the compiler that will compile our files from .tsx down to .js with information such as what we targeting such as ES6 and other settings.

CSS Preprocessors: Sass/SCSS

Cascading Style Sheets (CSS) is a core functionality in HTML, and you need to familiarize yourself with CSS if you are not already. This goes for working with HTML in particular and in React specifically. On large projects, CSS preprocessors are often used to complement CSS and add functionality. We will discuss these later in this book.

In terms of CSS preprocessors, there are four main CSS preprocessors that are often used with React projects: Sass/SCSS, PostCSS, Less, and Stylus.

Note   CSS is used to represent the visual layout of the web page on different devices. CSS preprocessors are used to enhance CSS functionality.

Sass/SCSS has the upper hand for the majority of today's projects, so that's what we will be using. In fact, Sass/SCSS is the most popular and will probably get you the best-paying job as a developer according to surveys (`https://ashleynolan.co.uk/blog/frontend-tooling-survey-2019-results`). If you want to see a comparison between the different CSS preprocessors, check out my article on Medium: `http://shorturl.at/dJQT3`.

We will be learning more about CSS and SCSS later in this book, but for now, install it with Yarn.

```
$ yarn add -D node-sass
```

Just like with CSS, if we want to use SCSS modules in TypeScript the same way we would use them in JavaScript, we need to install Webpack's loader for Sass/SCSS. It's called `scss-loader`.

Since we are using TS, we need a replacement for `scss-loader` that works with TS and generates typings for Sass/SCSS. Install the loader with Yarn.

```
$ yarn add -D scss-loader typings-for-scss-modules-loader
```

Redux Toolkit/Recoil

The Redux toolkit is the standard way to organize React app data and user interaction so your code doesn't get messy.

Note   Redux is an open source JavaScript library for managing application state. It is most commonly used with React for building user interfaces. See `https://redux.js.org`.

We will be going over Redux and Redux Toolkit later in this book. For now, let's install the Redux Toolkit libraries and types.

```
$ yarn add -D redux @reduxjs/toolkit react-redux @types/react-redux
```

Recoil is another state management library created by the Facebook team that I believe will take over Redux Toolkit. We will work with both of these libraries later in this chapter. To install Recoil, use this:

```
$ yarn add recoil@^0.0.13
```

Material-UI CSS Framework

A CSS framework (or CSS libraries) is based on the concept of bringing a more standardized practice to your web development. Using a CSS framework, you can speed up your web development effort versus just using CSS (or other style sheets) as it allows you to use predefined web elements.

Yes, we could create all of our custom components and style them, but most times it isn't worth the effort, and besides writing the components, we would need to test them on all browsers and devices. Can you imagine?

```
import 'bootstrap/dist/css/bootstrap.css';
```

Both Bootstrap and Material-UI are great CSS frameworks in certain projects to get started right away, without spending hours creating your own components.

To install it, I will be setting up Material-UI core as well as the icons bundle.

```
$ yarn add -D @material-ui/core @material-ui/icons
```

To get Material-UI to work seamlessly with TS, we also need to update some settings in our tsconfig.json file so that the TS page on React doesn't encounter any errors.

Open tsconfig.json with a text editor and update it.

```
// tsconfig.json
{
  "compilerOptions": {
    "target": "es5",
    "lib": [
      "es6", "dom",
      ...
      ...
    ],
    "noImplicitAny": true,
    "noImplicitThis": true,
    "strictNullChecks": true,
```

Styled Components

Styled Components go hand in hand with Material-UI. Styled Components is a styling solution, and it can also be used beyond Material-UI.

To add Styled Components and types to our project, use this:

```
$ yarn add -D styled-components @types/styled-components
```

Also keep this link handy, in case you need to install fonts:

```
https://medium.com/r/?url=https%3A%2F%2Fgithub.com%2Ffontsource%2Ffontsource
```

React Router

React is based on a single-page application; however, most applications need multiple views in React's single-page application paradigm.

Building an application on a single component is not ideal as the code and complexity can grow and it can become a developer's nightmare to maintain and test. We will learn more about creating components and subcomponents in the next chapter.

To handle routing, there are many tools to choose from: React Router, Router5, Redux-First Router, and Reach Router, to name a few.

The standard for React projects at the time of writing is React Router. To add React Router and types for Webpack, follow this command:

```
$ yarn add -D react-router-dom @types/react-router-dom
```

Jest and Enzyme + Sinon

Jest is a JavaScript unit testing framework and the standard for React applications. It was built to be used with any JavaScript project, and it comes with CRA out of the box. However, we do need Jest-dom and Enzyme to enhance the capabilities of Jest.

For Enzyme we want to install the React 16 adapter (that's the latest version at the time of writing but likely to change to 17). Also, we need to install `react-test-renderer` so we can render React components to pure JavaScript objects without depending on the DOM or a native mobile environment. Later in the book, we will be using Jest's snapshot testing feature to automatically save a copy of the JSON tree to a file and use tests to check that it hasn't changed.

To install these tools, use this command:

```
$ yarn add -D enzyme enzyme-adapter-react-16 react-test-renderer
```

We also want to make our life easier by installing the `enzyme-to-json` library so our code will be simplified when we use these libraries later in the book.

```
$ yarn add -D enzyme-to-json
```

Sinon

Another must-have library that we should be aware of and add to our toolbox is Sinon (`https://github.com/sinonjs/sinon`). Here's the command you can use to add it:

```
$ yarn add sinon @types/sinon
```

Jest and Sinon serve the same purpose, but there are times that you may find one framework more natural and easier to work with for the specific test. We will cover Sinon later in this book.

E2E Testing: Jest and Puppeteer

Testing is at the core of delivering quality software. There is a hierarchy in testing, and E2E is usually only considered after unit testing and integration testing are done.

End-to-end testing (E2E testing) is a testing method that includes testing our app workflow from beginning to end. What we are doing in E2E is replicating real user scenarios so our app is validated for integration and data integrity.

The solutions for E2E testing are Jest and Puppeteer. Puppeteer is the most popular E2E solution, and it integrates with Jest. To get this started, use this:

```
$ yarn add puppeteer jest-puppeteer ts-jest
```

Don't forget to also add the types for TS.

```
$ yarn add yarn add @types/puppeteer @types/expect-puppeteer @types/jest-
environment-puppeteer
```

That's all you need to get set up with Jest and Puppeteer and to configure everything and see an example of E2E testing for `App.tsx`. You'll learn more about E2E later in the book.

Component Folder Structure

When you work on a React project and the code keeps growing in size, it can become overwhelming with the number of components you may have, and then it can be hard to find them.

A neat way to organize your components so it makes them easier to find is to split the components into a separated component type like in Figure 2-8.

Figure 2-8. *A suggested React folder structure for Redux and TS*

This is my recommended folder structure to get started; however, feel free to use it as a suggestion only.

To follow this structure, create these folders:

- `src/components`

- `src/features`

- `src/layout`

- `src/pages`

- `src/redux`

- `src/recoil/atoms`

If you on a Mac, you can use this one-liner in the Terminal:

```
$ mkdir src/components src/features src/layout src/pages src/redux src/
recoil/atoms
```

Generate Templates

As developers, we don't like writing code again and again. `generate-react-cli` is a helpful utility we can use. It is based on templates, so we don't need to write our code again and again.

If you come from Angular, you probably love the Angular CLI and that it can generate templates for your project.

You can generate your project templates using the `generate-react-cli` project in a similar way in React. To install, we will be using the NPX task script.

```
$ npx generate-react-cli component Header
```

Because it's the first time running the script, it will install and create `generate-react-cli.json` with the options you chose the first time you used the tool, but feel free to change these manually.

A cool feature is that we can create our own template. Here is an example of creating a custom template for React pages.

Don't dig into the template code at this time. We just set these templates, and we will be going over the code and what it means in the next chapter as we build our components.

Change `generate-react-cli.json` to point to the template files we will be creating.

```
{
  "usesTypeScript": true,
  "usesCssModule": false,
  "cssPreprocessor": "scss",
  "testLibrary": "Enzyme",
  "component": {
    "default": {
      "path": "src/components",
      "withStyle": true,
      "withTest": true,
      "withStory": false,
      "withLazy": false
    },
    "page": {
      "customTemplates": {
        "component": "templates/page/component.tsx",
        "style": "templates/page/style.scss",
        "test": "templates/page/test.tsx"
      },
      "path": "src/pages",
      "withLazy": false,
      "withStory": false,
```

```
      "withStyle": true,
      "withTest": true
    },
    "layout": {
      "customTemplates": {
        "component": "templates/component/component.tsx",
        "style": "templates/component/style.scss",
        "test": "templates/component/test.tsx"
      },
      "path": "src/layout",
      "withLazy": false,
      "withStory": false,
      "withStyle": true,
      "withTest": true
    }
  }
}
```

Create a template file for the TypeScript class page components with a React router and a hook to the pathname: templates/component/component.tsx. In the next chapter, we will create a custom React component, and this template component will make sense. You can change the author name to your own name and website, of course.

```
/*
Author: Eli Elad Elrom
Website: https://EliElrom.com
License: MIT License
Component: src/component/TemplateName/TemplateName.tsx
*/

import React from 'react';
import './TemplateName.scss';
import { RouteComponentProps } from 'react-router-dom'

export default class TemplateName extends React.PureComponent<ITemplateName
Props, ITemplateNameState> {
```

```
constructor(props: ITemplateNameProps) {
  super(props);
  this.state = {
    name: this.props.history.location.pathname.substring(
      1,
      this.props.history.location.pathname.length
    ).replace('/', '')
  }
}

// If you need 'shouldComponentUpdate' -> Refactor to React.Component
// Read more about component lifecycle in the official docs:
// https://reactjs.org/docs/react-component.html

/*
public shouldComponentUpdate(nextProps: IMyPageProps, nextState:
IMyPageState) {
  // invoked before rendering when new props or state are being received.
  return true // or prevent rendering: false
} */

static getDerivedStateFromProps:
  React.GetDerivedStateFromProps<ITemplateNameProps, ITemplateNameState>
  = (props:ITemplateNameProps, state: ITemplateNameState) => {
  // invoked right before calling the render method, both on the initial
    mount and on subsequent updates
  // return an object to update the state, or null to update nothing.
  return null
}

public getSnapshotBeforeUpdate(prevProps: ITemplateNameProps, prevState:
ITemplateNameState) {
  // invoked right before the most recently rendered output is committed
  // A snapshot value (or null) should be returned.
  return null
}
```

```
  componentDidUpdate(prevProps: ITemplateNameProps, prevState:
  ITemplateNameState, snapshot: ITemplateNameSnapshot) {
    // invoked immediately after updating occurs. This method is not called
       for the initial render.
    // will not be invoked if shouldComponentUpdate() returns false.
  }

  render() {
    return (
      <div className="TemplateName">
        {this.state.name} Component
      </div>)
  }
}

interface ITemplateNameProps extends RouteComponentProps<{ name: string }>
{
  // TODO
}

interface ITemplateNameState {
  name: string
}

interface ITemplateNameSnapshot {
  // TODO
}
```

Create an SCSS file template: templates/component/style.scss.

```
.TemplateName {
  font-family: 'Open Sans', sans-serif;
  font-weight: 700;
}
```

Create a test file with Enzyme: templates/component/test.tsx.

```
import React from 'react'
import { shallow } from 'enzyme'
import TemplateName from './TemplateName'

describe('<TemplateName />', () => {
    let component

    beforeEach(() => {
        component = shallow(<TemplateName />)
    });

    test('It should mount', () => {
        expect(component.length).toBe(1)
    })
})
```

At this point, you should have a template folder with the files shown in Figure 2-9.

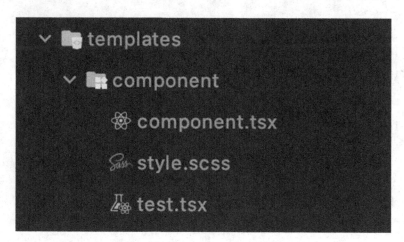

Figure 2-9. *Template folder structure and files*

You can repeat the same steps for components of the type page or anything you like.

Linting: ESLint and Prettier

How neat would it be to have a code review and have someone formatting your code to make sure it's consistent?

All code in any code base should look like a single person typed it, no matter how many people contributed.

—Rick Waldron, creator of Johnny-Five

Luckily, this can be done.

Lint is a tool for analyzing your code. It is a static code analysis tool created to identify problematic patterns found in code. Prettier is an opinionated code formatter.

Note   Linting is the process of running a program to analyze your code to find potential errors.

Lint tools can analyze your code and warn you of potential errors. For it to work, we need to configure it with specific rules.

It's not wise to get into a debate about whether there should be two spaces in every newline or a tab, there should be single quotes or double quotes, etc. The idea is to have some sort of a style guide and follow it for consistency. As was nicely said:

Arguments over style are pointless. There should be a style guide, and you should follow it.

—Rebecca Murphey

Airbnb, as part of its style guide, provides an ESLint configuration that anyone can use as their standard.

ESLint is already installed on Create-React-App, but it's not optimized with a styling guide and for TypeScript.

To set up your project with ESLint and Prettier for TypeScript using Airbnb's styling guide (which is considered the standard), use the following:

```
$ yarn add -D --save-exact eslint-config-airbnb eslint-config-airbnb-
TypeScript eslint-config-prettier eslint-config-react-app eslint-import-
resolver-TypeScript eslint-loader eslint-plugin-flowtype eslint-plugin-
import eslint-plugin-jsx-a11y eslint-plugin-react eslint-plugin-react-hooks
babel-eslint eslint-plugin-jest @TypeScript-eslint/parser @TypeScript-
eslint/eslint-plugin$ yarn add -D --save-exact prettier prettier-eslint
prettier-eslint-cli eslint-plugin-prettier
```

Read my article (https://medium.com/react-courses/react-create-react-app-v3-4-1-a55f3e7a8d6d) for more information.

Follow the instructions at shorturl.at/otuU8 to update the following files or just copy them from the CRA MIIL template project.

There are three files that we will configure.

- .eslintrc: ESLint run commands configuration file.

- .eslintignore: ESLint ignore files

- .prettierrc: Prettier run commands configuration file

Lastly, we can update the package.json file's run scripts so that we can run Lint and format utilities and even run the app build (the production build we will cover later in this book) with just one command.

```
"scripts": {
    ..
    ..
    ..
    "lint": "eslint --ext .js,.jsx,.ts,.tsx src --color",
    "format": "prettier --write 'src/**/*.{ts,tsx,scss,css,json}'",
    "isready": "npm run format && npm run lint && npm run build"
}
```

We are ready to let Lint do its job and change our code (see Figure 2-10).

```
$ yarn run lint
```

```
/Users/eli/Desktop/starter-project/src/serviceWorker.ts
   52:11   warning   Unexpected console statement                                    no-console
   69:7    error     Assignment to property of function parameter 'registration'     no-param-reassign
   88:15   warning   Unexpected console statement                                    no-console
   93:15   warning   Unexpected console statement                                    no-console
  105:7    warning   Unexpected console statement                                    no-console
  133:7    warning   Unexpected console statement                                    no-console
  146:9    warning   Unexpected console statement                                    no-console
```

Figure 2-10.   Output after running Lint

To run the formatter to clean our code, we can use Yarn as well.

```
$ yarn run format
```

Now confirm we can still compile by checking port 3000 or running `yarn start` if you stopped the process (see Figure 2-11).

```
$ yarn start
```

```
Compiled successfully!

You can now view starter-project in the browser.

  Local:            http://localhost:3000
  On Your Network:  http://10.241.0.97:3000

Note that the development build is not optimized.
To create a production build, use yarn build.
```

Figure 2-11. *Compiling our code after formatting and linting it*

Other Useful Libraries

We will install a couple of useful libraries that will come in handy later in the development exercises in this book.

Classnames

Classnames (`https://github.com/JedWatson/classnames`) is a simple JavaScript utility for conditionally joining `classNames` together.

```
$ yarn add -D classnames @types/classnames
```

Here is an example of its usage:

```
import classNames from 'classnames'
const footerClasses = classNames('foo', 'bar') // => 'foo bar'
```

Prop-types

Prop-types is a great little utility (`https://github.com/facebook/prop-types`) for runtime type checking for React props and similar objects. We are setting our starter project with TypeScript, so we really don't *need* this utility, because we will pass

TypeScript objects and get type checking. However, just because we are using TS doesn't mean we are never going to need JS. There are cases such as importing a component from a different project that we may need this little utility.

```
$ yarn add -D prop-types
```

You can download the code from here:

```
https://github.com/Apress/react-and-libraries/tree/master/01/starter-
project
```

Here is an example of its usage:

```
import PropTypes from "prop-types";
whiteFont: PropTypes.bool
```

To have Yarn use `package.json` and download all the dependencies, run the following:

```
$ yarn start
```

Additional Useful Utilities

Here are some additional useful utilities:

- *Lodash* (`https://github.com/lodash/lodash`): This makes JS easier by taking the hassle out of working with arrays, numbers, objects, strings, etc.

- *Moment* (`https://github.com/moment/moment`): For working with dates, this is a must-have.

- *Serve* (`https://github.com/vercel/serve`): Install this with `$ yarn add serve`. It adds a local server. CRA scripts include a run script to publish your app. It will generate a folder called `build`. We want to be able to test our build code before going to production. You'll learn more about production build in later chapters.

- *Precache React-snap to working offline*: This is an optimizing library that we will use to configure our app to work offline. See Chapter 11.

- *react-helmet change header metadata*: This updates a header of each page for SEO; you'll learn more in Chapter 11.

- *Analyzer Bundle*: You can install the `source-map-explorer` and `cra-bundle-analyzer` tools to look inside our JS bundle chunks (more in Chapter 11).

Summary

In this chapter, we learned about the Create-React-App project and set up our starter project and development environment with essential libraries we will be learning about through this book. We installed the CRA MHL template project that already includes everything we need, as well as learned about vanilla CRA and the TypeScript template.

We also learned about libraries such as NPM, Yarn, Webpack, NPM scripts, TypeScript, Sass/SCSS, Redux Toolkit, Material-UI, Styled Components, Router, Jest and Enzyme, Generate templates, and ESLint and Prettier as well as other useful libraries.

In the next chapter, we will be building React custom components and subcomponents.

CHAPTER 3

React Components

In this chapter, I will give you an overview of React components and what you can use them for in React. You need to understand what React components are because they are at the core of React.

In previous chapters, we created our first React project, we set up our environment, and we created a starter project that includes many of the libraries we will be using in this book.

Our simple project already included components and subcomponents. In this chapter, we will dive deeper into the components and create more complex components and subcomponents. We will also look at the related libraries that can help us speed up development as well as maintain our project.

What Are React Components?

React components are like functions. They let you build your front-end implementation by breaking down a complex UI into small, stand-alone pieces. In fact, the heart of React is nothing more than a compilation of components working together in harmony. Take a look what React.org has to say about components:

> *Components let you split the UI into independent, reusable pieces, and think about each piece in isolation.*
>
> —React.org docs, `https://reactjs.org/docs/components-and-props.html`

There are three types of components.

- Functional components
- Class components
- Factory components

E. Elrom, *React and Libraries*, https://doi.org/10.1007/978-1-4842-6696-0_3

Writing components in the correct way can help you reduce the complexity of your app, ensure you select the right type of component for the job, avoid pitfalls, and increase performance.

This section is broken down into these parts:

- JavaScript (JS) functions and class components

- TypeScript (TS) functions and class components

- Exotic components such as factory components

- Complex TS factory components

- `React.PureComponent` versus `React.Component`

JavaScript Function and Class Components

Function components (also called *functional stateless components*) are nothing more than JavaScript functions. They go hand in hand with functional programming (FP). FP means building our software with pure functions and avoiding shared state, mutable data, and side effects.

FP is declarative rather than imperative, and the application state flows through pure functions. Because React is a declarative language (it does not actually manipulate the DOM itself directly), it integrates great with React, because we want to use a declarative architecture.

Note   Declarative programming is a paradigm that expresses the logic of a computation without describing its control flow. The imperative paradigm uses statements that change a program's state such as changing the DOM directly.

If we want to write the most basic React component by creating a React component inside a JavaScript tag of an HTML file, the code would look like the following. In the application we wrote in Chapter 1, we wrote the most basic React component by creating a React component inside an HTML file with a JavaScript tag.

```
<div id="app"></div>
<script type="text/babel">
    ReactDOM.render(
    <h1>Hello World</h1>,
    document.getElementById('app')
    );
</script>
```

Taking that simple "Hello World" example, say we want to pass user-defined properties. We can set a function and assign a user-defined property and then pass that to the React DOM render to be executed as a JSX code. See the following example:

```
function WelcomeUser(props) {
    return <h1>Hi {props.userName}</h1>;
}
const element = <WelcomeUser userName="John" />;

ReactDOM.render(
    element,
    document.getElementById('app')
);
```

props stands for the properties we pass and the functions returned by the React Element. Here we pass a userName that will display on our user interface.

Open this example in your favorite browser, as shown in Figure 3-1.

Figure 3-1. *WelcomeUser.html output example*

You can download this code from the book GitHub location.

https://github.com/Apress/react-and-libraries/tree/master/03/ WelcomeUser.html

JavaScript Functional Components

When we write our components, we normally would not use one component and include our subcomponents inside a parent component.

We can see that, for example, in the Create-React-App (CRA). The App subcomponent is nested inside of our main component index.

```
ReactDOM.render(<App />, document.getElementById('root'))
```

We can then create a subcomponent and code the subcomponent using pure JavaScript. Take a look at this basic example that gives us the same "Hi John" results, but this time in our CRA starter project instead of the stand-alone HTML page:

```
function Welcome(props) {
  return <h1>Hi {props.userName}</h1>;
}
```

Javascript Class Component

Creating a class component with props using pure JavaScript to produce the same output of Hello userName is similar. With ES6 syntax, a JS class component that produces the same output looks like this:

```
class Welcome extends React.Component {
  render() {
    return <h1>Hi {this.props.userName}</h1>;
  }
}
```

React Hooks

In both function and class components, we can use hooks to access the state and the component lifecycle features. The class component extends React.Component, if we use the Hook function by importing the feature from React.

Note   Hooks are functions that allow us to "hook into" React state and lifecycle features.

You can find good resource about hooks on the ReactJS.org website.

```
https://reactjs.org/docs/hooks-overview.html
```

For the next step, you can use the `starter-project` you created in the previous step or start fresh with one command, as shown here:

```
$ yarn create react-app starter-project --template must-have-libraries
```

Next, we can change the directory to the new project and start the project.

```
$ cd starter-project
$ yarn start
```

The app should be running on port 3000 if that port is not in use by another app, in other words, `http://localhost:3000`. Refer to the previous chapter for more details.

CRA generates a component called `src/index.tsx` that wraps another component app inside the React Render function.

```
ReactDOM.render(
  <React.StrictMode>
    <App />
  </React.StrictMode>,
  document.getElementById('root')
)
```

If we look at the `src/App.tsx` subcomponent, we find the JSX code, which includes the code we see once we run the Yarn start script (`yarn start`).

```
import React from 'react'

function App() {
  return (
    <div className="App">
    ..
    </div>
  )
}

export default App
```

If we want to tap into the state feature of React, we need to import the useState feature from the React library.

```
import {useState} from 'react'
```

Next, we can write JSX code inside our function component that will render a button that on a click event will increase the values of a counter. The counter variable is our state.

```
function App() {
  const [count, setCount] = useState(0);
  return (
  ..
  ..
  <p>You clicked {count} times</p>
  <button onClick={() => setCount(count + 1)}>
    Click me
  </button>
  ..
  ..
  )
}

export default App
```

useState is a state hook; it returns a state with the current state of the app, in this case, the state of our counter (count). Notice that there is a second parameter that is a function to update the state (setCounter).

Once the user clicks the button, we call the function to update the state of the app via the setCounter, and there we can increment the value of Count + 1. That updates the variable count, which increases the value by one. Using reflection {count}, the data inside the paragraph tag ends up on the user interface.

The complete updated code of src/App.tsx will look like this:

```
import React, { useState } from 'react'
import logo from './logo.svg'
import './App.scss'
```

```
function App() {
  const [count, setCount] = useState(0)
  return (
    <div className="App">
      <header className="App-header">
        <img src={logo} className="App-logo" alt="logo" />
        <p>You clicked {count} times</p>

        <button type="submit" onClick={() => setCount(count + 1)}>
          Click me
        </button>

        <p>
          Edit <code>src/App.tsx</code> and save to reload.
        </p>
        <a
          className="App-link"
          href="https://github.com/EliEladElrom/react-tutorials"
          target="_blank"
          rel="noopener noreferrer"
        >
          Learn React
        </a>
      </header>
    </div>
  )
}

export default App
```

If you are still running the yarn start command, you can just go to the
http://localhost:3000 page, and you will see the changes (Figure 3-2); otherwise, use
the yarn start command.

Once you click the button, you will see the counter variable changes as expected. See
Figure 3-2.

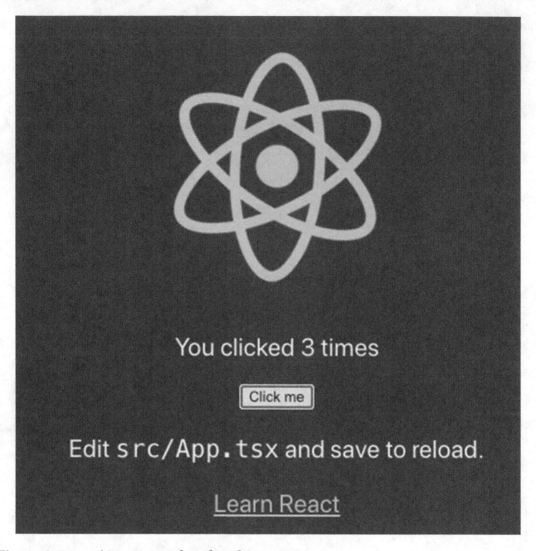

Figure 3-2. *src/App.tsx updated with a counter state*

TypeScript Components

So far so good. We are able to create JavaScript functions and class components. Notice that in the previous example, we used a .tsx file extension; however, we didn't really write any specific TypeScript code. The code is still good ol' JavaScript.

In this book, we set up our project with TypeScript. Using functions and class components is similar to how we set up our JavaScript function with the ES6 class; however, there are additional syntax-specific methods, as well as type checking, that are unique just to TypeScript. Let's take a look.

60

Pure Functions

This goes to the core of React. FP is declarative rather than imperative, and the application state flows through pure functions. Because React is a declarative language (it does not actually manipulate the DOM itself directly), we want our React components to be pure functions.

Take this example:

```
const Component = (props: IProps) =>
  render() {
    return
  }
}
```

It will compile and work, but it's not ideal because it's not pure. To turn it into a pure component, write your pure functions like so:

```
const Component = (props: IProps) =>
```

Pure Functions with Side Effects

Note   A side effect is a state change that is observable outside the called function other than its return value. Examples of a side effect include the following: changing the value of an external variable or object property (global variable, or a variable in the parent function scope chain), an `import` statement with no specifiers (i.e., `import someLib`), logging to the console, data fetching, setting up a subscription, or manually changing the DOM.

Our pure functions can handle side effects (also known as *effects*). To do that, we wrap our side effects inside `useEffect` and ensure they won't render on every change. For instance, look at the following component to scroll to the top that uses the browser API:

```
export default function ScrollToTop() {
  const { pathname } = useLocation()
  useEffect(
    () => () => {
      try {
```

```
        window.scrollTo(0, 0)
    },
    [pathname]
  )
  return null
}
```

TypeScript Function Components

For TypeScript, we can specify the type of our `props` interface. We can use the `useState` functionality, just as we did with the pure JavaScript example.

```
// src/components/MyCounter/MyCounter.tsx
import React, { useState } from 'react'

export const MyCounter: React.FunctionComponent<IMyCounterProps> =
(props: IMyCounterProps) => {
  const [count, setCount] = useState(0)
  return (

      <p>You clicked MyCounter {count} times</p>
      <button type="submit" onClick={() => setCount(count + 1)}>Click
      MyCounter</button>

  )
}
interface IMyCounterProps {
  // TODO
}
```

You can download this from GitHub.

https://github.com/Apress/react-and-libraries/tree/master/03/starter-project/src/components/MyCounter/MyCounter.tsx

---

Tip   In JSX, `<div></div>` is the equivalent of `<></>`.

Now we can take this subcomponent and include it inside of our `src/App.tsx` component.

```
import {MyCounter} from './components/MyCounter/MyCounter'

function App() {
  return (
    <div classname="App">
      <header className="App-header">
      ...
      <MyCounter />
      ...
      </div>
    </div>
  )
}
```

That will produce the results in Figure 3-3.

Figure 3-3. *src/App.tsx updated with MyCounter subcomponent*

TypeScript Class Components

To create the same subcomponent as in `MyCounter` as a TypeScript class, we don't need to use the `useState` method.

Instead, we can create a state interface (`IMyClassCounterState`) and set our variable count as the type number.

Then inside our constructor we set our initial component state. We can set the counter equal to zero.

Lastly, when we need to change the state of our component, we can use the `this.setState` function and update our counter. See the complete code here:

```tsx
// src/components/MyCounter/MyClassCounter.tsx

import React from 'react'

export default class MyClassCounter extends React.
Component<IMyClassCounterProps, IMyClassCounterState> {
  constructor(props: IMyClassCounterProps) {
    super(props)
    this.state = {
      count: 0,
    }
  }

  render() {
    return (
      <div>
        <p>You clicked MyClassCounter {this.state.count} times</p>
        <button type="submit" onClick={() => this.setState({ count: this.
        state.count + 1 })}>
          Click MyClassCounter
        </button>
      </div>
    )
  }
}

interface IMyClassCounterProps {
  // TODO
}

interface IMyClassCounterState {
  count: number
}
```

This code can be downloaded from GitHub.

https://github.com/Apress/react-and-libraries/tree/master/03/starter-project/src/components/MyClassCounter/MyClassCounter.tsx

To view these changes in our user interface, include our subcomponent inside the src/App.tsx component so we can visually see our subcomponent (Figure 3-4).

```
import { MyCounter } from './components/MyCounter/MyCounter'
import MyClassCounter from './components/MyCounter/MyClassCounter'

function App() {
  const [count, setCount] = useState(0)
  return (
    <div className="App">
      <header className="App-header">
        ...
        <p>You clicked {count} times</p>
        <MyCounter />
        <MyClassCounter />
        ...
      </header>
    </div>
  )
}
export default App
```

Figure 3-4. *src/App.tsx updated with MyClassCounter subcomponent*

This example works fine, but there is a problem here. Run the linter that we set up in our project to check for potential coding mistakes.

$ yarn lint

You will get an error message error Use callback in setState when referencing the previous state.

```
starter-project/src/components/MyCounter/MyClassCounter.tsx
 15:69 error Use callback in setState when referencing the previous state
react/no-access-state-in-setstate
✖ 1 problem (1 error, 0 warnings)
```

When using states in React, we can simplify our code by updating the current state based on the previous state, and the code will compile and work as expected for many use cases; however, that's really breaking the React architecture and should be avoided.

Let's revise our code.

```
// src/components/MyCounter/MyClassCounter.tsx

  handleClick(e: React.MouseEvent) {
    this.setState(prevState => {
      const newState = prevState.count+1
      return ({
        ...prevState,
        count: newState
      });
    })
  }

  render() {
    return (
      <div>
        <p>You clicked MyClassCounter {this.state.count} times</p>
        <button type="submit" onClick={this.handleClick}>
          Click MyClassCounter
```

```
      </button>
    </div>
  )
 }
}
```

Run Lint again, and we are now error-free.

```
$ yarn lint
yarn run v1.22.10
$ eslint — ext .js,.jsx,.ts,.tsx ./
✦ Done in 7.31s.
```

Read my article (`shorturl.at/cmRWO`) for common linting mistakes and how to avoid them.

Exotic Components: Factory Components

The last type of component I would like to talk about is factory components. React allows you to create components that look like functional components; however, functional components use React hooks to access the lifecycle events.

Take a look at this code:

```
function Hello(props) {
  return {
    componentDidMount() {
      alert('wow')
    }
    render() {
      return <div>Hi, {this.props.name}</div>
    }
  };
}
```

You can write that code in React 16; however, in React version 17, the code will generate an error message if you do that.

Tip   In React 17, the access to the previous events such as
`componentDidMount` was deprecated, and you should be using hook features
to access the component lifecycle events `getDerivedStateFromProps`,
`getSnapshotBeforeUpdate`, and `componentDidUpdate`. You'll learn more
about these hooks later in this chapter.

Take a look at the issue on GitHub where the React Core team is asking to create
a warning for developers using this type of components; see `https://github.com/`
`facebook/react/issues/13560`.

Complex TS Function Components

Extending the function components' `props` interface gives our functions superpowers. In
this section, I will show you two examples of extending the interface for React Router and
for Material-UI styles as well as creating your own interface extension.

When extending a class, there are three options.

- Inheritance

- Interface

- Composition

Inheritance is when one class inherits the features of another class. An *interface* is
just the signature (blueprint) of the class. *Composition* means creating small functions
and then creating bigger and more complete functions and using both of them together.

When we extend our interface, it's better to avoid inheritance as a rule of thumb
because the object is an interface.

Generally speaking, when it comes to component inheritance, the React team
promotes using composition over inheritance when possible; however, here we
are doing a `props` inheritance. See `https://reactjs.org/docs/composition-vs-`
`inheritance.html`.

Using this type of pattern gives us the ability to reuse code as well as implement
pure JavaScript or TypeScript code. There is somewhat of a disagreement about what
is the best practice. Whatever you do, you want to avoid tons of boilerplate code and
complexity so your code is more readable and more testable.

This is a larger discussion that is beyond the scope of this book, but if you find yourself with a need to extend the interface, note that there are a few approaches.

Extending props for Router

If you recall in Chapter 2, we set up the project to be able to generate the project templates using the `generate-react-cli` library, and we set up a custom template file called `starter-project/ templates/component/component.js`.

Now that we understand the React function and class component as well as hooks, we can examine the code again.

We have here a class component with two interfaces, `ITemplateNameProps` and `ITemplateNameState`. They are not implemented yet.

Inside our class, we call the constructor of the class, pass the `props`, and set the state of the app.

The parent component will set the properties, and we will set the state of the app just as we have done with `useState`. Because we extend `React.Component`, we don't need to import that feature from React; it's available to us automatically.

In addition, we get these hook features to access the component lifecycle: `getDerivedStateFromProps`, `getSnapshotBeforeUpdate`, and `componentDidUpdate`.

These have to do with the order of the components being mounted, rendered, and unmounted, and if we need to do operations such as to avoid memory leaks, that can be done here.

Take a look at our template file we are using for `generate-react-cli` to generate components. It includes the interfaces `ITemplateNameProps`, which extends `RouteComponentProps` to get the component name, and `ITemplateNameSnapshot` for the `componentDidUpdate` hook and interface for the state (`ITemplateNameState`). You can read about when to use which hook in the React docs: `https://reactjs.org/docs/react-component.html`.

```
import React from 'react';
import './TemplateName.scss';
import { RouteComponentProps } from 'react-router-dom'

export default class TemplateName extends React.
Component<ITemplateNameProps, ITemplateNameState> {
```

```
constructor(props: ITemplateNameProps) {
  super(props);
  this.state = {
    name: this.props.history.location.pathname.substring(
      1,
      this.props.history.location.pathname.length
    ).replace('/', '')
  }
}

// Read more about component lifecycle in the official docs:
// https://reactjs.org/docs/react-component.html

public shouldComponentUpdate(nextProps: ITemplateNameProps, nextState:
ITemplateNameState) {
  // invoked before rendering when new props or state are being received.
  return true // or prevent rendering: false
}

static getDerivedStateFromProps:
  React.GetDerivedStateFromProps<ITemplateNameProps, ITemplateNameState>
  = (props:ITemplateNameProps, state: ITemplateNameState) => {
  // invoked right before calling the render method, both on the initial
     mount and on subsequent updates
  // return an object to update the state, or null to update nothing.
  return null
}

public getSnapshotBeforeUpdate(prevProps: ITemplateNameProps, prevState:
ITemplateNameState) {
  // invoked right before the most recently rendered output is committed
  // A snapshot value (or null) should be returned.
  return null
}

componentDidUpdate(prevProps: ITemplateNameProps, prevState:
ITemplateNameState, snapshot: ITemplateNameSnapshot) {
```

```
    // invoked immediately after updating occurs. This method is not called
      for the initial render.
    // will not be invoked if shouldComponentUpdate() returns false.
  }

  render() {
    return (
      <div className="TemplateName">
        {this.state.name} Component
      </div>)
  }
}

interface ITemplateNameProps extends RouteComponentProps<{ name: string }>
{
  // TODO
}

interface ITemplateNameState {
  name: string
}

interface ITemplateNameSnapshot {
  // TODO
}
```

Note   componentWillMount, componentDidUpdate, and
componentWillUpdate were deprecated in React 16.9.0 (https://reactjs.
org/blog/2019/08/08/react-v16.9.0.html).

The props interface extends RouteComponentProps and asks us to pass the name,
which will be passed from the parent component when we include this component
inside a Route tag. You will see that later in this chapter.

```
interface ITemplateNameProps extends RouteComponentProps<{ name: string }>
```

Then we have access to the Router APIs via hooks.

```
this.state = {
        name: this.props.history.location.pathname.substring(1, this.
        props.history.location.pathname.length)
    }
```

My parent component will need to wrap my component with the Router tag. The React Router can pass data to our subcomponent.

```
function AppRouter() {
  return (
    <Router>
      <Switch>
        <Route exact path="/" component={App} />
      </Switch>
      <div className="footer">
      </div>
    </Router>
  )
}
```

Extending props for Material-UI Styles

If I want to create a component that is using Material-UI and I want to keep the styles in a separate class, I can give my props special powers by extending the class with WithStyles, and the props classes and properties will be available to me.

For instance, if I want to create a layout component that will center content for other components, I can create a component called Centered.tsx.

```
// src/layout/Centered/Centered.tsx

import * as React from 'react'
import { withStyles, WithStyles } from '@material-ui/core/styles'
import styles from './Centered.styles'

const CenteredViewInner: React.FunctionComponent<Props> = (props) => (
  <div className={props.classes.container}>{props.children}</div>
)
```

```
interface Props extends WithStyles<typeof styles> {}

export const Centered = withStyles(styles)(CenteredViewInner)
```

Then create a style class called `ClassName.styles.ts` that `Centered.tsx` can access.

```
import { createStyles, Theme } from '@material-ui/core/styles'

export default (theme: Theme) =>
  createStyles({
    '@global': {
      'body, html, #root': {
        paddingTop: 40,
        width: '100%',
      },
    },
    container: {
      maxWidth: '400px',
      margin: '0 auto',
    },
  })
```

We will learn more about this type of component later in this book.

Extending props Inheritance on Your Own

To extend `props` using inheritance and create our own component, we can create a base class that extends an interface. Then our class will extend our base child and can enforce properties from both the base and the child.

It is easier to understand with an example. For instance, say I want to create a custom button. Instead of the button, I just use the label to give the name of the button. My custom button is called `SpecialButton`. The button will use both a label and a name variable to show the button name to the user. I will need to implement logic to handle the name of the button as well as set a click event so the user can interact with my button. Take a look at the following code:

```
// src/components/SpecialButton.tsx

// eslint-disable-next-line max-classes-per-file
import React from 'react'
```

```
interface IBaseProps {
  name: string
}

// eslint-disable-next-line react/prefer-stateless-function
class Base<P> extends React.Component<P & IBaseProps, {}> {
  // TODO
}

interface IChildProps extends IBaseProps {
  label: string
  className: string
  handleClick: () => void
}

export class SpecialButton extends Base<IChildProps> {
  render(): JSX.Element {
    return (
      <div>
        <button type="submit" className={this.props.className}
        onClick={this.props.handleClick}>
          {this.props.label} - {this.props.name}
        </button>
      </div>
    )
  }
}
```

Notice   I am using disabling Lint in two places, because we set our Lint to have only one class for each class. This is just for illustration purposes, so I want to keep this simple. For production code, this should be broken down into two files where each file holds one class.

Now, to implement our SpecialButton, our parent component will need to pass on classname, label, name, and event handler. Take a look:

```
<SpecialButton
  className='specialButton'
  label='Special'
  name='Button'
  handleClick={() => setCount(count + 1)}
/>
```

We can place this code right in App.tsx. Since my event handler is placed inside the App.tsx code that holds the count state, it will increment the state on every click of our special button, as shown in Figure 3-5.

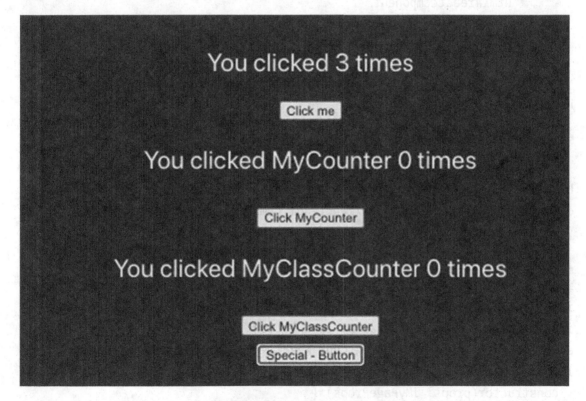

Figure 3-5. *src/App.tsx updated with SpecialButton subcomponent*

In this section, we will create function and class components both with JavaScript and with TypeScript. We also learned how to extend the prop interface to implement specific functionality.

Understanding function and class components help us know when to use what. If we need full access to the React component lifecycle events for various reasons such as cleanup and setup, it's wise to use class components. Functional components are meant to be used more when we don't need the full hooks set up. Using TypeScript helps us prevent the wrong data from creeping in and will come handy during testing.

Using Pure Components As Much As Possible

Last but not least, in the previous examples, we used React.Component when creating class components. It gave us access to the component's shouldComponentUpdate. However, keep in mind that there are two options.

- React.Component: See https://reactjs.org/docs/react-api. html#reactcomponent.

- React.PureComponent: See https://reactjs.org/docs/react-api. html#reactpurecomponent.

When you don't need shouldComponentUpdate, it's better to use PureComponent instead.

extends React.PureComponent

React.PureComponent gives a performance boost in some cases in exchange for losing the shouldComponentUpdate lifecycle. You can read more about it in the React docs (https://reactjs.org/docs/react-api.html#reactpurecomponent).

Here's an example:

```
import React from 'react'
import './MyPage.scss'
import { RouteComponentProps } from 'react-router-dom'
import Button from '@material-ui/core/Button'
export default class MyPage extends React.PureComponent<IMyPageProps,
IMyPageState> {
  constructor(props: IMyPageProps) {
    super(props)
    this.state = {
      name: this.props.history.location.pathname
        .substring(1, this.props.history.location.pathname.length)
```

```
        .replace('/', ''),
      results: 0
  }
 }
 render() {
    return (
      <div className="TemplateName">
        {this.state.name} Component
      </div>)
    )
  }
}
interface IMyPageProps extends RouteComponentProps<{ name: string }> {
  // TODO
}
interface IMyPageState {
  name: string
  results: number
}
```

Re-re-re-re-render

With that being said, there are times where shouldComponentUpdate is needed because
we can use that method to let React know that the component is not affected by a state
change from a parent component and there's no need to rerender.

```
public shouldComponentUpdate(nextProps: IProps, nextState: IState) {
  return false // prevent rendering
}
```

Summary

In this chapter, we covered React component basics and moved to more complex
exercises. We looked at JS and TS functions and class components, exotic components,
complex TS function components, and more.

Understanding functions and class components help us know when to use what. If we need full access to the React component lifecycle events for various reasons such as cleanup and setup, it's wise to use class components. Functional components are meant to be used more when we don't need the full hooks setup. Using TypeScript helps us prevent the wrong data creeping in and will come in handy during testing.

While learning about the ways you can write component, you learned about using React hooks, avoiding side effects, and extending the prop interface.

In the next chapter, we will learn about React Router and the Material-UI framework.

CHAPTER 4

React Router and Material-UI

In this chapter, you will learn how to integrate two useful libraries to help you speed up your development efforts and make your code more readable, testable, and maintainable. They are React Router and Material-UI.

In this book, we will create a completely functional app, test a portion of it, and even publish it to production. The app will be a site that sells products, with a logged-in members area and other elements that are common in many apps.

In this chapter, we will get started on this app project by doing two exercises. Specifically, we will create a usable project that includes a top menu, and then we will add drop-down menus and a drawer.

Figure 4-1 shows the final result after working through this chapter. In the next chapters, we will continue adding more subcomponents, style sheets, and other libraries. While learning more about all the libraries and elements of React, we will continue building our app.

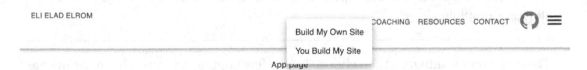

Figure 4-1. *Final app result of Chapter 4*

Integrate React Router

In this section of this chapter, we will be integrating a common feature that is needed in most apps: routing. We will be integrating the latest version of React Router, v5.2.0, into a React TypeScript project.

© Elad Elrom 2021
E. Elrom, *React and Libraries*, https://doi.org/10.1007/978-1-4842-6696-0_4

Why Do We Need a Router?

Why do we need a router anyway? Isn't React all about a single-page paradigm? Most applications need multiple views in React's single-page application (SPA) paradigm. Even if your application is simple and doesn't include many components, if it's just a single web page that does not need to change, or if it can be built into a one single main component, in the future that may change, so it's better to integrate the router code into the app in the early stages of your project.

Building an application on a single component is not ideal as the code and complexity will grow, and it can become a developer nightmare to maintain and test.

If you recall from Chapter 1, we looked at how DOM manipulation happens in React. The content of the web page is dynamically changed by methods such as `getElementById` and `removeChild` on the DOM.

What we really do during routing is take a single-page app in React and dynamically switch out the different tree objects in the browser using the React virtual DOM. The changes happen faster than in a traditional HTML paradigm as only the changes are updated on the actual DOM.

During this "reconciliation," React figures out which objects have changed with a diffing process. Then React updates only the objects in the "real" HTML DOM that need to be changed. This speeds up the process.

In this section, I will show you how to work with the latest version of React Router with TypeScript and implement routing.

Note   React is built on the concept of an SPA, but most applications are actually built using multiple views.

To implement routing, you can choose from a few popular options. The following are the most popular routing libraries:

- React Router

- Router5

- Redux-first router

- Reach Router

Reach Router (also known as @reach/route) is suited for a smaller number of routes, and it should be easily migrated back and forth between React Router and Reach Router. In fact, Reach Router and React Router were built by the same team. React Router is considered a must-know and is the most popular project with more than 61,000 stars on GitHub.

Note that React Router was drastically changed in version v5.x.

"with the introduction of hooks, React has fundamentally changed how we can compose state and behavior, and we want to take advantage of it."

—Ryan Florence, cofounder/CEO at React Training

The benefits of React Router include performance and exposing APIs to React hooks such as the location and navigate hooks.

You can read more about React Router at https://reacttraining.com/blog/reach-react-router-future/. You can also check out the React API at https://reactrouter.com/web/api/.

How Can We Integrate React Router into the ReactJS Project?

We'll break down the process into two steps.

- *Step 1*: Scaffolding, where we create menus and pages

- *Step 2*: Showing views, where we create the route logic and linking

Step 1: Scaffolding

We will be sectioning our app into a header, body, and footer. See Figure 4-2.

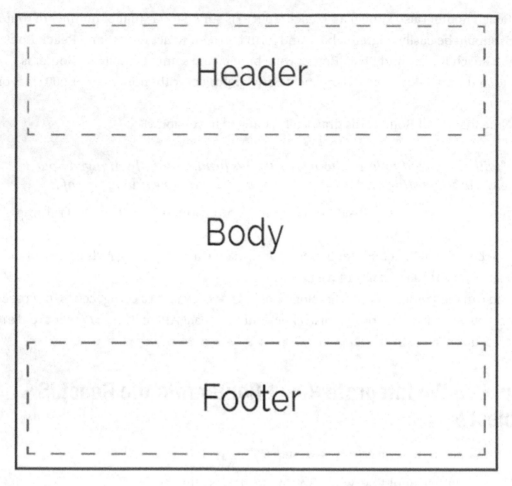

Figure 4-2. *Sectioning our app into a header, footer, and body*

We are also going to include a drawer menu that will be open with a menu icon. Let's get started.

Create a new CRA project using `must-have-libraries` and name it exercise-4-1.

```
$ yarn create react-app exercise-4-1 --template must-have-libraries
```

Next, we can change the directory to the new project and start the project.

```
$ cd exercise-4-1/
$ yarn start
```

You can find and download the complete code for this exercise here:

```
https://github.com/Apress/react-and-libraries/exercise-4-1
```

First, we will change `src/App.tsx` to just show a `div` that will output "App page" instead of the default CRA welcome page. We will use that page inside our router later when we set up our router. The new `App.tsx` page will look like this:

```
// src/App.tsx

import React from 'react'
import './App.scss'

function App() {
  return (
    <div className="App">
      <div>App page</div>
    </div>
  )
}

export default App
```

Since the `index.tsx` component is already including the App subcomponent, if you run `yarn start,` you should see the changes we made. See Figure 4-3.

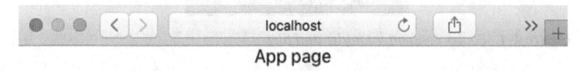

Figure 4-3. *Our app after changing App.tsx to output "App page"*

We will be using the `generate-react-cli` library included with the CRA MHL to create our pages and to lay out elements. We can create the `Header` and `Footer` components with `generate-react-cli` using the custom template we set. Run the following command while in the project's root folder:

```
$ npx generate-react-cli component Footer --type=layout
```

The output will give you the components that were created for you. It generated SCSS, a Jest test file, and the component file. For instance, here's the Footer component:

```
Stylesheet "Footer.scss" was created successfully at src/layout/Footer/
Footer.scss
Test "Footer.test.tsx" was created successfully at src/layout/Footer/
Footer.test.tsx
Component "Footer.tsx" was created successfully at src/layout/Footer/
Footer.tsx
```

If you open the src/layout folder, you will see our files created for us. See Figure 4-4.

Figure 4-4. *Footer component folder and files*

The project set up the initial testing Jet file for us (you will learn more about testing later in this book). We talked about that in Chapter 2. Now we actually put run script commands to work and use Lint. Then we will format and test them to ensure that our project is passing certain coding criteria.

- *ESLint*: We will do code analysis and flag programming errors, bugs, stylistic errors, and any other suspicious constructs.

- *Jest testing*: We will ensure our tests run and our tests pass.

- *Format*: We will ensure our code is formatted using the best practices we set (in our case, we set the Airbnb style).

To do that, run these commands, which are the run scripts we have set up in package.json:

```
$ yarn format
$ yarn lint
$ yarn test
```

Tip   If you get any Lint errors and warnings, you can run $ `yarn lint --fix` to automatically fix them as well as adjust the `.eslintrc` file, if needed.

You can compare your results with mine, as shown in Figure 4-5.

```
✦ Done in 1.37s.
eli@Elis-MacBook exercise-4-1 % yarn lint
yarn run v1.22.10
$ eslint --ext .js,.jsx,.ts,.tsx ./
✦ Done in 6.77s.
eli@Elis-MacBook exercise-4-1 % yarn test
yarn run v1.22.10
$ react-scripts test
 PASS  src/AppRouter.test.tsx
 PASS  src/App.test.tsx
 PASS  src/layout/Footer/Footer.test.tsx


Test Suites: 3 passed, 3 total
Tests:       3 passed, 3 total
Snapshots:   0 total
Time:        5.367s
Ran all test suites related to changed files.
```

Figure 4-5. *Format, lint, and test results*

Note   In the next chapters of this book, we will get more detailed into tests and how to set up the automated development and deployment process as well as optimize your app. Here I wanted to at least show you these tasks that I highly recommend you do every time you code to ensure your code quality.

Similarly, to create our Header layout component, run the following command to generate the component files:

```
$ npx generate-react-cli component Header --type=layout
```

If you open the template file, you can see it's set as React.PureComponent. Add the Hooter and Footer components to the render JSX output.

```
import React from 'react'
import './Header.scss'

export default class Header extends React.PureComponent<IHeaderProps,
IHeaderState> {
  constructor(props: IHeaderProps) {
    super(props)
    this.state = {}
  }

  render() {
    return Header
  }
}

interface IHeaderProps {
  // TODO
}

interface IHeaderState {
  // TODO
}
```

In our app, I am including different pages that are common for a site that sells digital content such as for contacts, books, courses, coaching services, and others. You can change these pages if you like; these are just suggestions.

```
$ npx generate-react-cli component HomePage --type=page
$ npx generate-react-cli component ContactPage --type=page
$ npx generate-react-cli component BooksPage --type=page
$ npx generate-react-cli component BuildSiteCoursePage --type=page
$ npx generate-react-cli component YouBuildMySitePage --type=page
$ npx generate-react-cli component CoachingHourlyPage --type=page
$ npx generate-react-cli component CoachingPackagePage --type=page
$ npx generate-react-cli component MembersPage --type=page
$ npx generate-react-cli component LoginPage --type=page
$ npx generate-react-cli component ArticlesPage --type=page
$ npx generate-react-cli component NotFoundPage --type=page
```

For sanity, run Lint and test it. You should be getting the following if you followed all the steps so far:

```
Test Suites: 15 passed, 15 total, and lint pass results
```

Step 2: Showing views, where we create the route logic and linking

If you open the pages component, as you saw in Chapter 1, the template file example we set includes a TypeScript class component with React Router and a hook to the path's name.

We import the React Router DOM, and then using a hook, we can access the URL location of the current browser location to display the name. For example, if the URL is http://localhost:3000/home or home/, the name variable would be home.

```
import { RouteComponentProps } from 'react-router-dom'

this.state = {
  name: this.props.history.location.pathname.substring(
    1,
    this.props.history.location.pathname.length
  ).replace('/', '')
}
```

`react-route` in this template class extracts the page name from the history API on `react-route`, using the hooks set up by the `react-route` API.

Notice that on the interface class of the template, the interface needed to extend `RouteComponentProps` for `this.props.history` to work. The other thing that is necessary is for the parent component to wrap this subcomponent in a `<Router>` tag for the hook to work.

We have created the pages, and we will be linking to these pages with a drawer component and menus. In this section, we will include all the pages we created and set up the page layout with a header and a footer.

To do all of this, we will create a subcomponent that we can include in our main `index.tsx` component.

We could just write all this code in `index.tsx`, but our code will be more readable, easier to test, and maintainable if we split this code into subcomponents.

That is why we already have a subcomponent in our template project called `src/AppRouter.tsx`. We can refactor the code to include imports to React and React Router as well as all the components pages. So, we will be using the following:

```tsx
// src/AppRouter.tsx

import React from 'react'
import { BrowserRouter as Router, Redirect, Route, Switch } from 'react-router-dom'
import App from './App'
import Home from './pages/HomePage/HomePage'
import Contact from './pages/ContactPage/ContactPage'
import Books from './pages/BooksPage/BooksPage'
import BuildSiteCourse from './pages/BuildSiteCoursePage/BuildSiteCoursePage'
import YouBuildMySite from './pages/YouBuildMySitePage/YouBuildMySitePage'
import CoachingHourly from './pages/CoachingHourlyPage/CoachingHourlyPage'
import CoachingPackage from './pages/CoachingPackagePage/CoachingPackagePage'
import Members from './pages/MembersPage/MembersPage'
import Login from './pages/LoginPage/LoginPage'
import Articles from './pages/ArticlesPage/ArticlesPage'
```

```
import NotFound from './pages/NotFoundPage/NotFoundPage'
import Footer from "./layout/Footer/Footer";
import Header from "./layout/Header/Header";
```

For the function `return` part, we need to wrap each component inside the Router tag to have access to the Router hooks. The `Header` and `Footer` components always will show up on a page, while the content will change.

To achieve that, each content page is set as a route with an exact path, as shown here:

```
function AppRouter() {
  return (
    <Router>
      <Header />
      <Switch>
        <Route exact path="/" component={App} />
<Route exact path="/Home" component={Home} />
<Route exact path="/contact" component={Contact} />
<Route exact path="/Books" component={Books} />
<Route exact path="/BuildSiteCourse" component={BuildSiteCourse} />
<Route exact path="/YouBuildMySite" component={YouBuildMySite} />
<Route exact path="/CoachingHourly" component={CoachingHourly} />
<Route exact path="/CoachingPackage" component={CoachingPackage} />
<Route exact path="/Members" component={Members} />
<Route exact path="/Login" component={Login} />
<Route exact path="/Articles" component={Articles} />
        <Route path="/404" component={NotFound} />
        <Redirect to="/404" />
      </Switch>
      <Footer />
    </Router>
  )
}
export default AppRouter
```

Notice that we have a `Redirect` tag to a 404 `NotFound` component. We will be using that component in case the user tries to go to a page that doesn't exist.

Next, notice that our project includes the AppRouter subcomponent in index.tsx already, so we don't need to do anything. I just wanted to point it out to you.

```
ReactDOM.render(<AppRouter />, document.getElementById('root'))
```

At this state, the final result should look like Figure 4-6.

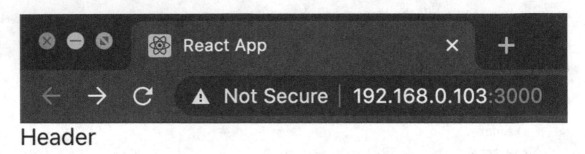

Header

App page

Footer

Figure 4-6. *Final results*

At this point, we don't have a menu to navigate between pages; however, if you change the URL of the browser address bar to one of the pages we set in our router, for instance if we navigate to http://localhost:300/Home, we will see the screen in Figure 4-7.

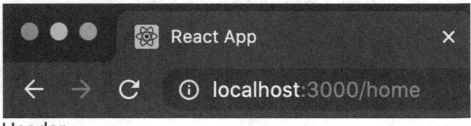

Header
home Component
Footer

Figure 4-7. *Final results for home page*

In this exercise, you learned about React Router. We sectioned our app into header, footer, and content sections. We generated subcomponents, and then we created a Router App subcomponent to create structure and be able to use the React Router APIs.

In the next section of this chapter, we will learn about Material-UI CSS framework so we can speed up development and create menus and a drawer that we can then link to the subcomponent pages we created.

Integrate the Material-UI CSS Framework

So far, you have learned about React and the DOM and what's happening behind the scenes. You even learned how to create simple and complex components as well as use React Router.

Now we need to link our pages. We could start building our own custom components; however, to speed up development, a common practice is to use a CSS framework.

In this section of this chapter, we will be building common elements that are needed in most websites.

To create a top menu with a drawer, we will be getting help from the Material-UI CSS framework.

The complete code of this exercise can be downloaded from here:

```
https://github.com/Apress/react-and-libraries/exercise-4-2
```

Why Do We Need a CSS Framework?

A CSS framework (or CSS library) brings a more standardized practice to your development. Using a CSS framework, we can speed up our development effort versus using just plain old CSS (or other style sheets), as it allows us to use predefined elements. Yes, we could create all these custom components from scratch, style them, and test them on all devices and even legacy browsers, but most of the time it isn't worth the effort. We are not looking here to reinvent the wheel. Instead, we can just use predefined elements.

Also, keep in mind that you can still use style sheets in your existing project, so it's not really that we are giving up style sheets or other styling options. A framework just offers additions.

Now, when it comes to CSS frameworks, there are a few popular options to choose from. The main ones used in React projects (based on GitHub stars) are as follows:

- *Bootstrap*: 143,000 stars

- *Material-UI*: 60,000 stars

- *Bulma*: 40,000 stars

- *Semantic UI*: 48.3,000 stars

There are also other great frameworks such as Tailwind, Picnic CSS, and PaperCSS as well as many others all suited to solving different challenges.

Although Bootstrap is the most popular framework, I believe that Material-UI is a better choice. Keep in mind that Bootstrap can be used with Material-UI, so we are not limited to using just one framework here.

The Material-UI framework (`https://material-ui.com/`) is based on Facebook's React framework and integrates well with React. Being built by the Facebook team is a big deal because we want to ensure that our code won't break when we upgrade our React project to future React versions. The GitHub page of Material-UI is here:

`https://github.com/mui-org/material-ui`

Note   The Material-UI project contains components that are made according to the Material-UI guidelines and that follow the Material-UI design principles.

How Can We Integrate Material-UI into Our ReactJS Project?

The functionality we will add will be a drawer menu that you can open with the links as well as a header top with a link that will collapse for small screen sizes.

Yes, we could use the same `Header` component we created in the previous exercise; however, this code would be complex and hard to test as well as maintain.

Because of that, it's better to break the `Header` component into subcomponents. I broke down the `Header` component into four subcomponents. Take a look at Figure 4-8.

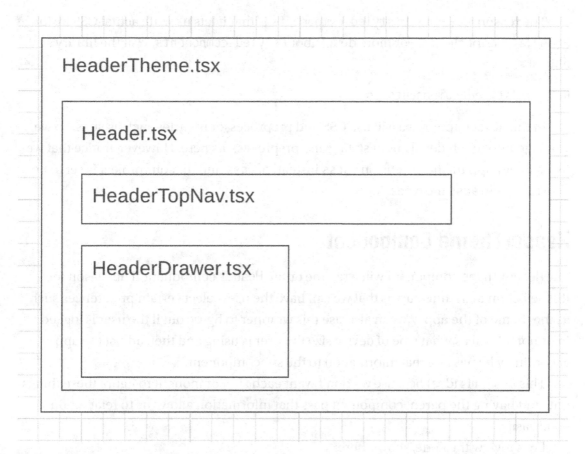

Figure 4-8. *Header component wireframes*

You can see this site out in the wild here: https://elielrom.com.

Let's Get Started

In terms of the libraries needed for Material-UI in Chapter 1, we already installed the libraries on top of the vanilla flavor of CRA, so we are ready to get started without any installation of any libraries.

Let's just review what we installed. We installed the Material-UI core, icons, and styled components in Chapter 1, and it's part of our starter project already. Feel free to visit that chapter if you want to review the libraries.

The reason we are using `styled-components` is that it lets us write actual CSS inside of our JavaScript classes. For more detail about `styled-components`, visit the library's official site here:

`https://styled-components.com/`

In the next chapters, we will use CSS and preprocessor libraries such as `scss`, so we won't go into much detail about styling and preprocessors here. However, notice that we using in our app the file extension `.scss` instead of `.css` and that our project is set to be able to handle `scss` file types.

HeaderTheme Component

The `HeaderTheme` component will wrap the entire `Header` component. The reason for this selection of architecture is that we can have the user select certain preferences such as the theme of the app. We can also use this wrapper to figure out if the user is logged in or not as well as what type of device size the user is using and then adjust the app accordingly by passing that information to the subcomponent.

This design is ideal because we don't want each subcomponent to figure these things out, and having the parent component pass that information allows us to refactor our code easily.

Let's review the code, shown here:

```
// src/layout/Header/HeaderTheme.tsx

import React, { FunctionComponent } from 'react'
import AppBar from '@material-ui/core/AppBar/AppBar'
import { useMediaQuery } from '@material-ui/core'
import HeaderComponent from './Header'

function appBarBackgroundStyle() {
  return {
    background: '000000',
  }
}
```

```
export const HeaderTheme: FunctionComponent = () => {
  const smallBreakPoint = useMediaQuery('(min-width: 0px) and (max-width:
  1100px)')
  return (
    <AppBar position="fixed" style={appBarBackgroundStyle()}>
      <HeaderComponent smallBreakPoint={smallBreakPoint} />
    </AppBar>
  )
}
```

Notice that I am using useMediaQuery from @material-ui/core to figure if we need to implement any logic for the small screen. The breaking point (smallBreakPoint) is set to a 1,100-pixel resolution, but this can be adjusted to a different value.

Then we use the AppBar component (https://material-ui.com/components/app-bar/) from Material-UI to wrap our component in a neat bar, and inside that we have our HeaderComponent where we pass the smallBreakPoint as a prop. The AppBar is ideal for displaying information and actions relating to the current screen.

We set our AppBar color to white using a function, and we can adjust the theme to a different color, from even the parent component.

Header Subcomponent

The Header subcomponent will wrap these two subcomponents:

- HeaderTopNav

- HeaderDrawer

```
// src/layout/Header/Header.tsx
import HeaderDrawer from './HeaderDrawer'
import HeaderTopNav from './HeaderTopNav'
```

On the code level, the import statements include the components we will be using as well as the Material-UI component. We will be using the Toolbar, Box, and Button components.

You can learn more about these Material-UI components at https://material-ui.com/.

```
import Toolbar from '@material-ui/core/Toolbar'
import Box from '@material-ui/core/Box'
import Button from '@material-ui/core/Button'
```

Import a style file and a font we will be using.

```
import './Header.scss'
```

There are few ways we can import the font; an easy way is to use Yarn.

```
$ yarn add fontsource-open-sans
import 'fontsource-open-sans'
```

We will import React and the style SCSS.

```
import React from 'react'
import './Header.scss'
```

For navigating the different pages, we can use the router link component. React Router supports Link and NavLink, so we can link our components to the different pages.

```
// router
import { Link } from 'react-router-dom'
```

In the class definition, we don't need any hooks, so it is better to use PureComponent as it gives us the best performance.

We don't need to store any state at this point, and for the prop we need to set smallBreakPoint that we are passing from the parent component.

```
interface IHeaderProps {
  smallBreakPoint: boolean
}

interface IHeaderState {
  // TODO
}
```

```
export default class Header extends React.PureComponent<IHeaderProps,
IHeaderState> {
  constructor(props: IHeaderProps) {
    super(props)
    this.state = {}
  }
}
```

Inside the render method we can define our components. We will wrap everything in a `Toolbar` component and set a box component with `position`, because we want to collapse the navigator with the media queries we set, and we want to ensure the top elements stay on the screen.

Take a look at the Material-UI elements we will be using:

```
<Toolbar>
    <Box>
            Logo
    </Box>
    <Box>
            <Nav />
    </Box>
     <Box>
            <Drawer />
    </Box>
</ToolBar>
```

Notice that I am using the material box (`https://material-ui.com/components/box/`), which suits our needs as we can set the layer. The `flexGrow` component keeps our navigation items on the same level (`https://material-ui.com/system/flexbox/#flex-grow`).

Let's implement it, as follows:

```
render() {
  return (
    <Toolbar>
      <div style={{ width: '100%' }}>
```

The button from Material-UI already includes properties that we can use to navigate to our pages. For example, when clicking our logo, we want to navigate back to the home page, /.

```
            <Box display="flex" p={1}>
              <Box p={1} flexGrow={1}>
                <Button component={Link} to="/">
                  ELI ELAD ELROM
                </Button>
              </Box>
```

Next, we can use inline logic and either display the HeaderTopNav or collapse it by showing the Nav component.

```
              <Box p={1}>
                {this.props.smallBreakPoint ? (
                  <nav />
                ) : (
                  <HeaderTopNav />
                )}
              </Box>
              <Box p={1}>
                <div
                  style={{
                    position: 'absolute',
                    right: '0.5rem',
                  }}
                >
```

The drawer code could have been places here; however, it would make the code harder to read, so I broke that down the code to another sub-component, named: HeaderDrawer.

```
                  <HeaderDrawer />
                </div>
              </Box>
            </Box>
          </div>
        </Toolbar>
      )
    }
  }
```

HeaderTopNav Subcomponent

The HeaderTopNav subcomponent will show the links for the pages in case the screen is big enough or will show just the drawer icon to open the drawer in cases where the user screen is small. We will be using Material-UI's Button and MenuItem.

For linking the pages, we will be using both Link and NavLink, as well as the styled-components library we introduced in Chapter 1 that allows us to create a styles object inside of our component.

```
// src/layout/Header/HeaderTopNav.tsx

import React from 'react'
import Button from '@material-ui/core/Button'
import Menu from '@material-ui/core/Menu'
import { Link, NavLink } from 'react-router-dom'
import MenuItem from '@material-ui/core/MenuItem'
import styled from 'styled-components'
```

Material-UI comes with predefined icons that we can use. So, we will import them as well.

You can view all the different Material-UI icons here: https://material-ui.com/components/material-icons/.

We will use the GitHub icon, and the IconButton API (https://material-ui.com/api/icon-button/)

```
import IconButton from '@material-ui/core/IconButton'
import GitHubIcon from '@material-ui/icons/GitHub'
```

Next, we will set up some CSS styles using the styled-components library for the hover state of our links. I am using a transition of 0.5 seconds to change the color to gray on hover.

```
const DetectHover = styled.div`
  transition-duration: 0.5s;
  :hover {
    color: grey;
    span {
      opacity: 1;
    }
  }
}
`
```

We are also going to take into account media queries. Media queries in CSS allow us to place specific logic for different screen sizes. In our case, we want to collapse the navigation links if the screen is too small because we have many pages and the links won't fit into a small screen. That's why we will be using a drawer that will open with the same links. I am setting the style for the navigation to `block` to hide the navigation on small screens up to 400px and show it on larger screens up to 1100px.

For `Nav`, we don't need any style; we just set the component.

```
const Nav = styled.nav``
```

We need to keep track of a few things, which we can set as the state of the app.

For instance, we need the location of the component anchor that we can use to align our drop-down menus as well as flags to indicate whether a drop-down menu is open.

To do that, let's set `anchorElement` that we will be using to keep track of the location of the anchor.

```
let anchorElement: HTMLButtonElement
```

For the flags, we have three flags because we will set three drop-down menus, one for each parent menu (the Build My Site, Coaching, and Resources parent menu items).

```
interface IHTNState {
  menuBuildItem1Flag: boolean
  menuBuildItem2Flag: boolean
  menuBuildItem3Flag: boolean
}
```

At this point, we don't need `props`, but we will define it anyway as our code is likely to change and there's a good chance it will need `props` in the future.

```
interface IHTNavProps {
  // TODO
}
```

As for the actual component, we are creating a React TypeScript class component, and we pass the `props` and `state` interfaces that defines and sets the initial state of the app, setting all the flags to false as all the menus will be closed.

```
export default class HeaderTopNav extends React.PureComponent<IHTNavProps,
IHTNState> {
  constructor(props: IHTNavProps) {
    super(props)
    this.state = {
      menuBuildItem1Flag: false,
      menuBuildItem2Flag: false,
      menuBuildItem3Flag: false,
    }
  }
```

Next, we need a mechanism to handle cases where the user clicks a top link and opens a drop-down menu with more links. We can do that with a mouse event handler and a switch. Inside the switch case, we will set the flag to open the drop-down menu as well as set the anchor so that drop-down menu is aligned to the correct component.

We are giving each switch case a number so we know who called this handler (which drop-down was clicked).

Next, we need three more handlers.

- When a user clicks a menu item, we want to close the toggle menu as expected after a menu item is selected.

- When the user clicks the menu close icon button, we want to close all the submenu drop-down menus.

- We want to have a drawer icon with a toggle to open and close the drawer.

Take a look:

```
handleMenuOpen = (event: React.MouseEvent, item: string) => {
  anchorElement = (event as React.MouseEvent<HTMLButtonElement>).
  currentTarget
  switch (item) {
    case '1':
      this.setState((prevState) => {
        return {
          ...prevState,
          menuBuildItem1Flag: true,
        }
      })
```

```
          break
        case '2':
          this.setState((prevState) => {
            return {
              ...prevState,
              menuBuildItem2Flag: true,
            }
          })
          break
        case '3':
          this.setState((prevState) => {
            return {
              ...prevState,
              menuBuildItem3Flag: true,
            }
          })
          break
      }
  }

  handleMenuClose = () => {
    this.setState((prevState) => {
      return {
        ...prevState,
        menuBuildItem1Flag: false,
        menuBuildItem2Flag: false,
        menuBuildItem3Flag: false,
      }
    })
  }

  render() {
    return (
      <Nav>
        <Button onClick={(event) => this.handleMenuOpen(event, '1')}>Build
        My Website</Button>
```

```
<Menu id="menu-appbar1" anchorEl={anchorElement} open={this.state.
menuBuildItem1Flag} onClose={this.handleMenuClose}>
```

Each drop-down menu parent item has a few links to other pages. We can set them by creating an array and then map that array to a NavLink React Router component that will navigate to the link we want.

The array with the map allowed us to create a loop with all the NavLink components instead of creating several NavLink components. That can come handy especially when you have an undefined number of items, or you want to connect the data to a back-end source.

```
{[
    { name: 'Build My Own Site', url: '/BuildSiteCourse' },
    { name: 'You Build My Site', url: '/YouBuildMySite' },
].map((itemObject, index) => (
    <NavLink exact to={itemObject.url} className="NavLinkItem"
    key={itemObject.name}>
        <MenuItem onClick={this.handleMenuClose}>{itemObject.name}</
        MenuItem>
    </NavLink>
))}
</Menu>
```

Each navigation item is mapped to an event handler to open the drop-down menu. We set the switch with a number to each menu item.

```
<Button onClick={(event) => this.handleMenuOpen(event, '2')}>
Coaching</Button>
<Menu id="menu-appbar2" anchorEl={anchorElement}
getContentAnchorEl={null} open={this.state.menuBuildItem2Flag}
onClose={this.handleMenuClose}>
    {[
        { name: 'Hourly', url: '/CoachingHourly' },
        { name: 'Packages', url: '/CoachingPackage' },
    ].map((itemObject, index) => (
        <NavLink exact to={itemObject.url} className="NavLinkItem"
        key={itemObject.name}>
```

```
        <MenuItem onClick={this.handleMenuClose}>{itemObject.name}
        /MenuItem>
      </NavLink>
    ))}
  </Menu>
```

We can repeat the same process for each parent button.

```
<Button onClick={(event) => this.handleMenuOpen(event, '3')}>
Resources</Button>
<Menu id="menu-appbar2" anchorEl={anchorElement} getContent
AnchorEl={null} open={this.state.menuBuildItem3Flag} onClose={this.
handleMenuClose}>
  {[
    { name: 'Books', url: '/Books' },
    { name: 'Articles', url: '/Articles' },
  ].map((itemObject, index) => (
    <NavLink exact to={itemObject.url} className="NavLinkItem"
    key={itemObject.name}>
      <MenuItem onClick={this.handleMenuClose}>{itemObject.name}
      </MenuItem>
    </NavLink>
  ))}
</Menu>
```

If we have a navigation item without children, we can just use the button and bind the Link in the component property. Take, for example, the contact link shown here:

```
<Button component={Link} to="/Contact">
  Contact
</Button>
```

We could also use the IconButton from Material-UI and use href. This behaves in JSX just as you expect in HTML and references an external URL.

> **Tip** The reason we use `Link` and not `href` is that we don't want our page refreshed, which will slow down the process of flipping through pages with this setup on an SPA.

```
<a href="https://github.com/EliEladElrom/react-tutorials"
target="_blank" rel="noopener noreferrer">
  <IconButton>
    <DetectHover>
      <GitHubIcon fontSize="large" />
    </DetectHover>
  </IconButton>
</a>
    </Nav>
  )
 }
}
```

React Event Handlers

If you are coming from the JavaScript world, you know about the event handlers that are used. React uses JSX and has its own event system.

That's why we can't use the events we are used to from JS such as the handleMenuOpen method called `MouseEvent`.

This code is wrong and will produce Lint errors:

```
onClickHandler = (e: MouseEventHandler)
```

> **Tip** We need to use `React.MouseEvent`; otherwise, we will get an error or just we won't be able to access methods. Generally speaking, most events are mapped with the same name as JavaScript used in HTML pages.

Luckily, React typings give you the proper equivalent of each event you might be familiar with from the standard DOM.

We can either use `React.MouseEvent` or import the `MouseEvent` typing from the React module.

Here is an example:

```
const onClickHandler = (e: React.MouseEvent) => {
  e.preventDefault()
}<Button type="submit" onClick={onClickHandler}>
```

HeaderDrawer Subcomponent

The `HeaderDrawer` subcomponent will provide a menu icon for the `HeaderTopNav` subcomponent plus the actual drawer that will include the same navigation links.

The reason we need both the `HeaderTopNav` and `HeaderDrawer` subcomponents is because when the user's screen is smaller than 1,100 pixels and we can fit all the navigation links, the user should still be able to use the menu item and use the drawer to navigate between pages. This is a user interface (UI) design that is common on mobile devices.

On the coding level, we will import the Material-UI components that we will be using, as well as `styled-components` and the `NavLink` and Material-UI icons.

```
// src/layout/Header/HeaderDrawer.tsx

import Drawer from '@material-ui/core/Drawer'
import Divider from '@material-ui/core/Divider'
import List from '@material-ui/core/List'
import { NavLink } from 'react-router-dom'
import ListItem from '@material-ui/core/ListItem'
import ListItemIcon from '@material-ui/core/ListItemIcon'
import WebIcon from '@material-ui/icons/Web'
import WebAssetIcon from '@material-ui/icons/WebAsset'
import ListItemText from '@material-ui/core/ListItemText'
import SupervisorAccountIcon from '@material-ui/icons/SupervisorAccount'
import SupervisedUserCircleIcon from '@material-ui/icons/
SupervisedUserCircle'
```

```
import MenuBookIcon from '@material-ui/icons/MenuBook'
import LibraryBooksIcon from '@material-ui/icons/LibraryBooks'
import MailIcon from '@material-ui/icons/Mail'
import IconButton from '@material-ui/core/IconButton'
import React from 'react'
import MenuIcon from '@material-ui/icons/Menu'
import styled from 'styled-components'
```

We will be using `styled-components` to set the style for the hover state.

```
const DetectHover = styled.div`
  transition-duration: 0.5s;
  :hover {
    color: grey;
    span {
      opacity: 1;
    }
  }
`
```

The interfaces for `props` and `state` will include a state of the `toggleMenuFlag` to indicate whether the drawer is open.

```
interface IHDProps {
  // TODO
}

interface IHDState {
  toggleMenuFlag: boolean
}
```

The default state is that the drawer is closed, and we need to bind the `handleToggle` method we will create so that it will be available in the render phase.

```
export default class HeaderDrawer extends React.PureComponent<IHDProps,
IHDState> {
  constructor(props: IHDProps) {
    super(props)
```

```
  this.state = {
    toggleMenuFlag: false,
  }
  this.handleToggle = this.handleToggle.bind(this)
}
```

Once a list item is clicked, we set the state of our subcomponent to false.

Note   The ...prevState maintains the previous state. We don't need it here
because we have only one variable in the state, but it's a good habit to always
write the code this way in case we add another state variable.

```
handleListItemClick = () => {
  this.setState((prevState) => {
    return {
      ...prevState,
      toggleMenuFlag: false,
    }
  })
}
```

On toggle, we just switch the state, and since the state is binding, it will close or open
the drawer.

```
handleToggle() {
  this.setState((prevState) => {
    const newState = !prevState.toggleMenuFlag
    return {
      ...prevState,
      toggleMenuFlag: newState,
    }
  })
}

render() {
  return (
```

As for the drawer, we need an icon button that will open and close (toggle) our drawer with an event handler to the `handleToggle` method we created.

The toggle icon on the click event is binded to `handleToggle`, which will switch the state.

```
<IconButton style={{ color: 'black' }} onClick={this.handleToggle}>
  <DetectHover>
    <MenuIcon fontSize="large" />
  </DetectHover>
</IconButton>
```

For the drawer itself, we will create a list of links. We will create them with the `List` Material-UI component and again use an array with a map to create several `NavLink` React Router components and link to these pages. I am only showing the first `List`, but the code in GitHub includes all of them. It's the same process. The `List` tag could also be wrapped in another array to avoid copying and pasting the same piece of code.

```
<Drawer anchor="left" open={this.state.toggleMenuFlag}
onClose={this.handleToggle}>
  <Divider />

  <List>
    {[
      { name: 'Build My Site', url: '/BuildSiteCourse' },
      { name: 'We Build Site', url: '/YouBuildMySite' },
    ].map((itemObject, index) => (
      <NavLink to={itemObject.url} className="NavLinkItem"
      key={itemObject.url} activeClassName="NavLinkItem-selected">
        <ListItem button key={itemObject.name} onClick={this.
        handleListItemClick}>
          <ListItemIcon>{index % 2 === 0 ? <WebIcon /> :
          <WebAssetIcon />}</ListItemIcon>
          <ListItemText primary={itemObject.name} />
        </ListItem>
      </NavLink>
    ))}
  </List>
  <Divider />
```

```
    )
  }
}
```

Header.scss

Lastly, in our `Header.scss` style file, we are not using any specific `scss` style feature. This is plain CSS. We set our font family and styles for `NavLinkItem` and `NavLinkItem-selected`. Take a look:

```
.Header {
  font-family: 'Open Sans', sans-serif;
  font-weight: 700;
}

.NavLinkItem {
  color: black;
  max-width: 360px;
  text-decoration: none;
}

.NavLinkItem-selected nav {
  background-image: linear-gradient(120deg, #a1c4fd 0%, #c2e9fb 100%);
}
```

Footer.scss

As for the `Footer` component, I want to align it relative 500px from the top and 20px padding from the left. This will do for now as our pages are empty.

```
.Footer {
  position: relative;
  padding-top: 500px;
  padding-left: 20px;
}
```

Pages scss

For the pages to align below the menu, we can either place a general CSS style or just set each page with padding so that they're aligned nicely.

```
.ArticlesPage {
  padding-top: 120px;
  padding-left: 20px;
}
```

AppRouter.tsx

Lastly, we need to switch the Header subcomponent to the HeaderTheme component we created.

```
function AppRouter() {
  return (
    <Router>
      <HeaderTheme />
      ...
    </Router>
  )
}
```

Figure 4-1 already showed the final result. If we toggle our drawer icon, we can see that the drawer opens up to the left with our drawer links. See Figure 4-9.

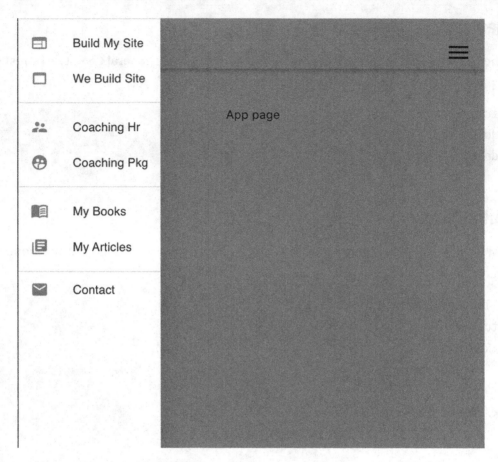

Figure 4-9. *Final result of drawer exercise*

You can downland the complete code of this exercise from here:

https://github.com/Apress/react-and-libraries/exercise-4-2

Summary

In this chapter, we completed two exercises while learning about the React Router and Material-UI frameworks. We also learned more about creating realistic components.

We started building an app that included a header, footer, and content area and created a top menu with navigation links with a drop-down menu and a drawer. We also adjusted the content with media queries to improve our navigation and content on different screen sizes.

In the next section, we will continue building our app, while starting to integrate state management, which will allow us to manage our state and communicate between different components without breaking the React architecture.

CHAPTER 5

State Management

In the previous chapter, we built a header component with a menu and a drawer with the help of Material-UI. We also connected the pages using React Router. We learned about React components and how to pass information from parent components down to a child component using `props`. We also learned about the component lifecycle and the component state. However, if we want to implement other common elements in most apps, such as store user's information, cart, or any other data-based state that multiple components or subcomponents may need, we need help from other libraries to build quality software.

In this chapter, I will introduce you to an important library that is a must-have in your React arsenal toolbox. It's a state management library, which can help ensure you write bullet-proof code that won't get messy over time, be hard to debug and test, and result in a nightmare to refactor and add new features.

Specifically, you will learn about the state management architecture introduced by Facebook, called Flux, and then you will learn about the most popular state management at the time of writing, called Redux. Lastly, you will graduate to using Redux Toolkit. In the process, we will implement Redux Toolkit in the app we started building in the previous chapter.

When you complete this chapter, you will have created the final results that you can see in Figure 5-1.

© Elad Elrom 2021
E. Elrom, *React and Libraries*, https://doi.org/10.1007/978-1-4842-6696-0_5

Figure 5-1. *Final results including a footer with a theme*

If you look at our footer, you will notice that it has special powers. Specifically, the user will be able to adjust the theme of our app from light to dark, or vice versa. The app color scheme will change accordingly, including the font colors on menus. Figure 5-2 shows the result of changing to the dark theme.

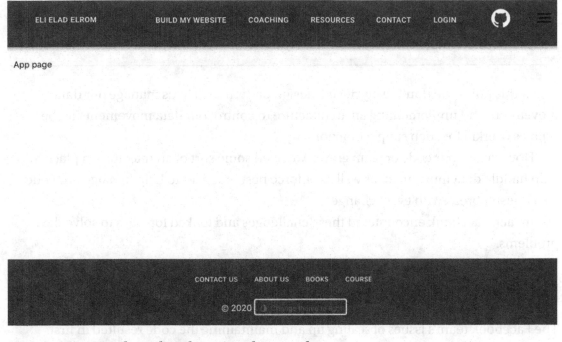

Figure 5-2. *Final results: changing the app theme*

State Management Architecture

When the user clicks the "Change theme" button (see the footer in Figure 5-2), we want to change the appearance of our app and all of our components and subcomponents accordingly. To achieve this, we can store the user's data in a user preference object.

The user preference of the decided theme color is the data, or in other words the "state" of our app, and we want that data to flow to our components and subcomponents in one direction, meaning the components don't need to send data back. They just need to receive a message saying that the data has changed. Once our view receives a message that the data has changed, we make changes in our components and subcomponents (our view).

Why Do We Need a State Management Architecture?

That change by itself sounds insignificant and easy to implement and manage. So, why do we need a state management library to achieve this task?

In layman's terms, state management helps organize data and user interaction of your app until the user's session ends. It also helps ensure your code doesn't get messy as more features are added. It makes life easier when it comes to testing and ensures the code is not dependent on a specific development and can scale up.

Note   State management is a method to maintain the state of our app until our user's session ends.

At this point, we don't really need a design pattern to help us manage our data movement, and implementing an architecture to control our data movement can be seen as overkill for such simple functionality.

However, as our code or team grows, we need some sort of architecture in place to help handle data movement, as well as enforce best practices to help manage our code so it doesn't break with every change.

In fact, Facebook encountered these challenges and looked for ways to solve these problems.

Facebook Solution: Flux

The Facebook team's issues of scaling up and maintaining the code resulted in first trying what was out there. They first implemented the Model-View-Controller (MVC) pattern; however, they found the architecture pattern caused issues as more and more features were added. A portion of the code was hard to maintain, and the code broke constantly.

What Is MVC and What Does It Solve?

In a complex app, it's advised to separate concerns (think of separating your clothes for laundry).

- *Model*: The model is the app data.

- *View*: The view is the front-end presentation layer. This is an implementation that should not be updated directly; ideally it should be updated by a reflection design pattern. Reflection means that once the data is changed, the view is changed "magically."

- *Controller*: This is the glow that binds the model and the view.

The Facebook team tried using MVC, but they experienced issues with the data flow that can cause a loop, which in turn can crash an app as it will become a memory leak (cascading effects by nested updates).

The Facebook team solved these issues by coming up with an architecture they called Flux and more recently with an experiment library called Recoil (which we will talk about and implement in the next chapter).

Note   Flux is an application architecture for building user interfaces. See `https://facebook.github.io/flux/`.

"Flux is the application architecture that Facebook uses for building client-side web applications. It complements React's composable view components by utilizing a unidirectional data flow. It's more of a pattern rather than a formal framework"

—https://facebook.github.io/flux/docs/in-depth-overview

Flux is a data management pattern used by the Facebook team. Flux can be broken down to three ingredients.

- *Dispatcher*: The central hub holds the callbacks that are registered with the dispatcher and sends data to the stores. The data is sent via actions.

- *Stores*: The stores, as the name suggests, hold the data. In other words, they hold the state of the app.

- *Views (our components)*: The view is the front-end implementation. Our components should aim at being as pure and stateless as possible and be updated automatically once the state changes (by using a reflection).

The data will flow through the app like so:

Action ➤ *Dispatcher* ➤ *Store* ➤ *View*

Using this type of architecture allows us to know where data is coming from and where it's going. That allows any developer to "jump in" and start coding, as they can watch the actions and figure things out fast, as well as help debug, test, and implement new features easily.

For example, say we want to change the state of our app. A user interaction on the view can invoke an action that will trigger a dispatcher callback, which will then update the state of our app in the store, and eventually these changes will be used in our view components. See Figure 5-3.

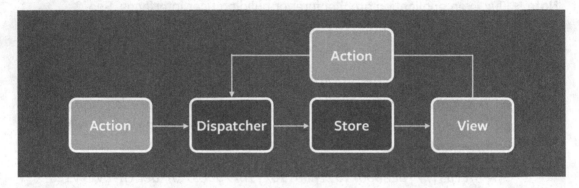

Figure 5-3. *Flux data flow (credit: https://facebook.github.io/flux/docs/ in-depth-overview)*

Flux, Facebook's proposed application architecture, aims to achieve its goals by doing the following:

- *Explicit data*: Use explicit data instead of derived data (explicit data is the original data unalerted).

- *Separate concerns*: Separate the data from the view just like in MVC.

- *Avoid cascading effects*: Prevent nested updates (that can happen in the MVC pattern), which is the biggest difference between Flux and MVC.

You can learn more about Facebook Flux mindset by watching this video: `https:// youtu.be/nYkdrAPrdcw`.

I have worked with many MVC-based applications small and large, and some were complex enterprise-level applications built on MVC. I have to somewhat disagree with the Facebook team. By enforcing good habits, MVC-based apps can work seamlessly. With that being said, there is a lot of boilerplate code involved in many of the MVC framework implementations out there, and code review is often necessary to enforce good habits and to maintain a separation of concerns.

Facebook's Flux architecture does simplify the process of separating concerns and is a fresh alternative to state management, while keeping less boilerplate code and our components loosely coupled.

Vanilla Redux

There are many state management libraries to choose from. Here are a few:

- Facebook's Flux (`https://github.com/facebook/flux`)

- Facebook's Recoil (`https://recoiljs.org/`)

- Flux-react (`https://github.com/christianalfoni/flux-react`)

- Reflux (`https://github.com/reflux/refluxjs`)

In fact, state management is significant enough that it can be the reason to pick one framework over another. Remember, React is not a framework but a library, and unlike other frameworks that compete with React like Angular or Vue, there is no separation of concerns out of the box.

At the time of writing, the most popular state management tool that implements Flux is Redux. The Facebook team also came up with its own state management library called Recoil (`https://recoiljs.org/`) in mid-2020. It is very promising, and I will cover it in the next chapter. However, it is still in its infancy and hasn't matured past the experimental phase as of the writing of this book.

Why Redux

As the Redux.js organization states,

> *Redux is an open-source JavaScript library for managing application state. It is most commonly used with libraries such as React or Angular for building user interfaces.*

The vanilla Redux version is unopinionated, meaning you can do as you please in terms of architecture and practices. However, the Redux team's official recommended approach is to use a separate add-on package called Redux Toolkit, which includes some opinionated defaults to help use Redux more effectively. It is the standard for using Redux with React.

Note   The vanilla flavor of Redux is not recommended, and this section is only to help you understand Redux. Redux Toolkit is easier to use and the recommended approach for most apps.

I will show you Redux first before moving on to Redux Toolkit.

It's easier to first learn Redux as it's based on the same components. You will get to Redux Toolkit soon.

How Can You Learn Redux?

To teach you Redux, I broke down the process into four steps.

1. Set up a CRA project.

2. Install Redux.

3. Create a Redux cycle: action, reducer, and store.

4. Invoke an action.

Let's get started.

You can download the code from the book's GitHub location.

```
https://github.com/Apress/react-and-libraries/tree/master/05/hello-redux
```

As always, remember to run the following if you are downloading this code from GitHub:

```
$ yarn install
$ yarn start
```

And check the app on port 3000, in other words, `http://localhost:3000/`.

Step 1: Set Up the Project

Now, let's create our project. Just as we did in the first chapter, we will create a new project based on CRA and name it `hello-redux`.

```
$ yarn create react-app hello-redux --template must-have-libraries
```

After installation is complete, ensure it's running correctly on port 3000, change the directory to `hello-redux`, and run it using the following:

```
$ yarn start
```

Next, we will install Redux with the -D flag, so it will add Redux to the `package.json` file. At the time of writing, Redux is at version ^4.0.5.

```
$ yarn add redux -D
```

The CRA MHL template project and what we installed in Chapter 2 was Redux Toolkit. That's why we need to install vanilla Redux.

Step 2: Create a Redux Cycle

Let's take an example of a simple user gesture. Let's say a user clicks a button and a data change is needed in the app. For instance, a user wants to log in to our app or log out. This means our app needs two states: with a user that is logged in and a user that is logged out.

This sounds simple and common; however, without a formalized mechanism to separate these concerns, this can turn messy quickly.

Our app may need to make data changes across the board, from changing menus to changing page information to changing a member's access and more.

Further, your app may be simple now, but as the code grows, you may add other states such as states for registered users, existing users logged in, user interaction timed out, and more.

That's where Redux can help. It can help make your app more readable and easy to refactor and maintain. Even if you don't need it now, by using Redux, you are preparing your app for future growth. Take a look at the 10,000-foot diagram of Redux in Figure 5-4.

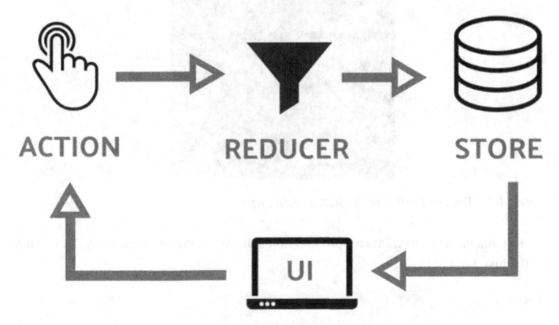

Figure 5-4. *10,000-foot diagram of Redux (credit: Medium.com)*

As you can see, it aligns neatly with the Flux architecture. Rather than this diagram explaining to you, let's just go through a login/logout state. Feel free to refer to this diagram whenever you want to better understand what's happening in the app and code. Look at the code, test it, and follow it, and it will make sense.

To start off, let's create our folder hierarchy. First, we'll create `actions`, `reducers`, and `store` folders. On a Mac, use this:

```
$ mkdir -p src/redux/actions src/redux/reducers src/redux/store
```

Note   I am using the `-p` flag. The `-p` flag creates each directory as well as the higher-level directory (`js`) that we are creating to avoid errors.

On Window Terminal for PC users, use this:

```
$ md src/redux/actions src/redux/reducers src/redux/store
```

At this point, the folder structure should look like Figure 5-5.

Figure 5-5.   *Folder structure for hello-redux app*

In Redux we need to create a store that holds our state. We will create the Redux store shortly; just hang tight.

Redux Actions

We will start with actions. Create a new file and call it `src/js/actions/MenuActions.ts`.

The store holds the state tree. Changing the state tree should be done only by emitting an action; it's a one-way direction.

An object describes what happened. In our case, we create two states, one for the user logging in and the other for the user logging out. Our reducer will have logic when the user logs in and logs out. Let's call these `showLogin` and `showLogout`.

```
// src/js/actions/MenuActions.ts

export const USER_LOGIN = 'USER_LOGIN'
export const USER_LOGOUT = 'USER_LOGOUT'

export function showLogin() {
  return { type: USER_LOGIN }
}

export function showLogout() {
  return { type: USER_LOGOUT }
}
```

Reducers

To specify how the actions transform the state tree, we write reducers. In our case, we will have a menu that gets updated on a state change. Create a new file and call it `src/js/reducers/MenuReducer.ts`.

Note   Our reducer holds the logic that controls the state of our app.

On the code level, let's create a default login state and a switch to handle the state change.

The data change will update the `is_login` from `true` to `false`. That will enable us to know if the user is logged in or not.

```
// src/js/reducers/MenuReducer.ts

import { USER_LOGIN, USER_LOGOUT } from '../actions/MenuActions'

const DEFAULT_LOGIN_STATE = {
  isLogin: false
}

export default (state = DEFAULT_LOGIN_STATE, action: { type: String }) => {
  switch (action.type) {
    case USER_LOGIN:
      return { is_login: true }
    case USER_LOGOUT:
      return { is_login: false }
    default:
      return state
  }
}
```

Unlike Redux Toolkit, which we will cover next, Redux is "unopinionated," so we are really allowed to do whatever we like here. We can design our app and put all the code in one file if that is what we want. Alternatively, we can stick to a better design by having each reducer use its own stand-alone, loosely coupled code.

What do you think? I prefer the latter.

As we build our app, we will have lots of logic, so it's better to split each logic piece into its own reducers. Since we will have lots of these reducers, what we can do is create a RootReducer object that will hold all these reducers. Go ahead and create a RootReducer.ts file with the following code:

```
// src/js/reducers/RootReducer.ts

import { combineReducers } from 'redux'
import MenuReducer from './MenuReducer'

export default combineReducers({
  MenuReducer,
})
```

In this design, we can add reducers to the root file, and the root file will serve as a table of content for our reducers.

Step 3: Redux Store

As I mentioned with the Flux architecture, the whole state of our app is meant to be stored in an object tree inside a single store. We are ready to create the store. Create a file called src/js/store/index.ts.

On the code level, create a store based on the reducers we created by just adding the root reducer, which holds all of our reducers.

```
// src/js/store/index.ts

import { createStore } from 'redux'
import rootReducer from '../reducers/RootReducer'

const index = createStore(rootReducer)

export default index
```

Step 4: Invoke an Action

Let's create the logic to handle our front-end code. I wanted to keep our example as minimalistic as possible, so let's use the window to access the DOM document. Create src/redux/store/index.ts.

The Window interface represents a window containing a DOM document. Our example is for learning only, so I am using the Window interface just to show the logic and not show it connecting to an actual component.

```
// src/redux/store/index.ts

import store from './store/index'
import { showLogin, showLogout } from './actions/MenuActions'

export interface StoreWindow extends Window {
  store: typeof store
  showLogin(): { type: string }
  showLogout(): { type: string }
}
declare let window: StoreWindow

window.store = store
window.showLogin = showLogin
window.showLogout = showLogout
```

127

Note   I am declaring `StoreWindow` because TS needs an interface. This is because TS needs types to be defined.

On the code level, what we have done is set up the store and our functions to show and hide the login state. Once we subscribe to the store's callbacks, we can use `dispatch` and see the state change.

In our case, we just use the alert to let you know the state changes, but anyone can subscribe to these events and update views.

Lastly, add our `import` statement to have our `src/index.js` run.

```
// src/index.js

import { StoreWindow } from './redux'

declare let window: StoreWindow
window.store.getState()
window.store.subscribe(() => window.alert(JSON.stringify(window.store.getState())))

window.store.dispatch(window.showLogin())
window.store.dispatch(window.showLogout())
```

In the browser, you will get two alerts as the state changes.

```
{"MenuReducer":{"is_login":true}}
{"MenuReducer":{"is_login":false}}
```

Figure 5-6 shows the final results.

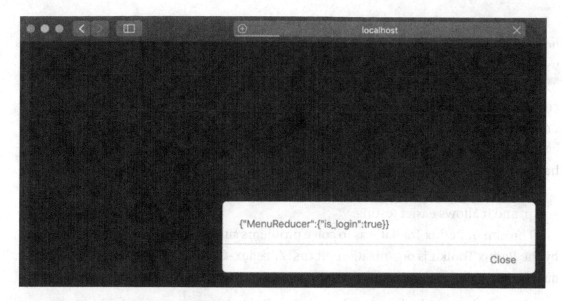

Figure 5-6. *Redux hello-world final result*

Let's Recap

We were able to quickly create Redux data movement and understand what Redux is all about. We set up our React project and installed Redux. We created a Redux cycle. Lastly, we invoked an action.

Redux Toolkit

As we saw, the original vanilla Redux flavor is a useful tool. It helps us organize the data and user interaction of our app so our code doesn't get messy.

We have the notion of a store that can hold our serialized key-value pairs and hold whatever values we want.

The Redux Toolkit architecture breaks each functionality into a feature slice, and as more and more features are added, we can then access each "slice" of data. If we think in terms of food, the Redux is a vanilla ice cream cone and then our store holds all the data or flavors.

In our Redux Toolkit, our store is more like a pizza. Our "slice" is like a slice of pizza, and all the slices make up our store. This is called the Ducks pattern ("re-dux" sounds like ducks, get it?), so each feature will be stored in a separate folder.

Redux Toolkit is opinionated, and we are encouraged to create a feature folder to hold all the different slices. The Redux toolkit includes some opinionated APIs to help us use Redux more effectively.

The Redux API consists of the following main functions: `createSlice`, `configureStore`, `createReducer`, `createAction`, `createAsyncThunk`, and `createEntityAdapter`.

The idea was to provide boilerplate tools that abstract over the setup process and handle the most common use cases and useful utilities that will let the user simplify writing code. It takes care of the middleware and DevTools without a need to do any setup, and it allows easier testing.

The aim of Redux Toolkit was to solve problems similar to the ones mentioned here by the Redux Toolkit.js organization (`https://redux-toolkit.js.org/introduction/quick-start`):

> *"Configuring a Redux store is too complicated*
>
> *- I have to add a lot of packages to get Redux to do anything useful*
>
> *- Redux requires too much boilerplate code"*

Redux Toolkit is used heavily in React enterprise-level apps, which makes it a must-have library for an advanced to expert React developer, and according to the React team, "These tools should be beneficial to all Redux users." I personally agree, but I will let you be the judge.

Redux Toolkit Under the Hood

If we get more technical, under the hood, the Redux Toolkit APIs reduce what code we need to write. By having boilerplate code, it prevents us from making common mistakes, because the code will minimize errors. For example, common mistakes can include mutating your state (changing data after creation and introducing potential bugs) or setting nonserializable data such as functions and promises inside the state (instead of handling them separately).

This is done with `redux-immutable-state-invariant` and `serializable-state-invariant-middleware`, as well as the `createAsyncThunk()` API, to handle nonserializable data asynchronous actions like interacting with your API. This goes hand in hand with functional programming (FP). As we saw in the previous chapters, functional components are one of the main building blocks of React.

FP means we are building our software with pure functions and avoiding shared state, mutable data, and side effects. FP is declarative rather than imperative, and the application state flows through pure functions. Because React is a declarative language (it does not actually manipulate the DOM itself directly), it integrates great with Redux Toolkit, because it helps enforce the declarative architecture.

Note   Declarative programming expresses the logic of a computation without describing its control flow. The imperative paradigm uses statements that change a program's state such as changing the DOM directly.

With that said, Redux Toolkit still has `getDefaultMiddleware()` if you want to create your own middleware, while utilizing the defaults. `getDefaultMiddleware()` will get called when we create the store.

The `redux-immutable-state-invariant, serializable-state-invariant-middleware` and `createAsyncThunk()` won't be called, and you will need to handle the logic yourself.

Redux Toolkit also runs the Immer library (`https://github.com/immerjs/immer`), which lets us write the code in a mutative way. We create the next immutable state tree by simply modifying the current tree. I will show it to you in the `createSlice()` code.

Really what we want is to use as many pure functional components as possible. Components without lifecycle methods require us to rely on a declarative, `props`-based approach and provide performance improvements as there will be no memory leaks anywhere.

In the purely functional approach, every call to the function produces the same result with no side effects. Does that make sense? It's just good programming practice overall.

Implementing a Theme Using the Redux Toolkit

Now that we have covered Redux Toolkit, we can start implementing logic. Let's create a preferences feature, where we can hold user-specific preferences such as app settings.

We will start where we left off in the previous chapter.

`https://github.com/Apress/react-and-libraries/04/exercise-4-2`

You can download the complete code of this chapter from the book's GitHub location.

```
https://github.com/Apress/react-and-libraries/05/exercise-5-1
```

Once you run the complete code, you can switch the theme of the app, as shown earlier in Figure 5-1 and Figure 5-2.

Model Enumeration Object: preferencesObject

Before we create our slice, let's create an enumeration file that will hold our preferences options. We can set a variable and call it ThemeEnum with two options: dark and light.

To get started, create src/model/preferencesObject.ts.

```
// src/model/preferencesObject.ts

export enum ThemeEnum {
  Dark = 'dark',
  Light = 'light',
}
```

Model Index File

When we access our model, there is an easy way to access these objects. We know that we need the entire object contents in our Bundle JS chuck, so we can create a class in the model folder that will include all the methods we created.

```
// src/model/index.ts
export * from './preferencesObject'
```

Next, as our model library grows, we can access any of them in a more intuitive way. Instead of this:

```
import { ThemeEnum } from '../../model/preferencesObject'
```

we can access our methods this way:

```
import { ThemeEnum } from '../../model'
```

There are pros and cons to this approach. You will learn more about techniques for optimizing the React app chunks in Chapter 12 when we optimize our app.

Set the Theme as a Global Style: index.scss

src/index.scss is a good spot to place the theme colors as they will relate to more than just one component and are a global style.

```scss
.dark {
  color: white;
  background-color: #2b2b2b;
}
.light {
  color: black;
  background-color: darkgrey;
}
```

Create a State Slice: preferencesSlice.ts

Next, create a file and call it preferencesSlice.ts. Inside the slice we set the initial state of our data. I am setting it to the light color (ThemeEnum.Light) as the initial state.

For the reducers, I am setting three types of actions.

- — *setThemeDark*: Setting our app theme to dark colors

- — *setThemeLight*: Setting our app theme to light colors

- — *switchTheme*: Switching to the opposite color scheme

Take a look:

```ts
// src/features/Preferences/preferencesSlice.ts

import { createSlice } from '@reduxjs/toolkit'
import { ThemeEnum } from '../../model'

interface SliceState {
  theme: ThemeEnum
}
```

createSlice is where the logic sits, and we create initialState as well as the reducers.

```
const preferences = createSlice({
  name: 'preferences',
  initialState: {
    theme: ThemeEnum.Light,
  } as SliceState,
```

Our reducers hold the actions. Although I only need to switch a theme using switchTheme and not the other methods, I am already creating reducers for other actions I may need. In terms of testing, when we get to Chapter X, you can see how this type of logic makes sense as each action can be tested separately.

```
  reducers: {
    setThemeDark: (state, action) => {
      state.theme = ThemeEnum.Dark
    },
    setThemeLight: (state, action) => {
      state.theme = ThemeEnum.Light
    },
    switchTheme: (state, action) => {
      state.theme = state.theme === ThemeEnum.Light ? ThemeEnum.Dark :
      ThemeEnum.Light
    },
  },
})
```

Lastly, export the actions.

```
export const { setThemeDark, setThemeLight, switchTheme } = preferences.
actions
export default preferences.reducer
```

Redux Toolkit Store

Now that we have our slice with specific actions, we can set up `Store.ts`. What we do is configure the store with the slice we set. That's all that we need. Take a look:

```ts
// src/redux/store.ts
import { configureStore, combineReducers } from '@reduxjs/toolkit'
import prefSlice from '../features/Preferences/preferencesSlice'

const store = configureStore({
  reducer: combineReducers({
    preferences: prefSlice,
  }),
})

export default store
```

Great. We have our state logic ready. We can now implement the view. In our footer view file, called `src/layout/Footer/Footer.tsx`, we can create a footer with a list of links and a button that will dispatch a callback to the action to switch the color theme.

Footer Architecture

So far, we have created a placeholder for the footer. Our footer needs to be aware of the user preference and be able to update the theme. To achieve that, we can wrap the `Footer` subcomponent with the parent component `FooterTheme.jsx`, just as we did for `Header`. Take a look at Figure 5-7.

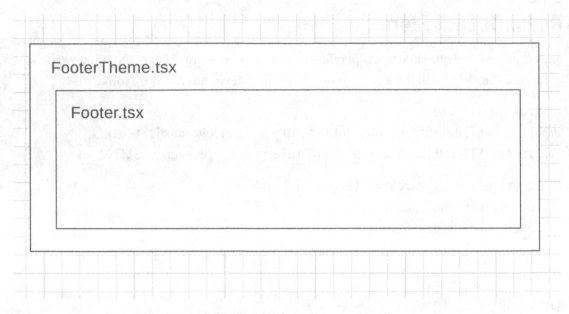

FooterTheme.tsx

Footer.tsx

Figure 5-7. *Footer component's high-level architecture*

Footer Subcomponent

We create a class of type `FunctionComponent` and pass the theme `prop`. Then we can wrap the view inside a navigation tag. This logic will set the background of our footer to change the entire container. We also use the `styled-component` library to extract the style for the component.

```
// src/layout/Footer/Footer.tsx

import React, { FunctionComponent } from 'react'
import classNames from 'classnames'
import { List, ListItem } from '@material-ui/core'
import { NavLink } from 'react-router-dom'
import InvertColorsIcon from '@material-ui/icons/InvertColors'
import { useStyles } from './Footer.styles'

// Redux Toolkit
import store from '../../redux/store'
import { ThemeEnum } from '../../model'
import { switchTheme } from '../../features/Preferences/preferencesSlice'

const Footer: FunctionComponent<TFooterProps> = ({ theme }) => (
```

```
  <nav className={theme === ThemeEnum.Dark ? 'dark' : 'light'}>
    <NestedGrid />
  </nav>
)

export type TFooterProps = {
  theme: ThemeEnum
}

export default Footer
```

Our NestedGrid function can take the theme prop and return the list of links.

```
function NestedGrid() {
  const classes = useStyles()
  const footerClasses = classNames({
    [classes.footer]: true,
  })
  const aClasses = classNames({
    [classes.a]: true,
  })
```

The updatePref method will use the Redux Toolkit slice to cause an action that will update the state of the preference.

```
  const updatePref = () => {
    store.dispatch(switchTheme(store.getState()))
  }
```

Then we can set these style classes in our render function return:

```
return (
  <footer className={footerClasses}>
    <div className={classes.container}>
      <div className={classes.left}>
        <List className={classes.list}>
          {[
            { name: 'Contact', url: '/Contact' },
            { name: 'About', url: '/About' },
```

```
            { name: 'Books', url: '/Books' },
            { name: 'Courses', url: '/BuildSiteCourse' },
          ].map((itemObject, index) => (
            <NavLink to={itemObject.url} className={classes.block}
            key={itemObject.url} activeClassName="NavLinkItem-selected">
              <ListItem className={classes.inlineBlock}>{itemObject.name}
              </ListItem>
            </NavLink>
          ))}
        </List>
      </div>
      <div className={classes.right}>
        &copy; {new Date().getFullYear()}{' '}
```

Here is our button to use the store and dispatch a callback to switch the theme action we created in our slice:

```
        <button type="submit" onClick={() => updatePref()}
        className={aClasses}>
          <InvertColorsIcon className={classes.icon} /> Change theme to
          {store.getState().preferences.theme === ThemeEnum.Dark ? 'light'
          : 'dark'}
        </button>
      </div>
    </div>
  </footer>
)
```

Footer.styles.ts Styled Component

Notice that we called Footer.styles.ts inside our Footer.tsx subcomponent. We separated our view from the style, and we placed our style in a separate file called Footer.styles.ts. Our code can import our style file.

import { useStyles } from './Footer.styles'.

Then using the class's object names, we can set the font color of our links. If the background is dark, we need bright color fonts, and if the background is bright, we need dark fonts.

In Footer.styles.ts, our code can set the styles for the links and even include media queries to adjust our footer container using the Material-UI core APIs createStyles, makeStyles, and Theme.

```
import { createStyles, makeStyles, Theme } from '@material-ui/core'

export const useStyles = makeStyles((theme: Theme) =>
  createStyles({
    block: {
      color: 'inherit',
      padding: '0.9375rem',
      fontWeight: 500,
      fontSize: '12px',
      textTransform: 'uppercase',
      borderRadius: '3px',
      textDecoration: 'none',
      position: 'relative',
    },
    left: {
      display: 'block',
    },
    right: {
      padding: '15px 0',
      margin: '0',
    },
    footer: {
      padding: '0.9375rem 0',
      textAlign: 'center',
      display: 'flex',
      zIndex: 2,
      position: 'relative',
    },
```

```
  a: {
    color: '#9c27b0',
    textDecoration: 'none',
    backgroundColor: 'transparent',
  },
  footerWhiteFont: {
    '&,&:hover,&:focus': {
      color: '#FFFFFF',
    },
  },
  container: {
    paddingRight: '15px',
    paddingLeft: '15px',
    marginRight: 'auto',
    marginLeft: 'auto',
    width: '100%',
    '@media (min-width: 576px)': {
      maxWidth: '540px',
    },
    '@media (min-width: 768px)': {
      maxWidth: '720px',
    },
    '@media (min-width: 992px)': {
      maxWidth: '960px',
    },
    '@media (min-width: 1200px)': {
      maxWidth: '1140px',
    },
  },
  list: {
    marginBottom: '0',
    padding: '0',
    marginTop: '0',
  },
  inlineBlock: {
```

```
      display: 'inline-block',
      padding: '0px',
      width: 'auto',
    },
    icon: {
      width: '18px',
      height: '18px',
      position: 'relative',
      top: '3px',
    },
  })
)
```

Lastly, we need to wrap our Footer subcomponent with a parent component called FooterTheme.tsx that will listen to a dispatch callback from the store in case the user decides to switch the theme. That architecture can allow us to dispatch that callback from any view instead of forcing that interaction from the footer.

FooterTheme Wrapper Parent Component

To achieve that, we create FooterTheme.tsx as a FunctionComponent and subscribe to the callback.

```
store.subscribe(() => {
  setTheme(store.getState().preferences.theme)
})
```

Here's the entire FooterTheme.tsx code;

```
// src/layout/Footer/FooterTheme.tsx

import React, { FunctionComponent, useState } from 'react'
import { ThemeEnum } from '../../model'
import store from '../../redux/store'
import FooterComponent from './Footer'

export const FooterTheme: FunctionComponent = () => {
  const [theme, setTheme] = useState<ThemeEnum>(ThemeEnum.Light)
```

```
store.subscribe(() => {
    setTheme(store.getState().preferences.theme)
  })
  return <FooterComponent theme={theme} />
}
```

HeaderTheme Parent Component

We need to do the same for the header. For the header, we have already set up the HeaderTheme wrapper parent components well as setting up the appBarBackgroundStyle method. For HeaderTheme.tsx, the code refactoring change is highlighted.

```
// src/layout/Header/HeaderTheme.tsx

import React, { FunctionComponent, useState } from 'react'
import AppBar from '@material-ui/core/AppBar/AppBar'
import { useMediaQuery } from '@material-ui/core'
import HeaderComponent from './Header'
import store from '../../redux/store'
import { ThemeEnum } from '../../model'

function appBarBackgroundStyle(color: string) {
  return {
    background: color,
  }
}
```

We set the state with the use of the React useState method. We than can set the style for the AppBar and pass the state to the HeaderComponent. Take a look:

```
export const HeaderTheme: FunctionComponent = () => {
  const smallBreakPoint = useMediaQuery('(min-width: 0px) and (max-width:
  1100px)')
  const [theme, setTheme] = useState<ThemeEnum>(ThemeEnum.Light)
  store.subscribe(() => {
    setTheme(store.getState().preferences.theme)
  })
```

```
return (
  <AppBar position="fixed" style={appBarBackgroundStyle(theme ===
  ThemeEnum.Dark ? '#2b2b2b' : 'white')}>
    <HeaderComponent theme={store.getState().preferences.theme} smallBreak
    Point={smallBreakPoint} />
  </AppBar>
)
}
```

Header Subcomponent

The Header component needs to be refactored to be able to hold a property with the state of the theme as well as pass the state to the different subcomponent and update the state of the Material-UI components.

Let's take a look. Refactor the IHeaderProps interface so we can pass the theme from the HeaderTheme parent component. The code changes are highlighted here:

```
import { ThemeEnum } from '../../model'

interface IHeaderProps {
  theme: ThemeEnum
  smallBreakPoint: boolean
}
```

To set the color of the button, we will be using a method called menuLabelBackgroundStyle where we can pass the color number.

```
function menuLabelBackgroundStyle(color: string) {
  return {
    color,
    padding: 20,
  }
}
```

Now our Material-UI button is able to switch colors on an update from the props.

```
<Button component={Link} style={menuLabelBackgroundStyle(this.props.theme
=== ThemeEnum.Dark ? 'white' : 'black')} to="/">
  ELI ELAD ELROM
</Button>
```

We also need to pass on the prop theme variable to the two Header subcomponents called HeaderTopNav and HeaderDrawer.

```
<HeaderTopNav theme={this.props.theme} />
<HeaderDrawer theme={this.props.theme} />
```

HeaderTopNav Subcomponent

For our HeaderTopNav subcomponent, we need to add the prop to the interface.

```
import { ThemeEnum } from '../../model'

interface IHTNavProps {
  theme: ThemeEnum
}
```

We will use the same approach as in the Header component to set the style of the Material-UI buttons. Since it's the same code as in the Header component, we could extract the code into a utility; however, since the code is small, I prefer to keep it duplicated so each component can be extracted as a stand-alone component without another dependency, but extracting duplicate code is not a bad idea.

```
function menuLabelBackgroundStyle(color: string) {
  return {
    color,
    padding: 20,
  }
}
```

Next, we can set the style for each parent button and repeat this process for each button: Contact, Resources, Coaching, and Build My Website. I am only showing one button but will repeat the same style property for each button.

```
<Button style={menuLabelBackgroundStyle(this.props.theme === ThemeEnum.Dark
? 'white' : 'black')} onClick={(event) => this.handleMenuOpen(event, '1')}>
  Build My Website
</Button>
```

HeaderDrawer Subcomponent

For the headerDrawer, I am not going to implement any style changes for now, but I would like to set the stage for later changes, so I will have the subcomponent be aware of the state via props, just as we did in HeaderTopNav.

```
import { ThemeEnum } from '../../model'

interface IHDProps {
  theme: ThemeEnum
}
```

AppRouter Refactoring

Now that we have refactored our footer, we need to change AppRouter.tsx to use the <FooterTheme /> subcomponent instead of <Footer />. Take a look:

```
const AppRouter: FunctionComponent = () => {
  return (
    <Provider store={store}>
      <Router>
        <HeaderTheme />
        <Switch>
          ...
        </Switch>
        <div className="footer">
          <FooterTheme />
        </div>
      </Router>
    </Provider>
  )
}
export default AppRouter
```

Congrats! We are code complete. If you check the app, you should see the results shown in Figure 5-1 and Figure 5-2.

Since our pages don't hold any content, we can just adjust the pages' SCSS with a height so it looks neat.

```scss
// src/App.scss
.App {
  text-align: center;
  padding-top: 120px;
  height: 350px;
}
```

We now have a scaffolding for our site with navigation, pages, a drawer, themes, and state management to be able to communicate the state between our component and subcomponents.

For quality, as we did in the previous chapter, you should get into the habit of running the following:

```
$ yarn format
$ yarn lint
$ yarn test
```

This will ensure we are getting tests that pass, linting, and working out any issues. The code from this example is passing all the tests, so you can compare your final results with mine.

Redux DevTools Extension

The last thing I want to show you that would be a great addition to add to your React toolbox is a plugin to keep track of what's happening in Redux Toolkit. It's called the Redux DevTools Extension. For Chrome you can download it from here:

```
https://chrome.google.com/webstore/detail/redux-devtools/lmhkpmbekcpmknklio
eibfkpmmfibljd?hl=en
```

Also, feel free to visit the project on GitHub for plugins for other browsers.

```
https://github.com/zalmoxisus/redux-devtools-extension
```

When we use the app we built, we can now see the action being dispatched on the plugin, as shown in Figure 5-8. Click the link to switch the theme of our app. In our case, the theme of the app changed from light to dark. This tool can come handy as you add more and more slices and the code grows.

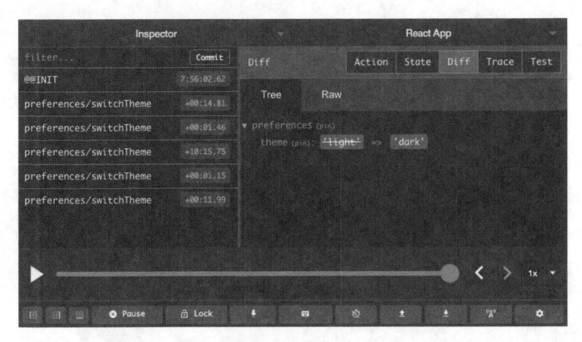

Figure 5-8. Redux DevTools extension for Chrome

Summary

In this chapter, you learned about state management and the state management architecture introduced by Facebook called Flux. You learned about the most popular state management at the time of writing called Redux by creating a `hello-redux` app using CRA. You then learned about Redux Toolkit and in the process implemented Redux Toolkit in the app we started building in the previous chapter. We added themes and the ability to communicate the state between the different components using Flux state management with the help of Redux Toolkit and styled components. Lastly, we installed the Redux DevTools Extension for Chrome.

In the next chapter, we will continue building our app and implement a login with an exclusive private member area using Recoil and the Mongo-Express-React-Node.js (MERN) stack.

CHAPTER 6

MERN Stack: Part I

In the previous chapter, you learned about state management and Facebook's Flux state management architecture. You learned about the most popular state management tools to date: vanilla Redux and Redux Toolkit. In this chapter, we will implement a login with an exclusive private member area using Recoil and the Mongo-Express-React-Node.js (MERN) stack. Specifically, we will be using React with Recoil to share the state across different components as the view layer and middleware. In the next chapter, we will implement Node.js, Express, and MongoDB as the back end.

Note Middleware provides services to our components beyond what's available in the React library. Think of middleware as the "software glue."

This chapter will contain a lot of hands-on coding. By the time you finish the chapter, you will have seen a full cycle of working with React and other related technologies. By the time you're done with the next chapter, you will have the tools to become a full-stack developer.

Again, the MERN stack is split into two chapters.

- In this chapter, we will set up the front end, the React part.

- In the next chapter, we will set up the back end.

This chapter is broken into two parts. In the first part, we will refactor the app we started in the previous chapters and refactor the state management to use Recoil. In the second part of this chapter, we will build an exclusive member area with a global toast messaging component that we can use across the app.

Figure 6-1 shows the final results where a user can log in and log out of an exclusive, secure, members-only area. Our components will change dynamically.

© Elad Elrom 2021
E. Elrom, *React and Libraries*, https://doi.org/10.1007/978-1-4842-6696-0_6

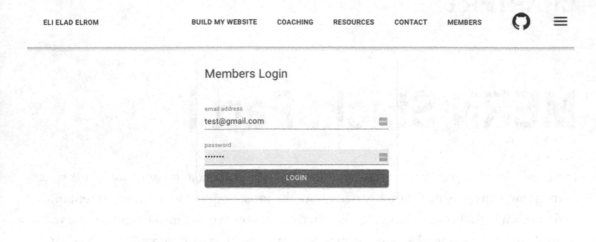

Figure 6-1. *Final results of this chapter*

Update Preferences with Recoil

In this section, we will refactor our app to use Recoil instead of Redux Toolkit to get our front end ready for the Recoil middleware integration with the back end that we will set up in the next chapter. First, though, let's talk about MERN and Recoil.

What Is the MERN Stack?

The MERN stack is a JavaScript stack that makes the development process easier as it is all based on JavaScript technologies. MERN includes four open source technologies: **M**ongoDB, **E**xpress, **R**eact, and **N**ode.js. These technologies provide us with a complete end-to-end cycle from the front end to the back-end frameworks. In this chapter, we will complete the React part of the MERN stack.

What Is Recoil?

To learn about Recoil, we will be refactoring the state of the preference component we created in the previous chapter, but this time instead of using Redux Toolkit we will be replacing the state management with the Facebook Recoil library.

Recoil (`https://recoiljs.org/`) is Facebook's life-changing state management experiment that is sweeping the React developer community. The Recoil team says the following:

> *"Recoil works and thinks like React. Add some to your app and get a fast and flexible shared state."*

Why Use Recoil?

As we saw in the previous chapter, there are many state management libraries, so why do we need yet another state management to share our app state? Can sharing state across multiple components and setting up middleware be done better and easier? The quick answer is yes!

If all you need to do is store values globally, any library you choose will work. However, things start to get complicated and messy when you start doing more complex stuff such as asynchronous calls or try to get your client in sync with your server state or reverse user interactions.

Ideally, and as mentioned many times in this book, we want our React components as pure as possible, and we want the data management to flow through the React hooks with no side effects. We also want the "real" DOM to be changed as little as possible for performance.

Keeping components loosely coupled is always a good place to be as a developer, so having a library that integrates well with React is a great addition to the React library as it puts React up there with other top JavaScript frameworks such as Angular.

Having a solid state management library will better promote React applications to serve enterprise-level complex applications as well as handle complex operations on both the front and middle tiers. Recoil simplifies state management, and we only need to create two ingredients: atoms and selectors.

Atoms are objects that are units of state that components can subscribe to. Recoil lets us create a data-flow graph that flows from these atoms (shared state) to the components. *Selectors* are pure functions that allow transforming the state either synchronously or asynchronously.

Unlike Redux or Redux Toolkit, there is no need to deal with a complex middleware setup and connect your components or use anything else to get the React components to play along nicely.

Did you know? The Recoil library is still at the experimental stage but has already gained some extraordinary popularity, passing Redux in popularity. The Recoil library clocked close to 10,000 stars on GitHub, passing Redux Toolkit's 4,100 stars!

It is my opinion and many others that Recoil will become the standard for state management and a much better investment of your time learning than continuing to utilize Redux Toolkit for the middleware. However, it is still good to know Redux Toolkit as you may be involved in a project that uses Redux. Additionally, Recoil is still an experiment and has not made it to the release stage as of the writing of this book, so it's not for the faint of heart.

Share the User's Preference State with Recoil

To get started with Recoil, I will make it easier for you by just refactoring our preference component that we built in the previous chapter, from sharing state through Redux Toolkit to utilizing Recoil. This will allow you to be able to compare the two libraries side by side. I broke down the process into two steps.

- *Step 1*: Implementing Recoil

- *Step 2*: Refactoring the view layer

On the project level, we will continue from where we left off in the previous chapter.

```
https://github.com/Apress/react-and-libraries/05/exercise-5-1
```

You can download the complete code for refactoring our preferences in Recoil here:

```
https://github.com/Apress/react-and-libraries/06/exercise-6-1
```

Implementing Recoil

To get started, we would normally first need to install Recoil (`yarn add recoil`). At the time of writing, Recoil is at version 0.0.13, but that could change by the time you read this chapter. However, our CRA MHL template already includes Recoil, so it is already set up without any extra work on your part.

Updating preferencesObject

Our first file that we will update is `preferencesObject.ts`, which we created in the previous chapter. The object holds an enumeration constant for the two app states. We will add to this object a way to hold a type for our preference object and a way to initialize the object. This will come handy in Recoil. Take a look:

```
// src/model/preferencesObject.ts
...

// eslint-disable-next-line @typescript-eslint/naming-convention
export interface preferencesObject {
  theme: ThemeEnum
}

export const initPreferencesObject = (): preferencesObject => ({
  theme: ThemeEnum.Light,
})
```

Notice that I am placing the `eslint-disable` code to have Lint ignore the signature line, because our ESLint is based on Airbnb style so is set not to use lowercase as a naming convention. I want to set the interface as lowercase. The other option is to change the ESLint configuration file.

Another thing to note (and some may dispute) is placing the enumeration inside an object model to keep it "purer." If you are coming from the Java world, you have heard of value objects (VOs) and data transfer objects (DTOs). I won't get into much detail, but the object can be refactored, and the enumeration can be extracted into an enumeration object and its own folder, if that's the design you want.

Creating a model folder with a type for our object lets us take full advantage of TypeScript, and using the object type can assist with writing our code and testing.

Preferences Atom

Next, we will create our Recoil object, called an *atom*. We will call the file `preferencesAtoms.ts`, and Recoil wants us to define a unique key for each atom as well as set a default value. The reason I am calling the file *atoms* as plural and not *atom* is that I may add other related atoms in that file. This is just a good habit.

Take a look:

```
// src/recoil/atoms/preferencesAtoms.ts

import { atom } from 'recoil'
import { initPreferencesObject } from '../../model'

export const preferencesState = atom({
  key: 'PreferencesState',
  default: initPreferencesObject(),
})
```

Notice that for the default value I am using the model's `initPreferencesObject` method to initialize the object with the default value (`ThemeEnum.Light`). We will use that later.

Session Atom

We are also going to create a `sessionAtoms.ts` file that will hold a user key that we can use to ensure the user is authorized to be logged into our secure member area. We won't implement that in this chapter, but feel free to create the logic and implement that functionality yourself after you complete the related chapters.

```
// src/recoil/atoms/sessionAtoms.ts
import { atom } from 'recoil'

export const sessionState = atom({
  key: 'SessionState',
  default: '',
})
```

Refactoring the View Layer

Now that we have our atoms `preferencesAtoms` and `sessionAtoms.ts`, we are ready to set our footer and header to get the shared state values from Recoil instead of Redux Toolkit as well as set the value through Recoil.

UserButton Subcomponent

We will start with creating a new subcomponent called UserButton.tsx.

UserButton will be aware of both the user's preferences and whether the user is logged into our app or not. The button will adjust the color and the information based on the state.

To achieve all of that, we will include in the interface the state of the theme, as well as a state of the login state that we can use later.

Our imports need to include the Material-UI button component, a link component, and the ThemeEnum as well as an interface that will hold a prop of the theme of the app that we will pass from the parent component. Take a look:

```
//src/components/UserButton/UserButton.tsx
```

```
import React from 'react'
import './UserButton.scss'
import Button from '@material-ui/core/Button/Button'
import { Link } from 'react-router-dom'
import { ThemeEnum } from '../../model'

export interface IUserButtonProps {
  isLoggedIn: boolean
  theme: ThemeEnum
}
```

Next we will create two constants that we can use to change the menu label style based on the user preferences.

```
const menuLabelsLight = {
  color: 'white',
  padding: 20,
}

const menuLabelsDark = {
  color: 'black',
  padding: 20,
}
```

For the class signature, we can use PureComponent. When you don't need the shouldComponentUpdate hook, use this:

```
export class UserButton extends React.PureComponent<IUserButtonProps, {}> {
  render() {
```

Inside the button style, we can have our switch decide which style element to use. In our case, the only difference between users logged in or not is either "members" or "login" displayed on the top menu, but the code is set up so that you can display any subcomponent you want. For instance, you may want to display the username or a picture when the user is logged in. Take a look:

```
    const { isLoggedIn } = this.props
    return isLoggedIn ? (
      <Button component={Link} style={this.props.theme === ThemeEnum.Dark ?
      menuLabelsLight : menuLabelsDark} to="/Members">
        Members
      </Button>
    ) : (
      <Button component={Link} style={this.props.theme === ThemeEnum.Dark ?
      menuLabelsLight : menuLabelsDark} to="/Members">
        Login
      </Button>
    )
  }
}
```

The inline conditional statement is the same as when writing it in pure JavaScript.

```
let value = isLoggedIn ? 'Members' : 'Login'
```

UserListButton Component

Similarly, we will create UserButton, which will be aware of the login state and use it in our drawer component. Our component will pass a user gesture of a click to the parent component, so our component will behave just like any other link component that's needed to be able to close the drawer without breaking encapsulation.

```
export interface IUserListButtonProps {
  isLoggedIn: boolean
  onClick: MouseEventHandler
}
```

For our imports, I picked a few icons from Material-UI that we can use to indicate that the user has logged in or out. We also need ListItem and ListItemText from Material-UI, as well as NavLink for the router.

```
import React, { MouseEventHandler } from 'react'
import { NavLink } from 'react-router-dom'
import ListItem from '@material-ui/core/ListItem/ListItem'
import ListItemIcon from '@material-ui/core/ListItemIcon/ListItemIcon'
import ListItemText from '@material-ui/core/ListItemText/ListItemText'
import VpnKeyIcon from '@material-ui/icons/VpnKey'
import CardMembershipIcon from '@material-ui/icons/CardMembership'
```

Our class signature can be PureComponent again, and the inline if/else statement will display either the member button or the login button.

```
export class UserListButton extends React.PureComponent<IUserListButtonPro
ps, {}> {
  render() {
    const { isLoggedIn } = this.props
    return isLoggedIn ? (
      <NavLink to="/Members" className="NavLinkItem" key="/Members"
      activeClassName="NavLinkItem-selected">
        <ListItem button key="Members" onClick={this.props.onClick}>
          <ListItemIcon>
            <CardMembershipIcon />
          </ListItemIcon>
          <ListItemText primary="Members" />
        </ListItem>
      </NavLink>
    ) : (
```

```
    <NavLink to="/Members" className="NavLinkItem" key="/Members"
    activeClassName="NavLinkItem-selected">
      <ListItem button key="Login" onClick={this.props.onClick}>
        <ListItemIcon>
          <VpnKeyIcon />
        </ListItemIcon>
        <ListItemText primary="Login" />
      </ListItem>
    </NavLink>
  )
 }
}
```

HeaderTheme Component Changes

Equipped with our atoms, we can move on and refactor HeaderTheme. We will update the component and pass a prop of the shared Recoil atom to the Header subcomponent via props.

We add useRecoilState as well as our preferencesState and sessionState to our import statement.

```
// src/layout/Header/HeaderTheme.tsx

import { useRecoilState } from 'recoil'
import { preferencesState } from '../../recoil/atoms/preferencesAtoms'
import { sessionState } from '../../recoil/atoms/sessionAtoms'
```

Next, we will utilize useRecoilState to get the values of our preferences and session token from Recoil. This integration of Recoil feels natural and better in line with the built-in state mechanism of the React component. You can see the power of Recoil in action here (the code changes are highlighted):

```
export const HeaderTheme: FunctionComponent = () => {
  const [preferences] = useRecoilState(preferencesState)
  const [session] = useRecoilState(sessionState)
  ...
}
```

Then we can use the shared value of preferences as well as pass data to the `Header` component. There's no need for Redux Toolkit's `store.getState()` anymore.

```
<HeaderComponent theme={preferences.theme} session={session} smallBreakPoin
t={smallBreakPoint} />
```

As you can see, I am keeping the subcomponents as pure as possible in terms of state by passing the shared state as `props`, which makes it easy not only to debug and test as the state will be passed on to the subcomponent from the parent state, but also to extract any component from one app to another.

Header Subcomponents

In our `Header` subcomponents (`Header`, `HeaderTopNav`, and `HeaderDrawer`), we can take the same theme `prop` approach and pass it to the other two subcomponents via `props`. Since the `Header` component doesn't have a set method and it only reads the theme state, our code is loosely coupled, and we could easily copy and paste our subcomponents from one project to another. Additionally, when we need to test that a component is not relying on another parent component, it is best to keep our components loosely coupled.

Header Subcomponent

We can start refactoring the `Header` subcomponent with the `Header` subcomponent code. In the `Header` `props`, we can set the theme and session variables.

```
// src/layout/Header/Header.tsx

interface IHeaderProps {
  theme: ThemeEnum
  session: string
  smallBreakPoint: boolean
}
```

For the render JSX side, we set the style using the theme and set the session key.

Notice that we are checking the session state directly on the component. The reason is that we need the component to be updated once the shared state is updated. We are checking the state of the session shared state as well as the localStorage. The reason we will set both is that we want both cases, as listed here:

- The app updating automatically through the hook

- The app updating once the user refreshes the browser

Note   localStorage, also known as DOM storage, is web storage that gives our web app the ability to store our client-side data, and when we refresh the browser, the data will be persisted.

```
<HeaderTopNav theme={this.props.theme} isLoggedIn={this.props.session ===
'myUniqueToken' || localStorage.getItem('accessToken') === 'myUniqueToken'} />
```

```
<HeaderDrawer theme={this.props.theme} isLoggedIn={this.props.session ===
'myUniqueToken' || localStorage.getItem('accessToken') === 'myUniqueToken'} />
```

Notice that on the code level I am creating baked code myUniqueToken for the session check. This can be connected to logic that checks the session via an encrypt/decrypt algorithm.

HeaderTopNav Subcomponent

For the HeaderTopNav subcomponent refactoring effort, we will import UserButton, which is aware of the preferences and login state we created.

```
// src/layout/Header/HeaderTopNav.tsx
```

```
import { UserButton } from '../../components/UserButton/UserButton'
```

Next, we need our subcomponent to be aware of whether the user logged in or not and the theme. We pass that information to the UserButton child.

```
interface IHTNavProps {
  theme: ThemeEnum
  isLoggedIn: boolean
}
```

Another item I want to refactor is the GitHub icon. The GitHub icon style needs to be based on the theme preference, so it matches the rest of the navigation items; otherwise, it stays the same color. Take a look:

```
function githubIconStyle(color: string) {
  return {
    color,
    width: 120,
  }
}
```

```
<IconButton style={githubIconStyle(this.props.theme === ThemeEnum.Dark ?
'white' : 'black')}>
```

Lastly, let's add the UserButton component under the existing Contact button.

```
<UserButton theme={this.props.theme} isLoggedIn={this.props.isLoggedIn} />
```

HeaderDrawer Subcomponent

The HeaderDrawer subcomponent refactoring effort is similar to the HeaderTopNav subcomponent. We set the import of the new button we created, UserListButton; update the props interface; and add the button. The rest stays the same. Take a look:

```
// src/layout/Header/HeaderDrawer.tsx
```

```
import { UserListButton } from '../../components/UserListButton/
UserListButton'
```

```
interface IHDProps {
  theme: ThemeEnum
  isLoggedIn: boolean
```

```
<UserListButton isLoggedIn={this.props.isLoggedIn} onClick={this.
handleListItemClick} />
```

Footer Component Refactoring

In our Footer component effort, the process is similar to what we are doing in the Header components. However, we don't just read the preference state; we also let the user change the state of the app theme. Once the user uses the onClick function, we can set the preference using setPreferences, so we need to refactor the code and remove Redux Toolkit.

FooterTheme Component

FooterTheme.tsx is a FunctionComponent wrapper that returns the FooterComponent. The reason we need a wrapper is that we are using the Recoil hooks, and we can only do that in pure functions.

As we did with the Header component, we will pass the preferencesAtom object to other subcomponents through props. We don't need to subscribe to the Redux Toolkit store. Take a look at the changes:

```
// src/layout/Footer/FooterTheme.tsx

import { useRecoilState } from 'recoil'

import { preferencesState } from '../../recoil/atoms/preferencesAtoms'
```

Next, we can set preferences to tie that to our state.

```
export const FooterTheme: FunctionComponent = () => {
  const [preferences] = useRecoilState(preferencesState)
  return <FooterComponent theme={preferences.theme} />
}
```

As you can see, I am using the useRecoilState Recoil function in the FooterTheme function to retrieve the atom, and then I am passing it to the FooterComponent.

Footer Subcomponent

We passed the preferences state from the Footer theme component, and it's tied to the Recoil shared state. When we use setPreferences, the state will be shared globally to any component and subcomponent that are using that state. Also, React will recognize automatically when to update the real DOM with any components and subcomponents that need change, all without any work on our end.

To do that, we need to first import Recoil.

```
// src/layout/Footer/Footer.tsx
```

```
import { useRecoilState } from 'recoil'
```

Next, our existing NestedGrid function can hold the state and binding the data that using Recoil.

```
function NestedGrid() {
  const [preferences, setPreferences] = useRecoilState(preferencesState)
  ...
}
```

The only other change we need to make is that when the user clicks to change the preference, we can now change setPreferences directly into the component state instead of using Redux Toolkit. This is much better and more intuitive.

```
const updatePref = () => {
  setPreferences({
    theme: preferences.theme === ThemeEnum.Light ? ThemeEnum.Dark :
    ThemeEnum.Light,
  })
}
```

AppRouter Component

Lastly, in the App component we need to wrap the router code inside RecoilRoot tags.

What Is RecoilRoot?

RecoilRoot provides context as an ancestor of all the components that use the Recoil hooks.

Suspense Tag

In Recoil, we also need to set a fallback suspense tag. A suspense tag sets a component that will display during the loading period.

In our case, we can set the suspense component to just display a loading message. Take a look at the code:

```tsx
// src/AppRouter.tsx

import React, { Suspense } from 'react'
import { RecoilRoot } from 'recoil'

function AppRouter() {
  return (
    <Router>
      <RecoilRoot>
        <Suspense fallback={<span>Loading...</span>}>
          <HeaderTheme />
          <Switch>
            ...
          </Switch>
          <div className="footer">
            <FooterTheme />
          </div>
        </Suspense>
      </RecoilRoot>
    </Router>
  )
}
```

Job well done! Now we can officially delete the redux and Preferences folders as we are not using them anymore.

- src/redux/store.ts

- src/features/Preferences/preferencesSlice.ts

As always, if you are not running the app, use yarn start. See the final results in Figure 6-2.

Figure 6-2. *Refactoring our app to use Recoil instead of Redux*

Go ahead and try to switch the theme using the footer button.

As you can see, Recoil acts and feels like it is an extension of the React library, and Recoil also gives us a shared state management without the hassle. Most importantly, the DOM updates only when it's needed. This is a speed boost. Imagine we are updating a list with thousands of results or maintaining a server-client state. React and Recoil play along nicely and separate our concerns.

Now we have our app refactored, and we are using Recoil instead of Redux Toolkit. Our app functionality so far is simple; it displays content pages and has a switch to change the user's theme preference.

However, say we want to add more functionality. For instance, a common functionality in an app is the ability to log in to a secure members-only area or submit a form, so we need to add more logic.

At this point, we are equipped with good knowledge of how to break down React components to subcomponents, separate concerns, and use the Recoil shared state library. We are ready to tackle more complex functionality.

Create a Members-Only Area with the MERN Stack

We'll now learn how to create a members-only area with the MERN stack.

How Do We Build a Members-Only Area with the MERN Stack?

To implement logic so we will be able to log in to a secure members-only area, I broke down the process into two main parts.

- Creating the front end

- Creating the back end

The front end will include the middleware and view layer of our application. The back end will include a server, a service, and a database.

In the next section, we will do just that using Recoil as the middleware, and then in Chapter 7, we will integrate Express, NodeJS, and MongoDB as the back end.

Let's get started writing our front end for our private member area.

Front End

You can download the complete code of this exercise from here:

https://github.com/Apress/react-and-libraries/06/exercise-6-2

We will be building two front-end components.

- Toast message component
- Login and member area components

The toast message component, as the name suggests, will pop up messages like a toaster. The messages can be used to notify the user of success, fail, info, and warning messages throughout the app, not just for this feature.

The login and member components will include a form that the user can submit to validate the user's name and password as well as get access to an exclusive members-only area.

Toast Message Component

To get started with our toast message component, we will start off with defining our data. This is a healthy start as we set the data first that we will be using in the component.

Each toast message needs to have a unique ID so we know what will be displayed. The toast also needs a message type such as `success` or `failed` and a description of the message that we want to display. We will accept four types of messages: success, fail, warning, and info. We will give each message a different style and icon.

You can see the final results in Figure 6-3.

Figure 6-3. *Testing the toaster components*

toastObject Model

A good place to start is with the data. The `toastObject` data object is a similar architecture design we used in the preference data object. We will include an interface and a method to initiate the toast message. I am also going to include a method to get a random ID number that we can use as our unique ID for each toast message.

It's a good idea to set an enum of message types so we don't need to constantly type them. It also won't hurt to set an enum of the different messages' background color so we can change them easily from one location. Create `toastObject.ts` and take a look at the code, shown here:

```
// src/model/toastObject.ts

// eslint-disable-next-line @typescript-eslint/naming-convention
export interface toastObject {
  id: number
  type: string
  description: string
}
```

```
export const initEmptyToast = (): toastObject => ({
  id: -1,
  type: '',
  description: '',
})
export const initToast = (id: number, type: string, description: string):
toastObject => ({
  id: id,
  type: type,
  description: description,
})
// eslint-disable-next-line @typescript-eslint/naming-convention
export const randomToastId = () => {
  return Math.floor(Math.random() * 101 + 1)
}
export enum notificationTypesEnums {
  Success = 'Success',
  Fail = 'Fail',
  Info = 'Info',
  Warning = 'Warning',
}
// eslint-disable-next-line @typescript-eslint/naming-convention
export enum backgroundColorEnums {
  Success = '#5bb85a',
  Fail = '#d94948',
  Info = '#55bede',
  Warning = '#f0a54b',
}
```

Notice that I am setting initEmptyToast and initToast. initEmptyToast sets the ID of the toast message to -1, which will indicate that the toast message is not set. initToast lets us decide the values of the toast object.

Remember to also add the toast model to the `src/model/index.ts` file for easy access.

```
// src/model/index.ts
export * from './toastObject'
```

Recoil: Toast Atom

Now that we have the model data, we can create the toast atom (`toastAtoms.ts`). We need to hold a unique key and default value, just as we did with the preference atom.

```
// src/recoil/atoms/toastAtoms.ts

import { atom } from 'recoil'
import { initEmptyToast } from '../../model'

export const toastState = atom({
  key: 'ToastState',
  default: initEmptyToast(),
})
```

Toast Component

In terms of component hierarchy design, our components design will have a `ToastNotification` component that will hold all the toasts we need to display. This design is healthy as we break down the functionality, and it will be easy to maintain. To help understand the hierarchy, take a look at Figure 6-4.

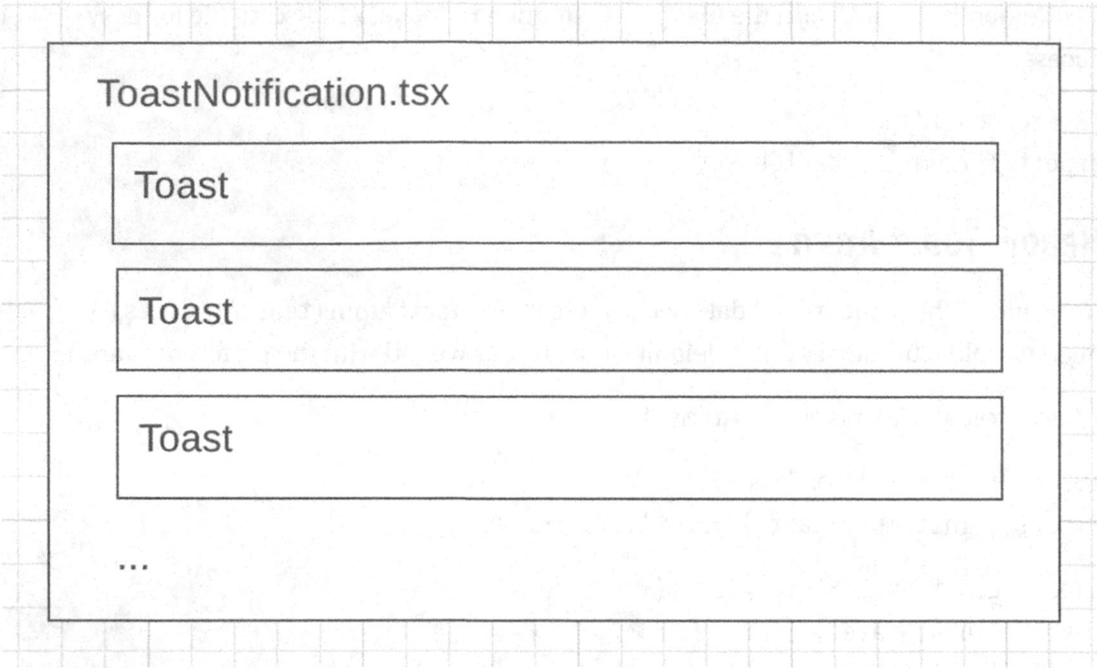

Figure 6-4. *Toast components architecture design*

Equipped with the Recoil toast atom and model, we can start and create our front-end components. We will start with a Toast component. That will be our subcomponent that will be used by our notification component to display a toast. It represents each toast we will dispatch.

Let's review the Toast component. Our import statements include the icons, recoil, suspense, and the notification enum.

```
// src/components/Toast/Toast.tsx
import React, { Suspense } from 'react'
import './Toast.scss'
import { useRecoilState } from 'recoil'
import { toastState } from '../../recoil/atoms/toastAtoms'
import checkIcon from '../../assets/toast/check.svg'
import errorIcon from '../../assets/toast/error.svg'
import infoIcon from '../../assets/toast/info.svg'
import warningIcon from '../../assets/toast/warning.svg'
import { backgroundColorEnums, initEmptyToast, notificationTypesEnums }
from '../../model'
```

Our import icons can be downloaded from GitHub's /assets/toast folder, or you can make your own SVG custom icons.

To tie our Recoil shared state in our Toast component, we will be using useRecoilState.

```
export const Toast = () => {
  const [toast, setToast] = useRecoilState(toastState)
```

The StyleDetails interface will hold the selected icon of the toast and the background's selected color code.

```
interface StyleDetails {
  background: string
  icon: string
}
```

Next, we will create a method (getToastStyle) that will hold a switch to assign an object with the icon and a background color. I am using a switch, but this can also be done with an object literal.

```
const getToastStyle = (toastType: string) => {
  let retVal: StyleDetails = {
      background: backgroundColorEnums.Success,
      icon: checkIcon,
  }
  switch (toastType)  {
    case notificationTypesEnums.Fail:
      retVal = {
          background: backgroundColorEnums.Fail,
          icon: errorIcon,
      }
      break;
    case notificationTypesEnums.Warning:
      retVal = {
          background: backgroundColorEnums.Warning,
          icon: warningIcon,
      }
      break;
```

```
    case notificationTypesEnums.Info:
      retVal = {
          background: backgroundColorEnums.Info,
          icon: infoIcon,
      }
      break;
  }
  return retVal;
}
```

On the render JSX side, we will ignore any toast that has an ID of -1 (remember, that is the initial value). That way, we can clear a toast that is being displayed on the screen that was not set or that needs to be removed.

```
return (

  {toast.id !== -1 && (
```

I am using the Suspense API that allows us to display a loading message while the component is being loaded. That loading message can be changed to a spinner if you like.

```
      <Suspense fallback={<span>Loading</span>}>
        <div className="notification-container top-right">
```

Each toast gets assigned its own random unique toast ID, and this design will allow us to delete a toast in case we want to implement multiple toasts to display at the same time or any other functionality we may want in the future.

```
        <div
          key={toast.id}
          className={`notification toast top-right`}
```

For the style of the background and icon, we will be using the getToastStyle we created. We pass the toast.type and get the background color. Take a look:

```
          style={{ backgroundColor: getToastStyle(toast.type).
          background }}
        >
```

Once the user clicks to close the toast, we set the toast with an ID of -1 to clear the toast using the `initEmptyToast` method we created in the model. That will delete the toast. Take a look:

```
                <button type="button" onClick={() => setToast(initEmpty
                Toast())}>X</button>
                <div className="notification-image">
                  <img src={getToastStyle(toast.type).icon} alt="" />
                </div>
                <div>
                  <p className="notification-title">{toast.type}</p>
                  <p className="notification-message">{toast.description}</p>
                </div>
              </div>
            </div>
          </Suspense>
        )}
      )
}
```

Toast.scss

As for `Toast.scss`, I won't display the entire code here, but you can download it from the GitHub repository. But I want to point out one feature.

In our code, we set the toast to the top-right corner of the user's screen, and we set up an animation to move the toast from right to left, but you can change the code to animate the toast from any corner of the screen. Take a look at the `Toast.scss` section of the code that handles the location:

```
.top-right {
  top: 12px;
  right: 12px;
  transition: transform 0.6s ease-in-out;
  animation: toast-in-right 0.7s;
}
```

```
@keyframes toast-in-right {
  from {
    transform: translateX(100%);
  }
  to {
    transform: translateX(0);
  }
}
```

ToastNotification Subcomponent

Now that we have our toast subcomponent ready, we will create the parent component ToastNotification.tsx. Recoil uses hooks, so to be able to use a React component instead of a pure function, we need to wrap our React component inside of a pure function and pass along the Recoil state through props. How this is done? Take a look.

We need to import the SCSS file, the recoil state and value, toast model, and toast atom, as well as the Toast component.

```
// src/components/Toast/ToastNotification.tsx
import React from 'react'
import './ToastNotification.scss'
import { SetterOrUpdater, useRecoilValue, useSetRecoilState } from 'recoil'
import { initEmptyToast, toastObject } from '../../model'
import { toastState } from '../../recoil/atoms/toastAtoms'
import { Toast } from './Toast'
```

Our pure function to retrieve the state of the toast as well as create a method to set a toast using the getToastState and useSetRecoilState APIs needs to be set in the ToastNotification wrapper. These are being passed through props to the ToastNotificationInner component we are wrapping.

```
// wrapper
export default function ToastNotification() {
  const setToastState = useSetRecoilState(toastState)
  const getToastState: toastObject = useRecoilValue(toastState)
  return <ToastNotInner setToastState={setToastState}
  getToastState={getToastState} />
}
```

Now that our `ToastNotification` wrapper is ready. The `ToastNotificationInner` React component implements the `setToastState` and `getToastState` interfaces.

```
interface IToastNotProps {
  setToastState: SetterOrUpdater<toastObject>
  getToastState: toastObject
}
```

```
interface IToastNotState {}
```

```
class ToastNotInner extends React.PureComponent<IToastNotProps,
IToastNotState> {
```

We want our toast to disappear automatically even if the user doesn't click to close the toast, so we can set an interval on the `componentDidUpdate` method with a 5,000-millisecond (half a second) timer.

The `componentDidUpdate()` method is good spot to place our code because it is invoked right after the most recently rendered output is committed.

Tip   The main difference is that `getDerivedStateFromProps` is invoked right before calling the render method. `getSnapshotBeforeUpdate` runs before the most recently rendered output is committed. `componentDidUpdate` runs after.

```
componentDidUpdate() {
  const interval = setInterval(() => {
    if (this.props.getToastState.id !== -1) {
      this.props.setToastState(initEmptyToast())
    }
  }, 5000)
  return () => {
    clearInterval(interval)
  }
}
```

You can increase the time from a half-second to a second (10,000 ms) if you want to leave the toast longer. On the JSX render side, we return the Toast subcomponent we created.

```
render() {
  return (
  <>
      <Toast />
  </>
  )
}
}
```

ToastNotification.scss

Lastly, for our ToastNotification.scss file, we need to set the toast button design properties.

```
.toast-buttons {
  display: flex;
}

.toast-buttons button {
  color: white;
  font-size: 14px;
  font-weight: bold;
  width: 100px;
  height: 50px;
  margin: 0 10px;
  border: none;
  outline: none;
}

.select {
  display: flex;
  width: 30%;
  margin-top: 10px;
}
```

```
.position-select {
  background-color: inherit;
  color: #fff;
  width: 100%;
  height: 30px;
  font-size: 16px;
}
```

AppRouter Component Refactoring

Now that we created the toast subcomponent and notification parent component, we can add logic to our AppRouter component to include the ToastNotification. It's good to place this code globally for two reasons.

- We need RecoilRoot because we are using the Recoil API.

- We can use the toast component with any of our pages.

Add <ToastNotification> to AppRouter.tsx inside the <RecoilRoot> tags.

```
<RecoilRoot>
  <ToastNotification />
  ..
  ..
</RecoilRoot>
```

We are all set. This architecture design allows our code to accept toast notifications on the global level from any components we want. Recoil provides us with a shared state that we can use to assign a toast any time we want.

Let's take the toast component for a test-drive. To dispatch a toast in App.tsx, for example, we set the toast state, and we imitate a toast of any type we like. See what the toast looks like once we refresh the page, as shown in Figure 6-3.

```
// src/App.tsx

import { useSetRecoilState } from 'recoil'
import { toastState } from './recoil/atoms/toastAtoms'
import { initToast, notificationTypesEnums, randomToastId } from './model'
```

```
function App() {
  const setToastState = useSetRecoilState(toastState)
  setToastState(initToast(randomToastId(), notificationTypesEnums.Success,
  'Hello World'))
  ...
}
```

Exclusive Members Area

In our last exercise for the chapter, we will be creating that exclusive password-protected members-only area section we talked about. The member area needs a login that will have an email and a password input box that the user can fill in so that they can log into an exclusive members-only area.

You can download the complete code of this exercise from here:

```
https://github.com/Apress/react-and-libraries/06/exercise-6-3
```

userObject Model

As always, a good place to start is to define our user object model file (userObject.ts). The user object holds the email and password and a method to initialize the object, just as we did with the previous models we added.

```
// src/model/userObject.ts

export interface userObject {
  email: string
  password: string
}
export const initUser = (): userObject => ({
  email: '',
  password: '',
})
```

Add an export to the index file;

```
// src/model/index.ts
export * from './userObject'
```

Login Recoil Logic

Let's look at the login logic.

User Atom

Next, just as we did in the preference and toast components, we need to set a Recoil atom. Create `userAtoms.ts`. The file will hold the user state with the default value set to the model object.

```
// src/recoil/atoms/userAtoms.ts
import { atom } from 'recoil'
import { initUser } from '../../model'

export const userState = atom({
  key: 'UserState',
  default: initUser(),
})
```

In addition to the user atom, we will need a session atom. If you recall earlier in the chapter when we set the preferences, we also created `sessionAtoms.ts` to hold a user key that we can use to ensure the user is authorized to be logged into our secure member area.

Recoil User Selector

For the user component, we need some middleware to make the service call. That will be achieved using the Recoil Selector API.

A Recoil selector share the state so all our React components can subscribe to the data. Selectors are pure functions that allow us to transform the state either synchronously or asynchronously.

In our case, we use a service call, so the call will be asynchronous. Take a look at the code level that shows the selectors' pure function `userSelectors.ts`:

```
// src/recoil/selectors/userSelectors.ts

import { selector } from 'recoil'
import { userState } from '../atoms/userAtoms'
```

For the service call, I will simply call the code by using a useful library called axios (https://github.com/axios/axios). Ensure you add that library to your project ($ yarn add axios).

```
import axios from 'axios'
```

In Recoil, we can use a selector or a selectorFamily and pass the user information. A selectorFamily is a pattern similar to a selector, but it allows passing parameters to the get and set callbacks of a selector. So, you could change the code and design it with a selectorFamily that will pass the user email instead of storing it in an atom. I am storing it in case other components need to know the selected user email, for instance, a newsletter component.

The Recoil selector, just like a Recoil atom, needs a unique key to be set. I am using async with the get method to be able to retrieve the userState. Take a look:

```
export const submitUserLoginSelector = selector({
  key: 'SubmitUserLoginSelector',
  get: async ({ get }) => {
    const payload = get(userState)
```

I can set another validation here to ensure the user filled out the form.

```
    if (payload.email === '' || payload.password === '') return `Error:
Please complete form`
```

Next, I am wrapping my service call in try and catch tags to ensure no errors got produced.

```
  try {
      const urlWithString = `http://localhost:8081/validate?email=$
      { payload.email }&password=${ payload.password}`
      const res = await axios({
        url: urlWithString,
        method: 'get',
      })
      return res?.data?.status
    } catch (err) {
      // console.warn(err)
      return `Error: ${ err}`
```

```
    }
  },
})
```

> **Note** I am using optional chaining (`res?.data?.status`). This lets us write
> code where TypeScript can immediately stop running our expression if it runs
> into a null value. It's healthy and helps avoid errors in case the service call fails or
> become malformed.

Login Components

Now that we have our atoms and selector, we can work on our view layer.

We will start with a form component for the login component.

We will be using the Material-UI style component libraries to speed up our development efforts. Just as we did before, we will use a wrapper component (`LoginForm`) and have our `LoginPage` wrapped inside a `LoginForm`. The `LoginForm` component will have another inner component that will hold the actual form. Look at Figure 6-5.

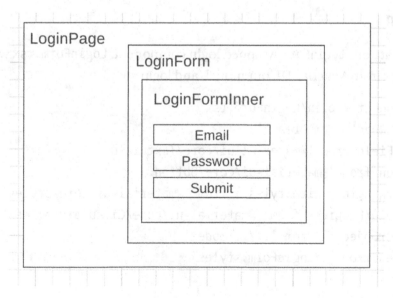

Figure 6-5. *Login components hierarchy*

In `LoginForm`, we will use a style file to separate the style from the view. Create `LoginForm.styles.ts` to center and set our component as a column container.

This added complexity is not necessary; however, it helps us separate the components better and keep them loosely coupled, and if we need to drop the `LoginForm` somewhere else in this app or drag it to another project, the extra step is worth it.

LoginForm.styles.ts

Our style sets the container type we will be using. It specifies how to lay out the form elements inside our component as a column and center of the page. Take a look:

```
// src/components/Login/LoginForm.styles.ts
import { createStyles, Theme } from '@material-ui/core/styles'

export default (theme: Theme) =>
    container: {
        display: 'flex',
        flexDirection: 'column',
        justifyContent: 'center',
    },
  })
```

LoginForm

Next, let's create our `LoginForm` wrapped login component. `LoginForm.tsx` will include form elements from Material-UI, our model, and login style.

```
// src/components/Login/LoginForm.tsx
import * as React from 'react'
import TextField from '@material-ui/core/TextField'
import Button from '@material-ui/core/Button'
import { withStyles, WithStyles } from '@material-ui/core/styles'
import CircularProgress from '@material-ui/core/CircularProgress'
import { userObject } from '../../model'
import styles from './LoginForm.styles'
```

To wrap `LoginForm.styles`, we will create an inner React function component and use the `withStyle` API to export the component that will connect our component with the style.

```
export const LoginForm = withStyles(styles)(LoginFormInner)
```

The `props` we will be setting includes extending the `withStyle` API and passing the `onLogin` and `onUpdateLoginField` functions from the parent component, passing the state of the user, and lastly passing a flag to show a loading progress once the form is submitted.

```
interface ILoginFormProps extends WithStyles<typeof styles> {
  onLogin: () => void
  onUpdateLoginField: (name: string, value: string) => void
  loginInfo: userObject
  loading: boolean
}
```

We will pass the values that the user updated the form with to the parent component using the `onTextFieldChangeHandler` and `onUpdateLoginField` that we will be setting in the `props`.

```
const LoginFormInner: React.FunctionComponent<ILoginFormProps> = (props:
ILoginFormProps) => {
  const onTextFieldChangeHandler = (fieldId: string) => (e: React.
  ChangeEvent<HTMLInputElement>) => {
    props.onUpdateLoginField(fieldId, e.target.value)
  }
```

On the JSX render side, we will set the email and password text field input with `onChange` ties to `onTextFieldChangeHandler` as well as tie the values to the state via `props.loginInfo`. Take a look.

```
return (
  <div className={props.classes.container}>
    <TextField label="email address" margin="normal" value={props.
    loginInfo.email} onChange={onTextFieldChangeHandler('email')} />
    <TextField label="password" type="password" margin="normal" value={props
    .loginInfo.password} onChange={onTextFieldChangeHandler('password')} />
```

Our submit button will use the callback from the props and the loading prop flag. Inside the submit button we will see a loading animation thanks to the Material-UI CircularProgress component.

```
<Button variant="contained" color="primary" disabled={props.loading}
onClick={props.onLogin}>
  Login
  {props.loading && <CircularProgress size={30} color="secondary" />}
</Button>
    </div>
  )
}
```

Great, our login form component is ready for usage.

Login Page

Our LoginPage component is the parent component that will include an inner component (LoginPageInner) to either show the form or handle the submission of the form and display the success or fail logic. To better understand what I am doing, take a look at Figure 6-6.

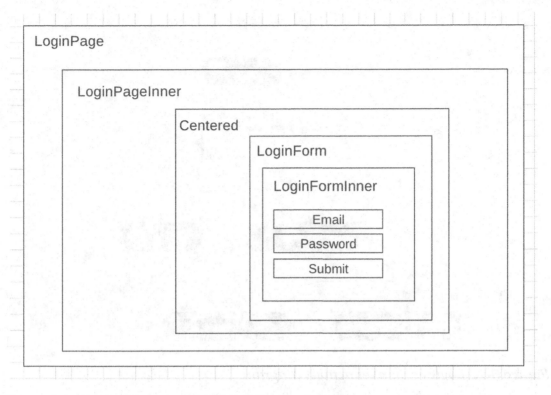

Figure 6-6. *LoginPage component and subcomponents*

As you can see, the LoginPage holds the inner page wrapper (LoginPageInner). Inside will be a subcomponent that will center our login form.

InnerPage will either display our form or use a subcomponent called SubmitUserFormComponent that will be used once the form is submitted and, based on the results, will set the state and display a message. In addition, it will initiate the toast component that we created previously.

In addition, take a look at the activity diagram in Figure 6-7 to better understand the process of submitting the login form.

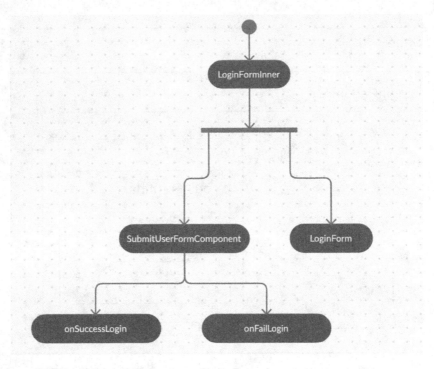

Figure 6-7. *LoginFormInner activity diagram*

Center Content Component

Let's start with the center component that can help us align our login form component. This component can be reused in other pages, so let's place it inside our layout folder for reuse.

We will separate the component from the style, as we usually do for clarity. Let's call the style component Centered.styles.ts.

```
// src/layout/Centered/Centered.styles.ts

import { createStyles, Theme } from '@material-ui/core/styles'

export default (theme: Theme) =>
  createStyles({
    '@global': {
      'body, html, #root': {
        paddingTop: 40,
        width: '100%',
      },
    },
```

```
  container: {
    maxWidth: '400px',
    margin: '0 auto',
  },
})
```

Next, we can create our wrapper component (Centered.tsx) that we will use as our container class that will center our child subcomponents.

```
// src/layout/Centered/Centered.tsx

import * as React from 'react'
import { withStyles, WithStyles } from '@material-ui/core/styles'
import styles from './Centered.styles'

const CenteredViewInner: React.FunctionComponent<Props> = (props) => <div
className={props.classes.container}>{props.children}</div>

interface Props extends WithStyles<typeof styles> {}

export const Centered = withStyles(styles)(CenteredViewInner)
```

Lastly, let's create an index.ts file for more intuitive access of this component so we can use it as JSX tag, like this: <Centered />.

```
// src/layout/index.ts
export { Centered } from './Centered'
```

LoginPage Component

For the LoginPage, we already have this component, but it is just displaying the name of the page. Let's start updating it. Our import needs to include the Material-UI components, Recoil elements, toast component, and our login form.

```
// src/components/Login/LoginPage.tsx

import './LoginPage.scss'
import { Card, CardContent, CardHeader } from '@material-ui/core'
import { useRecoilState, useRecoilValue, useSetRecoilState } from 'recoil'
import { Centered } from '../../layout/Centered'
import { LoginForm } from '../../components/Login/LoginForm'
```

```
import { initToast, initUser, notificationTypesEnums, randomToastId } from
'../../model'
import { userState } from '../../recoil/atoms/userAtoms'
import { toastState } from '../../recoil/atoms/toastAtoms'
import { submitUserLoginSelector } from '../../recoil/selectors/
userSelectors'
import { sessionState } from '../../recoil/atoms/sessionAtoms'
```

LoginPage needs to include the LoginPageInner component, which is where the heavy lifting happens.

```
export default LoginPage

const LoginPage = () => {
  return <LoginPageInner />
}
```

LoginPageInner and Subcomponents

As I mentioned, the LoginPageInner component sets the component's local login page state (userLoginPageState) as well as the Recoil page state (user).

The reason that we need both a local state and a shared state is that we don't need to update the global shared state on any keystroke update from the user but only once the user completed the form. We will also set the loading state flag here and pass it to the form, so we can control it from the parent component and keep subcomponents clean.

```
function LoginPageInner() {
  const [userLoginPageState, setUserLoginPageState] = useState(initUser)
  const [loading, setLoading] = useState(false)
  const [user, setUser] = useRecoilState(userState)
```

Once the user clicks the onLogin button, we set the loading state of the form as well as set the Recoil user state values.

```
const onLogin = () => {
  // console.log(`LoginPage.tsx :: onLogin :: userLoginPageState :: ${JSON.
  stringify(userLoginPageState)}`)
  setLoading(true)
  setUser(userLoginPageState)
```

```
  // eslint-disable-next-line no-console
  console.log(JSON.stringify(user))
}
const onUpdateLoginFieldHandler = (name: string, value: string) => {
  // console.log(`LoginPage.tsx :: Update name: ${name}, value: ${value}`)
  setUserLoginPageState({
    ...userLoginPageState,
    [name]: value,
  })
  // console.log(`LoginPage.tsx :: onUpdateLoginFieldHandler :: user ::
${JSON.stringify(user)}`)
}
```

On the JSX side, we check whether the form is loading via our state flag. We use the SubmitUserFormComponent, where we will put logic to make the service call or display the form depending on whether the form was submitted. The reason for this if/else conditional logic is that we don't want to show the LoginForm. If the user submits the form and it's being processed, we could create another page component to navigate to or split the code even more to more components. However, this design is sufficient for now as the code to show the results is simple.

```
  return (
    <Centered>
      {loading ? (
        <SubmitUserFormComponent />
      ) : (
        <Card>
          <CardHeader title="Members Login" />
          <CardContent>
            <LoginForm onLogin={onLogin} onUpdateLoginField={onUpdateLogin
            FieldHandler} loginInfo={userLoginPageState} loading={loading} />
          </CardContent>
        </Card>
      )}
    </Centered>
  )
}
```

SubmitUserForm Subcomponent

Lastly, our SubmitUserFormComponent is where the logic that uses the Recoil selector happens. We use the useRecoilValue pattern to call our selector.

```
function SubmitUserFormComponent() {
  const results = useRecoilValue(submitUserLoginSelector)
  const setSessionState = useSetRecoilState(sessionState)
  const setToastState = useSetRecoilState(toastState)
```

Once the results are retrieved from the selector, we need to set two methods to handle the success and fail logic. Here we can set our baked session state token that we can use in other components. In our case, the token is hard coding, but in real life we need to encrypt and decrypt a key and store it in a database whatever the business logic requires.

onSuccessLogin Logic

Here is the onSuccessLogin logic:

```
const onSuccessLogin = () => {
  localStorage.setItem('accessToken', 'myUniqueToken')
  setSessionState('myUniqueToken')
}
```

Notice that I am also using the localStorage browser API. That way, I can have the user come back to the page without the need to log in again, so I am setting the token on the localStorage.

onFailLogin Logic

For the failure logic, we can call the custom toast component we created and pass the failure message, for example a network error when our service is down.

```
const onFailLogin = () => {
  setToastState(initToast(randomToastId(), notificationTypesEnums.Fail,
  results))
  localStorage.removeItem('accessToken')
  setSessionState('')
}
```

Then we can use logic to check whether the value of retrieving the results from the server side is a success or fail.

```
results === 'success' ? onSuccessLogin() : onFailLogin()
```

On the JSX render level, we return a success message or a failure message, depending on the results retrieved from the service call. This can expand to be its own subcomponent if needed instead of just a text message.

```
return (
  {results === 'success' ? Success : We were unable to log you in please
  try again}
)
}
```

We have all our logic in place for the view of the login components including an atom and a selector that acts as our middleware and makes a service call.

Next, we will create a member component that can check the session token and display either the secure member area or the login component if the user did not log in.

Members Page

For our members area, we will update the member page component so that it will either show the login page or the exclusive member area home page. Take a look at the activity diagram in Figure 6-8.

MemberPage
LoginPage
MemberHome

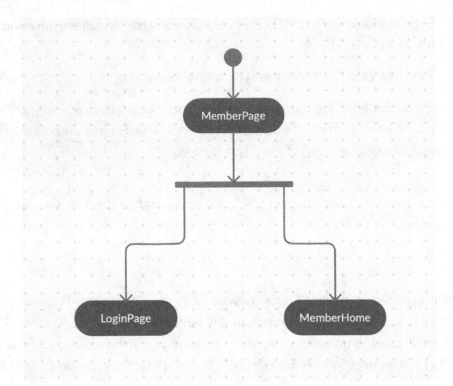

Figure 6-8. *Activity diagram for members area*

Let's start by creating a home page for the secure area that members can log in to called `MembersHome.tsx`. For now, that component just has a logout button that the code is set to clear the local storage. I am also going to empty the session state. That way, the other components will be updated automatically once the session state is changed, as shown in Figure 6-9.

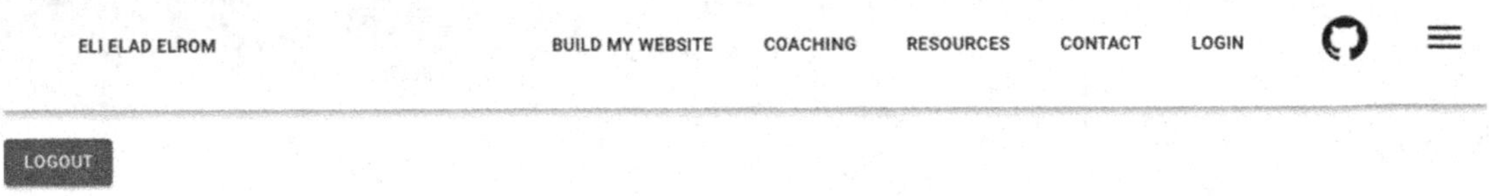

ELI ELAD ELROM
BUILD MY WEBSITE
COACHING
RESOURCES
CONTACT
LOGIN
LOGOUT

Figure 6-9. *Members exclusive area with a logout button*

MembersHome

On the code level, the MembersHome component will start by showing you the import libraries.

```
// src/page/MembersPage/MembersHome.tsx

import Button from '@material-ui/core/Button'
import React from 'react'
import { useSetRecoilState } from 'recoil'
import { sessionState } from '../../recoil/atoms/sessionAtoms'
```

Next, our pure function utilizes the useSetRecoilState pattern to be able to set the session state. We include the onClickHandler logic to log the user out. When we log out the user, we need to clear both the session shared atom and the localStorage.

```
const MembersHome = () => {
  const setSessionState = useSetRecoilState(sessionState)
  const onClickHandler = (e: React.MouseEvent) => {
    e.preventDefault()
    localStorage.removeItem('accessToken')
    setSessionState('')
  }
```

For the render, we only display a logout button at this point. This can be expanded to more subcomponents if we need a more complex view in the future.

```
  return (

      <Button type="submit" variant="contained" color="primary"
      onClick={onClickHandler}>
        Logout
      </Button>

  )
}

export default MembersHome
```

MembersPage

Lastly, we need a parent component for the members page called MembersPage.tsx that will hold a switch to either display the member secure area or the login page based on the token state.

```
// src/page/MembersPage/MembersPage.tsx

import React from 'react'
import './MembersPage.scss'
import { useRecoilValue } from 'recoil'
import LoginPage from '../LoginPage/LoginPage'
import MembersHome from './MembersHome'
import { sessionState } from '../../recoil/atoms/sessionAtoms'
```

The logic for the switch checks the session state if it equals a baked-in value of myUniqueToken. Later, we can create the logic to encrypt and decrypt the session and even store it inside our database.

I am checking whether both the Recoil shared state and localStorage is set to that value. We need both in case the user comes back to the page or the page was refreshed.

```
const MembersPage = () => {
  const isMemberHasAccess = useRecoilValue(sessionState) === 'myUnique
  Token' || localStorage.getItem('accessToken') === 'myUniqueToken'
  return <MembersPageInner isMemberHasAccess={isMemberHasAccess} />
}
```

For our inner component that displays the members page, we pass a prop called isMemberHasAccess that can tell the component whether the user should have access or not to the component, and that's what will be used as the condition to display the members or login component.

```
const MembersPageInner = (props: IMembersPageInnerProps) => (

    {props.isMemberHasAccess ? <MembersHome /> : <LoginPage />}

)
```

```
interface IMembersPageInnerProps {
  isMemberHasAccess: boolean
}
```

```
export default MembersPage
```

We are code complete. Bravo!

I will cover Jest testing in Chapter 9, but for now delete the Jest test for the member page, as we changed the code so our test won't pass: `MembersPage.test.tsx`.

Remember to run `format`, `lint`, and `test` to ensure the code quality.

```
$ yarn format & yarn lint & yarn test
```

We can finally run our code, if you are not running it already (`$ yarn start`), and take a look at our logic working with the preferences and the login system. See Figure 6-1.

If you try to log in, you will get an error message "We were unable to log you in please try again." That is expected since we did not set up our service call yet (Figure 6-10).

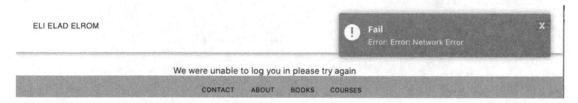

Figure 6-10. *Form fail toast and message*

Summary

This chapter drilled down into the coding. You learned more about how to structure your functions, classes, components, and subcomponents. You also learned about the MERN stack. We started the chapter by introducing you to Recoil. We changed the share user preference state from Redux Toolkit to Recoil, and you saw the differences between the two tools. You also saw how Recoil plays nicely with React with very little effort and how it feels out of the box compared to an imported library.

You also learned how to build an exclusive members-only area by creating a login system with React as the MERN stack front end, and we even created a custom toast message component to display messages to the user globally. Recoil has many functionalities to maintain the state throughout our component's lifecycle and even between the client and server sides. We only touched the surface with Recoil. I encourage you to visit the Recoil site (`https://recoiljs.org/`) and learn more about the possibilities. Now that our front end is ready, in the next chapter, you will learn how to set up the back end using Node.js, MongoDB, and Express.

CHAPTER 7

MERN Stack: Part II

In the previous chapter, you learned more about how to structure your React functions, classes, components, and subcomponents. You were introduced to the MERN stack. You learned about Recoil and how to build an exclusive members-only area by creating a login system with React as the MERN stack's front end. We even created a custom front-end toast message component to display messages.

In this chapter, we will pick up where we stopped in the previous chapter and start creating our back end with Node.js, Express, and MongoDB—the other parts of the MERN stack. In this chapter, you will see the full development cycle, from coding your front end to completing the back end so you have a working app. This app is capable of not just including components but actual functionality to log in to a secure members-only area and interacting with a database. It even provides the foundation to connect to a socket to receive live messages.

In the second part of this chapter, we will add a register component and complete the login cycle by encrypting and decrypting the user's password as well as updating the login selector so we can actually register a user and log into our exclusive member area.

What We'll Be Building

At this point in our app, if we try to actually log in to the exclusive members-only area we built in the previous exercise, we will get a network error, as shown in Figure 7-1.

© Elad Elrom 2021
E. Elrom, *React and Libraries*, https://doi.org/10.1007/978-1-4842-6696-0_7

Figure 7-1. *Attempting to log in to our app*

That's not an error. That is the correct behavior at this point. We get this message because we haven't set up our back-end service yet. In this chapter, we will set up our back-end logic and get the login system to work as well as complete the cycle by adding a register component and the backend API.

You can download the complete backend code that we will be creating from here:

`https://github.com/Apress/react-and-libraries/07/exercise-7-1`

Why Node.js?

Node.js should not be new to you. In fact, we already installed Node.js and have been using NPM, the Node.js package manager, since Chapter 1. We have been installing and using libraries from NPM.

Note   Node.js is a single-threaded, nonblocking framework based on Google's V8 JS engine.

Node.js makes code execution superfast. Node.js is a nonblocking, event-driven input/output approach that allows a significant number of fast concurrent connections. This is done with the JavaScript event loop.

When I say many, how many concurrent connections can we create? It really depends on the server we are running as well as the internal configuration settings of the server we are running.

In fact, Node.js can run 1,000 concurrent connections of Node.js at the same time on a standard Ubuntu server, without freezing up the CPU, and even that can be increased by libraries such as Posix (`https://github.com/ohmu/node-posix`). This is usually sufficient for small and medium-size apps, without setting a complex set of server stacks, load balancer, etc.

In fact, did you know that Node.js is being used by companies such as PayPal, LinkedIn, and Yahoo?

Why Express?

We can use the Node.js HTTP module and write our web server from scratch, so why do we need Express on top of Node.js?

Express is built on top of Node.js and utilizes the Node.js HTTP/HTTPS modules. There are many frameworks that are built on top of Node.js. Express is one of the oldest and widely used Node.js frameworks because it provides a separation of concerns. Express is used by companies such as Myspace, Twitter, Stack, and Accenture.

Note   Node.js is a fast, low-level input/output mechanism with an HTTP/HTTPS module built-in. Express is a web application framework that sits on top of Node.js. Express is light-weight and helps organize your server-side web application.

Why Should You Use MongoDB?

MongoDB is a document-oriented NoSQL database intended for high-volume data storage. Instead of storing data in tables and rows using traditional relational databases, MongoDB offers collections and documents. Documents consist of key-value pairs. Here is an interesting fact: more than 3,000 companies reportedly use MongoDB in their tech stacks, including Uber, Lyft, and the delivery service Hero.

Building the Back End

For the back-end service, we will be using Express to interact with MongoDB using a library that I created called `rooms.js` (https://github.com/EliEladElrom/roomsjs).

rooms.js is aimed at speeding up our development effort. rooms.js provides a way to send and receive messages and switch to different transporters to create rooms and stream data between users, stream data from a database, and even stream from a third-party CDN.

At the end of this process, we will be able to call the service file we will be creating on our localhost.

```
http://localhost:8081/validate?email=youremail@gmail.com&password=isDebug
```

In the next chapter, we will be publishing both our front ends and back ends in a project to a remote Ubuntu server so we can see the app running live.

I broke the process down in this chapter to these coding steps:

- Database schema
- Validate Service API
- Express framework
- MongoDB

You can download the complete code of the back-end code from here:

```
https://github.com/Apress/react-and-libraries/07/exercise-7-1
```

Database Schema

To get started, if you recall from our previous chapter when we learned about Recoil, our first step was to set up a model and then an atom. Our first step with our back-end project is going to be similar: setting up the data model on the back end. Go ahead and create a `database.js` file that we will be using to set up our database schema for our user. That schema will come in handy when we need to interact with the MongoDB database later. Our user object has an email and password of type `String`. Our database will include other variables that will come handy to when we want to register our user such as an encryption hash and salt (more about encryption later in the chapter), the last time the user logged in, the signup date, a login token, a phone number, a username, and how many times the user tried to log in but couldn't. Take a look:

```
// models/database.js
let usersSchema = {
    username: 'String',
    email: 'String',
    passwordHash: 'String',
    passwordSalt: 'String',
    lastLoginDate: 'String',
    attempt: 'Number',
    signDate: 'String',
    emailEachLogin: 'Boolean',
    loginToken: 'String',
    phone: 'String'
};

if (typeof exports != 'undefined' ) {
    exports.usersSchema = usersSchema;
}
```

Validate Service API

Next, we need to create a service API that we can use to validate our user. It needs to have an input of the user data and output an authentication response of success or fail. I am not showing here the register service API to set up a user register yet, but the login system usually needs to include encryption and decryption for security. Part of the code is implemented already and will come handy in our second part of this chapter.

At this point, I am allowing users to bypass all the encryption and decryption logic with a baked-in password of isDebug. I am also setting up a mechanism to check how many times the user tried to log into the system, so we can block users in case a hacker launches an assault robot on our login system to try to crack a user password. Security should always be your first priority.

To get started with our service API, we will create a service file and call it validate.js. Take a look at the code:

```
// src/services/validate.js
'use strict';
```

At the top of the file, it's good practice to use use strict to indicate that the code should be executed in strict mode, meaning we can't, for instance, use undeclared variables.

Next, we will use the database schema we created for the users in the previous step and define the libraries and variables we will be using.

```
let usersSchema = require("../models/database").usersSchema,
logger = require('../utils/log.js').logger,
moment = require("moment"),
CryptoJS = require('crypto-js'),
async = require('async'),
connector,
users,
isUserExists = false,
params,
user;
```

Our main function validate will take the data that we pass from our server file and the connection to the database we set.

```
function validate(data, dbconnectorCallBackToRooms) {

    connector = this.getConnector();
    params = data.query || data.params;
    params.member_id = -1;
```

We will be using async series logic. Node.js is an event-based loop, and we cannot stop Node.js; however, there are cases when we need to build logic that is based on an async call, and sometimes each operation relies on a previous operation or operations.

That can be done using the async.series library (https://github.com/hughsk/async-series). The library allows one or multiple operations that can be executed one after the other.

In our case, we just do one operation of checkUserInfo, but in future iterations we probably will expand this and include other operations, such as sending an email to the user that they have logged into our system or other required logic.

```
    let operations = ;
    operations.push(checkUserInfo);
```

```
async.series(operations, function (err, results) {

    let retData = {
        "exist_member_id": params.member_id,
        "isUserExists": isUserExists,
        "user": user
    };

    users = null;
    user = null;
    isUserExists = false;
    params = null;
```

Once the results are in from the async operations, we can pass them back to the output to display.

```
    if (err) {
        dbconnectorCallBackToRooms(data, {status: 'error', error_
        message: JSON.stringify(err), params: []});
    } else {
        dbconnectorCallBackToRooms(data, {status: 'success', params:
        retData});
    }
    });
}
```

For the checkUserInfo operation, we need to validate the user against the MongoDB database.

```
function checkUserInfo(callback) {

    logger.info('validate.js :: checkUserInfo');

    if (connector.isModelExists('users')) {
        users = connector.getModel('users');
    } else {
        let schema = connector.setSchema(usersSchema);
        users = connector.setModel('users', schema);
    }
```

```
let findObject = {
    email: (params.email).toLowerCase()
};
```

`users.find` is using the Mongoose library to sort through the MongoDB document, searching any document that has the object we define. In our case, this is the user's email address.

```
users.find(findObject)
    .then((doc) => {
        if (doc.length > 0) {
            user = doc[0]._doc;
            params.member_id = (user._id).toString();
```

Once we have the results, we can use `Hash` and `Salt` to decrypt the user information.

```
let passwordParam = (params.password).toString(),
    password = user.passwordHash,
    salt = user.passwordSalt,
    attempt = user.attempt,
    lastLoginDate = user.lastLoginDate;

let databaseTime = moment(lastLoginDate),
    now = moment().format(),
    diff = moment(now).diff(databaseTime, 'minutes');
```

If there are three bad attempts, we lock the user out for 60 seconds.

```
// don't even attempt to login - 3 attempts
if (diff < 60 && attempt >= 3) {
    callback('three_attempts_wait_one_hour', null);
} else {
    let decryptedDatabasePassword = (CryptoJS.AES.
    decrypt(password, salt)).toString(CryptoJS.enc.Utf8),
        decryptedURLParam = (CryptoJS.AES.
        decrypt(passwordParam, "SomeWordPhrase")).
        toString(CryptoJS.enc.Utf8),
```

```
loginSuccess = (decryptedDatabasePassword ===
decryptedURLParam && decryptedDatabasePassword
!== ''),
new_attempt_count = (loginSuccess) ? 0 :
attempt + 1;
```

For now, I am overwriting the entire encryption and decryption logic here, so we can test the service using a password of isDebug, but later I will expand how we can encrypt and decrypt. That is a standard protocol. The reason I broke it down into two steps is that first we just want to see our system working. Then we implement security, which is just good practice to ensure our code is working.

```
if (params.password === 'isDebug') {
    loginSuccess = true;
}

users.updateOne({"email": params.email}, {
    $set: {
        attempt: new_attempt_count,
        lastLoginDate: now
    }
}).then((doc) => {
    if (loginSuccess) {
        isUserExists = true;
        callback(null, null);
    } else {
        isUserExists = false;
        callback('No login success', null);
    }
}).catch((err) => {
    logger.info(err);
    callback(err.message, null);
});
}
```

```
            } else {
                callback('no user found', null);
            }
        })
        .catch((err) => {
            logger.info(err);
            callback(err.message, null);
        });
}

module.exports.validate = validate;
```

Express Framework

Now that we have our validate service API ready, we want to be able to access that logic and send data and display results.

To do that, we will be using Express, with the help of my own library called roomsjs (https://github.com/EliEladElrom/roomsjs). This library simplifies creating services, via SSL or HTTP, and the library can connect to any database (including MongoDB). We will set up MongoDB to use the default settings, but we could easily change the database to use MySQL or any other data source.

In Node.js, we can utilize the Express server using a server.js file that sets up our database and service library. We start by first importing the libraries we need.

```
// server.js
let os = require('os'),
    rooms = require('roomsjs'),
    roomdb = require('rooms.db'),
    bodyParser = require('body-parser'),
    port = (process.env.PORT || 8081),
    logger = require('./utils/log.js').logger,
    log = require('./utils/log.js'),
    isLocalHost = log.isLocalHost();
```

Next, we create the Express server.

```
let express = require('express'),
    app = express().use(express.static(__dirname + '/public'));
```

We need the logic to allow cross domain.

```
// will overcome the No Access-Control-Allow-Origin header error
let allowCrossDomain = function(req, res, next) {
    res.header("Access-Control-Allow-Origin", "*");
    res.header("Access-Control-Allow-Headers", "Origin, X-Requested-With,
    Content-Type, Accept");
    next();
};
app.use(allowCrossDomain);
Parse any 'url' encoded 'params';
app.use(bodyParser.urlencoded({ extended: false }));
app.use(bodyParser.json());
```

For now, we only need the HTTP module as we will be running this logic on a local box, but in the next chapter when we publish to production, we will add logic for HTTPS.

```
// create server
let server = require('http').createServer(app).listen(port, function () {
    logger.info('Listening on http://' + os.hostname() + ':' + port);
});
```

roomdb (https://github.com/EliEladElrom/roomsdb) is the roomjs companion library. It sets a connector to any database, as well as iterates through any service files that we set.

```
// services
roomdb.setServices('services/', app, 'get');

logger.info('hostname: ' + os.hostname());
let roomsSettingsJSON;

logger.info('*** Listening *** :: ' + os.hostname() + ', localhost: ' +
isLocalHost);
roomsSettingsJSON = (isLocalHost) ? require('./roomsdb-local.json') :
require('./roomsdb.json');

roomdb.connectToDatabase('mongodb', 'mongodb://' + roomsSettingsJSON.
environment.host + '/YourSite', { useNewUrlParser: true,
useUnifiedTopology: true });
```

The library sets a transporter using a socket. We don't need a socket at this point, and HTTP is sufficient in our logic, but it's good to have. Sockets can be used in case we want to create an app that needs live messages, for instance, a chat app.

```
// set rooms
rooms = new rooms({
    isdebug : true,
    transporter : {
        type: 'engine.io',
        server : server
    },
    roomdb : roomdb
});
```

This is beyond the scope of this chapter, but I wanted you to be aware of what's possible.

Lastly, we want to catch any uncaughtExceptions and display them so we can work out any issues with our code.

```
process.on('uncaughtException', function (err) {
    logger.error('uncaughtException: ' + err);
});
```

Local MongoDB

The last piece of the puzzle is to set up MongoDB on our local box. In the next chapter, we will create our MongoDB on a remote server as well as publish our code, but for now we need a working local build first.

We can create a local MongoDB using the following commands on a Mac. To get started, we can install MongoDB with Homebrew.

Note   Homebrew is open source package management to simplify the installation of software on macOS and Linux. brew is the core command of Homebrew.

First install Brew with Ruby and then update it.

```
$ ruby -e "$(curl -fsSL https://raw.githubusercontent.com/Homebrew/install/
master/install)"
$ brew doctor
$ brew update
```

Next, use the brew command to install MongoDB and set the location and permission of the MongoDB data we are storing.

```
$ brew install mongodb
$ sudo mkdir /data
$ sudo mkdir /data/db
$ sudo chown -R `id -un` /data/db
$ cd /Locally run mongodb
```

That's it. We have MongoDB installed and ready to be used.

Now, we can run Mongod and Mongo; see Figure 7-2 and Figure 7-3.

```
$ mongod
```

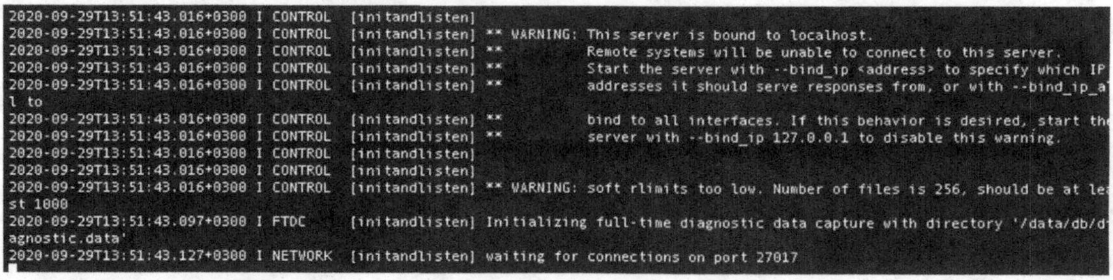

Figure 7-2. *Mongod process running in Mac terminal*

```
$ mongo
```

```
---
Enable MongoDB's free cloud-based monitoring service, which will then receive and display
metrics about your deployment (disk utilization, CPU, operation statistics, etc).

The monitoring data will be available on a MongoDB website with a unique URL accessible to you
and anyone you share the URL with. MongoDB may use this information to make product
improvements and to suggest MongoDB products and deployment options to you.

To enable free monitoring, run the following command: db.enableFreeMonitoring()
To permanently disable this reminder, run the following command: db.disableFreeMonitoring()
---

>
```

Figure 7-3. *mongo shell command*

Why two commands? What do these commands mean?

Mongod will start the MongoDB process and run it in the background. Mongo will give us a command-line shell that is connected to the Mongod process we are running. Inside the Mongo shell, we can execute commands.

This depends on the MongoDB version you have installed. Some MongoDB versions run as services in the background, and the terminal does not need to stay open.

Note   Mongod ("Mongo daemon") is the daemon process for MongoDB. Mongod handles the MongoDB data requests, manages the data access, and runs management operations. mongo is a command-line shell to connect to Mongod.

Now inside the Mongo shell terminal window, we need to create our database name.

```
$ use YourDatabaseName
```

Then we insert our user.

```
db.users.insert({"username": "user", "email":"youremail@gmail.
com", password:"123456", passwordHash: "someHash", passwordSalt:
"someSalt", attempt: 0, lastLoginDate: "2020-01-15T12:10:00+00:00",
"signDate":"2020-01-15T11:50:12+00:00" })
```

You can confirm this worked by using the following:

```
db.users.find();
```

This command will return the user we inserted. Although you can type all the commands in the Mongo shell, there are many graphical user interfaces (GUIs) to help manage the MongoDB database. Two good GUIs that I recommend and that can help are Compass (`https://www.mongodb.com/try/download/compass`) and nosqlbooster (`https://nosqlbooster.com/downloads`).

These tools can help back up, export, import, and run commands. See the download page of MongoDB Compass provided by the MongoDB team, as shown in Figure 7-4.

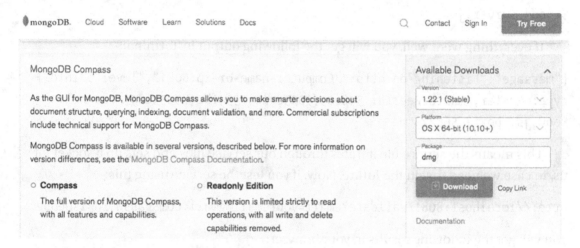

Figure 7-4. *MongoDB Compass GUI download page*

There are many tools, paid and free, so feel free to do your own research (DYOR). Each tool offers different sets of features based on the subscription and supports different platforms. I am not recommending any tools, and you don't have to use any GUI. The Mongo command-line shell could be all that you need.

To connect and set up these GUI tools, the process is the same: we connect to MongoDB on our local or remote box. Since we did not change the default MongoDB, the port of MongoDB should be 27017.

```
GUI Client > local localhost:27017 > connect
```

Many GUIs also support pasting in a URI. The URI for localhost without security in place will look like this:

URI: mongodb://localhost:27017

> **Note**   The URI value represents a uniform resource identifier (URI) to create a Mongo instance. A URI describes the hosts and options.

Now that we have our MongoDB database set up, we have created our service API, and we have a Node.js server file that utilizes Express, we are ready to run our back-end service. In a separate window, call this:

```
$ node server.js
```

If everything went well, you will get the following output in Terminal:

```
{"message":"Listening on http://Computer-name-or-ip:8081","level":"info"}
type: master, masterPeerId: 548e09f70356a1237594fbe489e33684, channel:
roomsjs, port: 56622
```

This means the service file iterates through our service files and sets up a socket for us, in case we need that in the future. Now, if you test the service using this:

```
http://localhost:8081/validate?email=youremail@gmail.com&password=isDebug
```

you will get the following results in your browser:

```
{"status":"success","params":{"exist_member_id":"5f58278c81cb4a742188d3c
b","isUserExists":true,"user":{"_id":"5f58278c81cb4a742188d3cb","user":
"user", "email":"YouEmail@gmail.com","password":"123456","passwordHash":"
someHash","passwordSalt":"someSalt","attempt":0,"lastLoginDate":"2020-01-
15T12:10:00+00:00","signDate":"2020-01-15T11:50:12+00:00"}}}
```

Next, if you check your front-end code, using the isDebug password and the email address you set, you can run your app again ($yarn start). You'll find we can log into our secure member area successfully. Figure 7-5 shows the member secure area that right now only has the logout button that we created in the previous chapter.

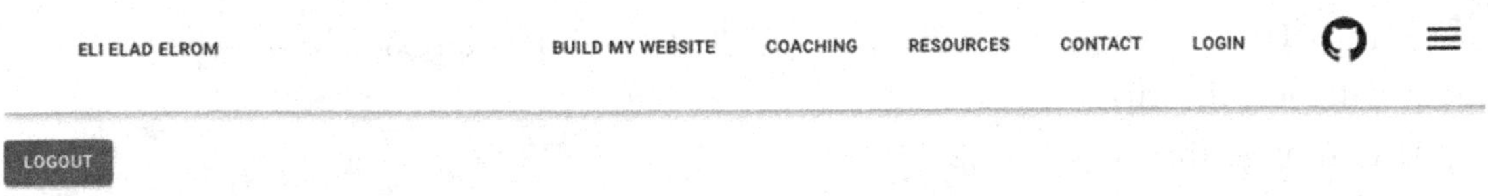

Figure 7-5. *Secure member area after user logged in successfully*

Now let's open our browser developer console. In Chrome DevTools, for instance, select View ➤ Developer ➤ Developer Tools from top menu.

We can see that our app created the accessToken inside our local storage, with the value we set, as shown in Figure 7-6. These values are used in our app to determine if the user can access the secure area.

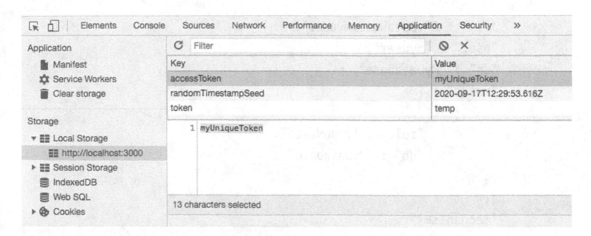

Figure 7-6. *Chrome developer tools local storage values*

Setting Up MongoDB Authentication

We have MongoDB set up on our local machine, so the next step is to create MongoDB authentication. Without authentication, any unauthorized user can just connect to your database and do as they please.

To set that up, in Terminal, connect to the Mongo shell terminal as an admin (ensure Mongod is running). Once we are connected to the database, we can create the user we will be using and set the roles of reading and writing. Here are the commands:

```
$ mongo admin
$ use MyDatabase
switched to db MyDatabase

$ db.createUser({ user: "myuser", pwd: "YOUR_PASSWORD", roles:
["readWrite"] })
Successfully added user: { "user" : "myuser", "roles" : [ "readWrite" ] }
```

For a sanity check, we can run the getUsers command to ensure our user was added correctly.

```
$ db.getUsers()
[
    {
        "_id" : "MyDatabase.myuser",
        "user" : "myuser",
        "db" : "MyDatabase",
        "roles" : [
            {
                "role" : "readWrite",
                "db" : "MyDatabase"
            }
        ],
        "mechanisms" : [
            "SCRAM-SHA-1",
            "SCRAM-SHA-256"
        ]
    }
]
```

Next, disconnect from the Mongo shell (Cmd+C).

We have our user with a secure password. Next, we can enable authentication in the Mongod configuration file. Enable security, if it's not already.

```
$ vim /usr/local/etc/mongod.conf
security: authorization: enabled
```

Great! Now connect to MongoDB with the username and password.

```
$ mongo MyDatabase -u myuser -p YOUR_PASSWORD
```

Bravo! Now our database is password-protected. In the Mongo shell or GUI, if you try to connect without credentials, you will get an error, as shown in Figure 7-7.

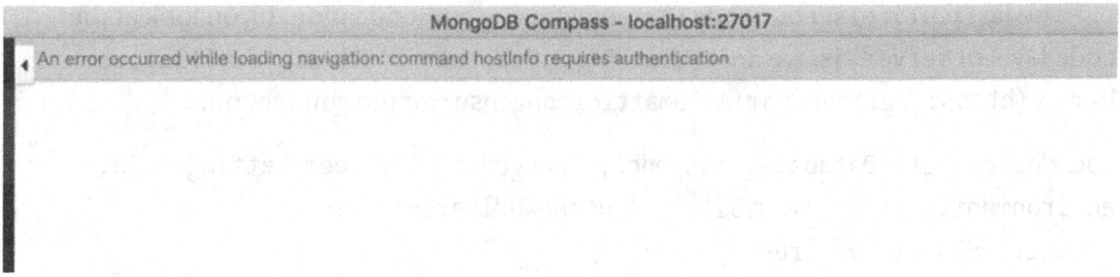

Figure 7-7. *Authentication error on MongoDB Compass*

To solve this authentication error, we need to connect with our credentials, as shown in Figure 7-8.

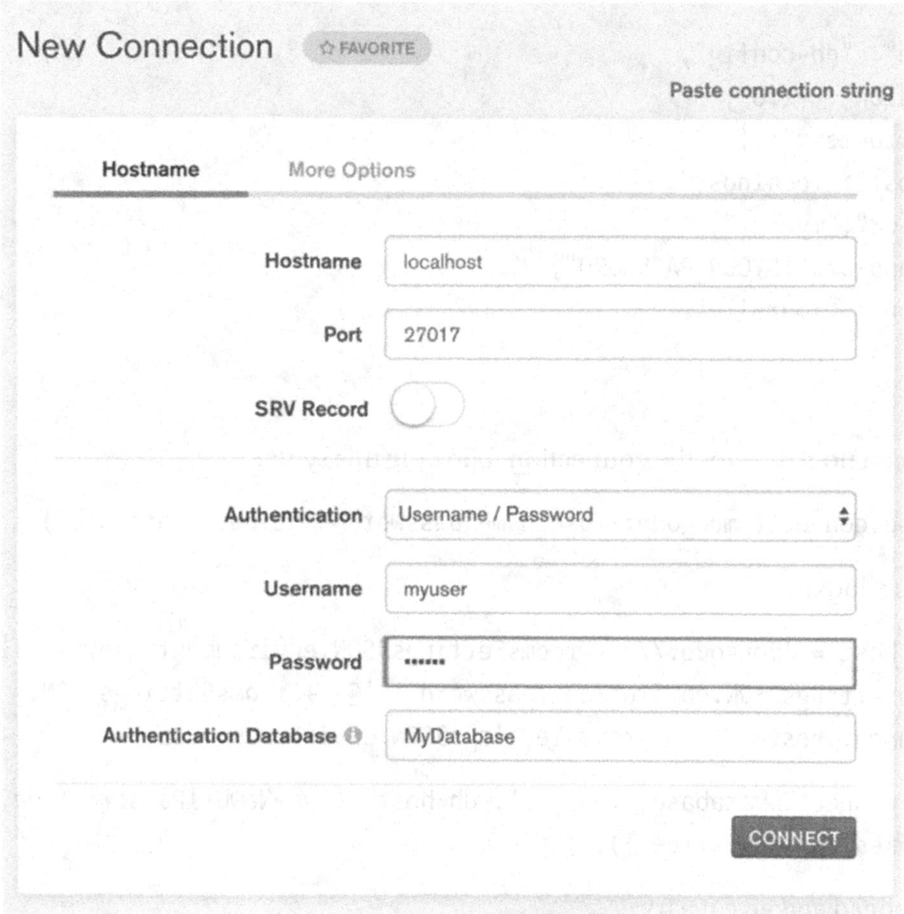

Figure 7-8. *Setting authentication in MongoDB Compass*

The last part is to set our code to connect using authentication. If you look at the code level of server.js, we are connecting with roomdb, which uses the Mongoose library (https://github.com/Automattic/mongoose) for the connection.

```
roomdb.connectToDatabase('mongodb', 'mongodb://' + roomsSettingsJSON.
environment.host + '/YourSite', { useNewUrlParser: true,
useUnifiedTopology: true });
```

The code is set to using a local file (roomsdb-local.json) on your local box and roomsdb.json on a remote box (which we will set in the next chapter).

If we set the new authentication information in our roomsdb-local.json file, we have this:

```
{
  "name": "db-config",
  "version": "1.0",
  "environment": {
    "host":"localhost",
    "user":"myuser",
    "password":"YOUR_PASSWORD",
    "dsn": "YourSite"
  }
}
```

We can now refactor the connection following this syntax:

```
mongoose.connect('mongodb://username:password@host:port/database')
```

Take a look:

```
let db_host = 'mongodb://' + roomsSettingsJSON.environment.user + ':'
+ roomsSettingsJSON.environment.password + '@' + roomsSettingsJSON.
environment.host + '/' + roomsSettingsJSON.environment.dsn;

roomdb.connectToDatabase('mongodb', db_host, { useNewUrlParser: true,
useUnifiedTopology: true });
```

Go ahead and give it a try:

```
$ node server.js
```

This design prepares us for production, as we have two files for development and production (`roomsdb-local.json` and `roomsdb.json`) holding the database information and the code switch between them based on where the code is running.

Full Login Register System

So far, we completed a full cycle from the front end to the back end for the login component, but we are still not code complete. Our code is not reading and writing into our MongoDB.

The reason is that in real life, we need to encrypt and decrypt the user's password instead of just passing in baked-in data. To do that, we need to add some register logic that can take the user's password string, encrypt the string, and then store it in our database. When the user wants to log in, we want to decrypt the user's password and match it with the password the user provided in the login input box. All of this is a normal security protocol for a secured login-register system.

In this part of this chapter, we will do just that. We will create a register component that encrypts the user's password and a service API to write the data into our MongoDB. Lastly, we will refactor our Recoil login selector to encrypt the password before sending it, so we can test reading the user's password and compare the results.

You can download the complete front-end code that we will be coding from here:

`https://github.com/Apress/react-and-libraries/07/exercise-7-2`

Let's begin.

Register Model

We can start off the same way we did with the login component, from the model object. Create a `registerObject.ts` with the register information we want to capture.

In our case, our form will capture the username, email, and password and will ensure the password was inserted correctly with a repeat password input. This can be expanded to any other information you would like to capture. We also will set the `initRegister` method to set our default values.

```
export interface registerObject {
  username: string
  email: string
```

```
  password: string
  repeat_password: string
}

export const initRegister = (): registerObject => ({
  username: '',
  email: '',
  password: '',
  repeat_password: '',
})
```

Remember to also add the register model to the `src/model/index.ts` file for easy access.

```
// src/model/index.ts
export * from './registerObject'
```

Register Atom

Next is setting up our Recoil atom. Create a new file and call it `registerAtoms.ts`. The file will use `initRegister` to set the default values.

```
// src/recoil/atoms/regsiterAtoms.ts
import { atom } from 'recoil'
import { initRegister } from '../../model'

export const registerState = atom({
  key: 'RegisterState',
  default: initRegister(),
})
```

Now that we have our atom ready, we can continue and create our register selector.

Register Selector

For encrypting and decrypting the user's password, we will be using a library called `crypto-js` (https://github.com/brix/crypto-js). It's a JavaScript library of crypto standards.

We will need both the library and the types installed.

```
$ yarn add crypto-js @types/crypto-js
```

Our registerSelectors.ts is going to be similar to our login selector.

```
// src/recoil/selectors/registerSelectors.ts

import { selector } from 'recoil'
import axios from 'axios'
import { registerState } from '../atoms/registerAtoms'
import * as CryptoJS from 'crypto-js'

export const registerUserSelector = selector({
  key: 'RegisterUserSelector',
  get: async ({ get }) => {
    const payload = get(registerState)
    if (
      payload.email === '' ||
      payload.password === '' ||
      payload.repeat_password === '' ||
      payload.username === '' ||
      payload.repeat_password !== payload.password
    ) {
      // eslint-disable-next-line no-console
      console.log(
        'registerSelectors.ts :: registerUserSelector :: ERROR incomplete
        form :: ' +
          JSON.stringify(payload)
      )
      return 'Error: Please complete form'
    }
    try {
      // console.log('registerSelectors.ts :: registerUserSelector :: start
      encrypt')
```

But we will add the encryption. To encrypt, we can create a secret passphrase that we can decide on and then use the `CryptoJS.AES.encrypt` method to encrypt our password. Take a look:

```
const secretPassphrase = 'mySecretPassphrase'
const passwordEncrypt = CryptoJS.AES.encrypt(payload.password,
secretPassphrase)
const passwordEncryptEncodeURI = encodeURIComponent(passwordEncrypt.
toString())
// console.log('passwordEncryptEncodeURI: ' +
passwordEncryptEncodeURI)
```

In addition, we can get prepared for publishing our code for production, which we will be doing in the next chapter. CRA accepts adding environment variables (`https://create-react-app.dev/docs/adding-custom-environment-variables/`). In fact, `process.env.NODE_ENV` is already baked into our app with the word `development` or `production`. We can use it to set our service API URL that we can set in our code.

```
const host = process.env.NODE_ENV === 'development' ? 'http://
localhost:8081' : ''
// console.log(
  `userSelectors.ts :: submitUserLoginSelector :: process.env.NODE_
  ENV: ${process.env.NODE_ENV}`
)
const urlWithString =
  host +
  '/register?name=' +
  payload.username.toLowerCase() +
  '&email=' +
  payload.email.toLowerCase() +
  '&password=' +
  passwordEncryptEncodeURI
// eslint-disable-next-line no-console
console.log('registerSelectors.ts :: registerUserSelector ::
url: ' + urlWithString)
const res = await axios({
  url: urlWithString,
```

```
    method: 'get',
  })
  // const status = `${res.data.status}`
  // console.log(`userSelectors.ts :: registerUserSelector :: results:
     ${JSON.stringify(status)}`)
  return res?.data?.status
} catch (err) {
  // console.warn(err)
  return `Error: ${err}`
}
},
})
```

Our register selector is complete and ready to be used. However, before we continue and build our view presentation layer, we can also adjust the login selector to send the encrypt string of our password for security. Let's take a look.

Refactor Login

In this section, we will refactor our login so it will adjust our userSelectors.ts logic so that it sends an encrypted version of our user's password.

From just passing the username and password, we have this:

```
const urlWithString = `http://localhost:8081/validate?email=${payload.
email}&password=${payload.password}`
```

To encrypt the username and password with the help of the crypto-js library (yarn add crypto-js), use this:

```
// src/recoil/selectors/userSelectors.ts

import * as CryptoJS from 'crypto-js'

const secretPassphrase = 'mySecretPassphrase'
const passwordEncrypt = CryptoJS.AES.encrypt(payload.password,
secretPassphrase)
const passwordEncryptEncodeURI = encodeURIComponent(passwordEncrypt.
toString())
```

```
// console.log('passwordEncryptEncodeURI: ' + passwordEncryptEncodeURI)
const urlWithString = `${host}/validate?email=${payload.email}&password=${p
asswordEncryptEncodeURI}`
```

Great! Now we have both our login and register selectors ready to pass the user's encrypted password to our service APIs.

In the next chapter, we will publish to production and set our app on an SSL server so the data is not only encrypted but also secured from hackers stealing our users' information. As you recall, we also placed some logic to check how many attempts the user tried to log in for extra security.

Register View Layer

For the register view layer, we will be using the same approach that we did with the login view layer. We will be creating the following:

- `RegisterForm.tsx` and `RegisterForm.styles.ts`

- `RegisterPage.tsx`, which includes `RegisterPageInner`, `SubmitUserFormComponent`, and `onFailRegister` as subcomponents

Take a look at the register component hierarchy, as shown in Figure 7-9.

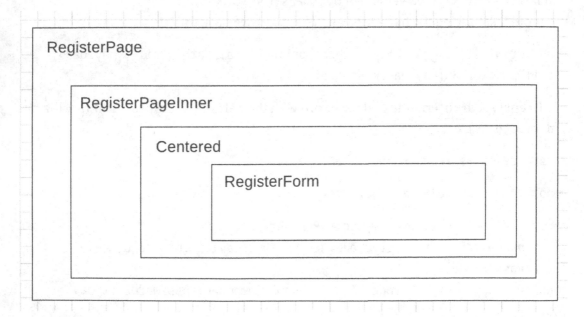

Figure 7-9. *Register view layer component hierarchy wireframe*

In `RegisterForm.tsx`, our `RegisterPage` will wrap the `RegisterPageInner` pure subcomponent for the React hooks to work. Once the user submits the atom, the form is updated, and the changes will be reflected in `SubmitUserFormComponent`, just as we did with the login component. The `onSuccessRegister` and `onFailRegister` methods handle what to do on success and failed login attempts. This is the same process we used for the `Login` view layer in the previous chapter. See Figure 7-10, which shows an activity flow diagram of this process.

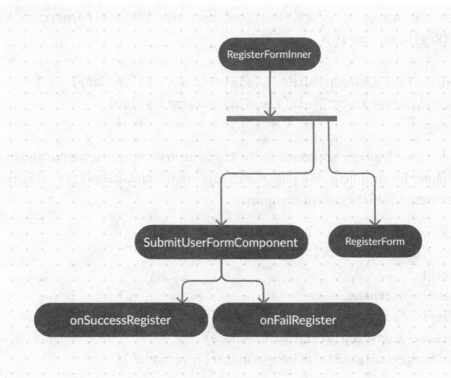

Figure 7-10. *Register activity flow diagram*

Register Form

Our register form is the subcomponent that holds the register form elements. We will start by showing the imported libraries.

```
// src/components/Register/RegisterForm.tsx
import * as React from 'react'
import TextField from '@material-ui/core/TextField'
```

```
import Button from '@material-ui/core/Button'
import { withStyles, WithStyles } from '@material-ui/core/styles'
import CircularProgress from '@material-ui/core/CircularProgress'
import styles from './RegisterForm.styles'
import { registerObject } from '../../model/registerObject'
```

RegisterFormInner is our wrapped React function component that we will be using to pass the styles and props.

```
const RegisterFormInner: React.FunctionComponent<IRegisterFormProps> = (
  props: IRegisterFormProps
) => {
  const onTextFieldChangeHandler = (fieldId: any) => (e: any) => {
    props.onUpdateRegisterField(fieldId, e.target.value)
  }
```

The code takes the same approach as the Login form component we created in the previous chapter for simplicity. We pass the changes to the onUpdateRegisterField and onRegister methods to the parent component.

```
  return (
    <div className={props.classes.container}>
      <TextField
        label="username"
        margin="normal"
        value={props.registerInfo.username}
        onChange={onTextFieldChangeHandler('username')}
      />
      <TextField
        label="email address"
        margin="normal"
        value={props.registerInfo.email}
        onChange={onTextFieldChangeHandler('email')}
      />
      <TextField
        label="password"
        type="password"
```

```
            margin="normal"
            value={props.registerInfo.password}
            onChange={onTextFieldChangeHandler('password')}
          />
          <TextField
            label="repeat password"
            type="password"
            margin="normal"
            value={props.registerInfo.repeat_password}
            onChange={onTextFieldChangeHandler('repeat_password')}
          />
          <Button
            variant="contained"
            color="primary"
            disabled={props.loading}
            onClick={props.onRegister}
          >
            Register
            {props.loading && <CircularProgress size={30} color="secondary" />}
          </Button>
        </div>
      )
    }
```

Our interface can tie to our registerObject to set the default values.

```
interface IRegisterFormProps extends WithStyles<typeof styles> {
  onRegister: () => void
  onUpdateRegisterField: (name: string, value: any) => void
  registerInfo: registerObject
  loading: boolean
}
```

Lastly, our Form subcomponent ties the style object.

```
export const RegisterForm = withStyles(styles)(RegisterFormInner)
```

Register Form Style

In our RegisterForm.styles.ts file, we set the container style to align our container in a flex column style.

```
// src/components/Register/RegisterForm.styles.ts
import { createStyles, Theme } from '@material-ui/core/styles'

export default (theme: Theme) =>
  createStyles({
    container: {
      display: 'flex',
      flexDirection: 'column',
      justifyContent: 'center',
    },
  })
```

Now that we have our Form subcomponent with the style set, we can create our parent component, which is the register page.

Register Page

We don't have the RegisterPage component created yet. You can create the register page using generate-react-cli.

```
$ npx generate-react-cli component RegisterPage --type=page
```

In our RegisterPage.tsx component, let's update the code. First set the import statements.

```
src/pages/RegisterPage/RegisterPage.tsx
import React, { useState } from 'react'
import { Card, CardContent, CardHeader } from '@material-ui/core'
import { useRecoilState, useRecoilValue, useSetRecoilState } from 'recoil'
import { Centered } from '../../layout/Centered'
import { RegisterForm } from '../../components/Register/RegisterForm'
import { initToast, notificationTypesEnums, randomToastId } from '../../
model'
import { registerState } from '../../recoil/atoms/registerAtoms'
```

```
import { toastState } from '../../recoil/atoms/toastAtoms'
import { registerUserSelector } from '../../recoil/selectors/
registerSelectors'
import { sessionState } from '../../recoil/atoms/sessionAtoms'
import { initRegister } from '../../model/registerObject'
```

Next, we set our RegisterPage to wrap the RegisterPageInner subcomponent for the React hooks.

```
const RegisterPage = () => {
  return <RegisterPageInner />
}
```

In RegisterPageInner we pass the props and get the register state object.

```
function RegisterPageInner(props: IRegisterPageProps) {
  const [userRegisterPageState, setUserRegisterPageState] =
  useState(initRegister)
  const [loading, setLoading] = useState(false)
  const [user, setUser] = useRecoilState(registerState)
  const onRegister = () => {
    setLoading(true)
    setUser(userRegisterPageState)
  }
```

Once the onUpdateRegisterFieldHandler is called from our form, we update the state.

```
  const onUpdateRegisterFieldHandler = (name: string, value: string) => {
    setUserRegisterPageState({
      ...userRegisterPageState,
      [name]: value,
    })
  }
```

On the JSX side, we set the `SubmitUserFormComponent` in case the form was submitted or display the form.

```
return (
  <Centered>
    {loading ? (
      <SubmitUserFormComponent />
    ) : (
      <Card>
        <CardHeader title="Register Form" />
        <CardContent>
          <RegisterForm
            onRegister={onRegister}
            onUpdateRegisterField={onUpdateRegisterFieldHandler}
            registerInfo={userRegisterPageState}
            loading={loading}
          />
        </CardContent>
      </Card>
    )}
  </Centered>
)
}
interface IRegisterPageProps {
  // TODO
}
export default RegisterPage
```

The `SubmitUserFormComponent` subcomponent is where we use the selector to make the service call and display the results.

```
function SubmitUserFormComponent() {
  console.log(`RegisterPage.tsx :: SubmitUserFormComponent`)
  const results = useRecoilValue(registerUserSelector)
  const setSessionState = useSetRecoilState(sessionState)
  const setToastState = useSetRecoilState(toastState)
```

The onSuccessRegister and onFailRegister methods handle what to do on a successful login attempt and on a failed login attempt. At this point, we just tie this to a baked-in token that we create, but later we can implement a logic to have our back-end system generate unique tokens and have these tokens interpreted by our front-end code; for instance, we can have them expire in 24 hours.

```
const onSuccessRegister = () => {
  localStorage.setItem('accessToken', 'myUniqueToken')
  setSessionState('myUniqueToken')
}
const onFailRegister = () => {
  setToastState(initToast(randomToastId(), notificationTypesEnums.Fail,
  results))
  localStorage.removeItem('accessToken')
  setSessionState('')
}
results === 'success' ? onSuccessRegister() : onFailRegister()
return (
  <div className="RegisterPage">
    {results === 'success' ? (
      Success
    ) : (
      We were unable to register you in please try again. Message:
      `{results}`
    )}

  )
}
```

For the style SCSS, we can set up some padding on the button so the page formats nicely, since we don't have content other than the logout button.

```
RegisterPage.scss
.RegisterPage {
  padding-bottom: 350px;
}
```

We have completed our front-end view for the register component.

Refactor AppRouter

To display the `RegisterPage` page we created, we need to include the page component in our `AppRouter` component. Take a look:

```
// src/AppRouter.tsx
```

```
import Register from './pages/RegisterPage/RegisterPage'

function AppRouter() {
  return (
    <Router>
      <RecoilRoot>
        <Suspense fallback={<span>Loading...</span>}>
          <ToastNotification />
          <HeaderTheme />
          <Switch>
            <Route exact path="/" component={App} />
<Route exact path="/Register" component={Register} />
            ...
          </Switch>
          <div className="footer">
            <FooterTheme />
          </div>
        </Suspense>
      </RecoilRoot>
    </Router>
  )
}
```

Register User Service API

Now that we have our front-end code complete, we can create our `register.js` service file in our Node.js app. The service is similar to `validate.js`.

Let's take a look. Our `imports` statements include the `crypto-js` library, so we can decrypt the password using the same library we used in the React app.

```
// src/services/register.js
'use strict';

let usersSchema = require("../models/database").usersSchema,
    logger = require('../utils/log.js').logger,
    moment = require("moment"),
    async = require('async'),
    CryptoJS = require('crypto-js'),
    params,
    user,
    isUserExists = false,
    connector,
    users;
```

Our main function, register, includes three operations: readUserInfoFromDB, insertUser, and getUserId.

```
function register(data, dbconnectorCallBackToRooms) {
    logger.info('---------- register ----------');
    connector = this.getConnector();
    params = data.query || data.params;
    params.member_id = -1;

    let operations = [];
    operations.push(readUserInfoFromDB);
    operations.push(insertUser);
    operations.push(getUserId);

    async.series(operations, function (err, results) {
        let retData = {
            "exist_member_id": params.member_id,
            "isUserExists": isUserExists,
            "user": user
        };

        user = null;
        users = null;
```

```
            isUserExists = false;
            params = null;

            if (err) {
                logger.info(err);
                dbconnectorCallBackToRooms(data, {status: 'error', error_
                message: err, params: retData});
            } else {
                dbconnectorCallBackToRooms(data, {status: 'success', params:
                retData});
            }
    });
}
```

The readUserInfoFromDB operation will check if the user already exists in the database because we don't want to have multiple users using the same email addresses.

```
function readUserInfoFromDB(callback) {
    logger.info('---------- register :: readUserInfoFromDB ----------');
    if (connector.isModelExists('users')) {
        users = connector.getModel('users');
    } else {
        let schema = connector.setSchema(usersSchema);
        users = connector.setModel('users', schema);
    }
    let findObject = {
        username: params.name,
    };
    users.find(findObject)
        .then((doc) => {
            if (doc.length > 0) {
                isUserExists = true;
                params.member_id = doc[0]._id;
                logger.info('isUserExists');
            } else {
                isUserExists = false;
            }
```

```
        callback(null, doc);
    })
    .catch((err) => {
        logger.info(err);
        params.member_id = -1;
        callback(err.message, null);
    });
}
```

Our `insertUser` operation will decrypt the password with the same secret string we created on our React front-end code. We are adding a random `salt` and `hash` to ensure that our user's password is stored securely in our database.

The reason is that we don't want to use the same password secret for all of our passwords, but a unique secret key for each password. This is a common secure protocol to ensure our users' personal information is protected.

```
function insertUser(callback) {
    logger.info('---------- register :: insertUser isUserExists :: ' +
    isUserExists + ', member_id: ' + params.member_id);
    if (isUserExists) {
        callback('error', 'user_exists_already');
    } else {
        let passwordEncrypt;
        let secretPassphrase = 'mySecretPassphrase';
```

With all the security in place, I am setting an override of the password, `isDebug`, which is used for testing purposes only and should be removed on a production build.

```
        if (params.password === 'isDebug') {
            passwordEncrypt = CryptoJS.AES.encrypt("123456",
            secretPassphrase);
            let passwordEncryptEncodeURI = encodeURIComponent
            (passwordEncrypt);
            logger.info('debug passwordEncryptEncodeURI: ' +
            passwordEncryptEncodeURI);
        } else {
            passwordEncrypt = params.password;
        }
```

```
let user_password = (CryptoJS.AES.decrypt(passwordEncrypt,
secretPassphrase)).toString(CryptoJS.enc.Utf8),
    pass_salt = Math.random().toString(36).slice(-8),
    encryptedPassword = CryptoJS.AES.encrypt(user_password,
    pass_salt),
    now = moment().format();

logger.info('---------- register :: insertUser :: user_password : '
+ user_password);

let newUsers = new users({
    username: (params.name).toLowerCase(),
    email: (params.email).toLowerCase(),
    passwordHash: encryptedPassword,
    passwordSalt: pass_salt,
    lastLoginDate: now,
    attempt: 0,
    signDate: now,
    emailEachLogin: true,
    loginToken: '',
    phone: ''
});

newUsers.save(function (err) {
    if (err) {
        logger.info('Error' + err.message);
        callback(err.message, null);
    } else {
        callback(null, 'success');
    }
});
    }
}
```

Lastly, the getUserId operation will retrieve the userId so we can pass that to our app and ensure our data was inserted correctly.

```
function getUserId(callback) {
    if (isUserExists) {
        callback('error', 'user_exists_already');
    } else {
        logger.info('register :: getUserId');

        users.find({
            username: params.name,
        })
        .then((doc) => {
            if (doc.length > 0) {
                params.member_id = doc[0]._id;
                callback(null, doc);
            } else {
                callback('error username return no results');
            }
        })
        .catch((err) => {
            logger.info(err);
            callback(err.message, null);
        });
    }
}

module.exports.register = register;
```

Tip   I left plenty of logging comments in the code to help you debug and understand the code better in both the front-end and back-end code.

Now run Node.js and Mongo in two Terminal windows.

```
$ node server.js
$ mongod
```

If you navigate to the register page at http://localhost:3000/Register, you will see the screen in Figure 7-11. You can now register a new user.

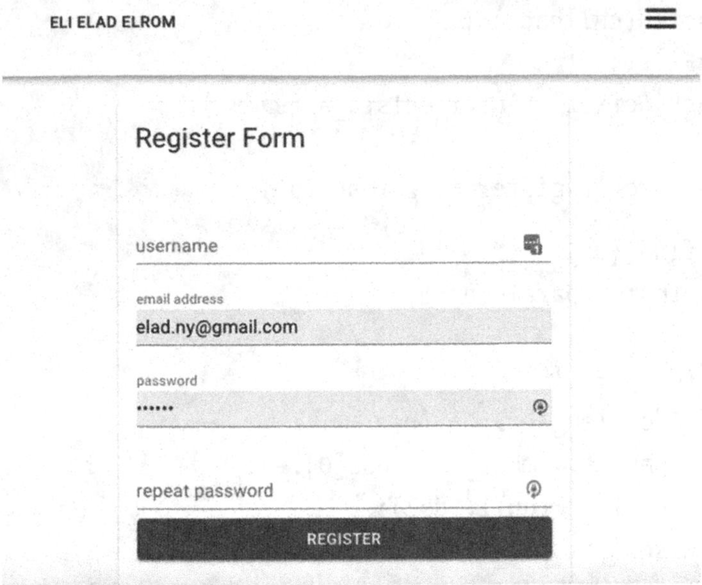

ELI ELAD ELROM ≡

Register Form

username

email address

elad.ny@gmail.com

password

••••••

repeat password

REGISTER

Figure 7-11. *Register page*

If everything went well, you can use a Mongo shell or other GUI of your liking to view the database and see the user we just entered. See Figure 7-12.

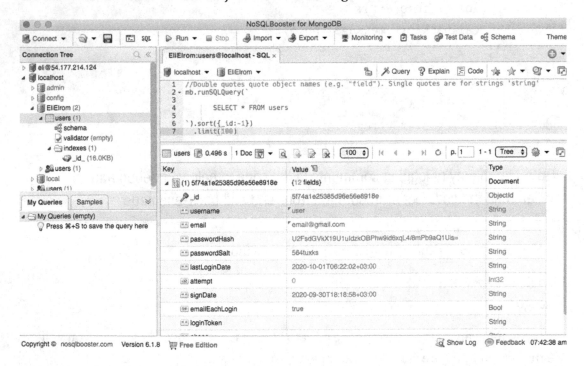

Figure 7-12. *GUI view of a user entered into the MongoDB database*

Summary

In this chapter, we created our back end with the help of Node.js, Express, and MongoDB. We started by creating our database schema and then created our validate service. We used the `rooms js` and `roomdb` libraries to expedite Express and Node.js development. We set up our local environment for our back end including creating authentication. In the second part of this chapter, we added a register component and completed the login cycle by encrypting and decrypting the user password as well as updating the login selector.

This chapter was exciting as all the previous chapters are coming together now to create a cycle. We were able to create a fully working website/app that allows users to not just view pages made out of React components but to have common features such as registration and login. We even implemented security measurements. In the process, you were able to learn about React, state management, browser local storage, dealing with data, and how to structure React components and subcomponents.

In the next chapter, you will learn how to publish your work to a deployment server.

CHAPTER 8

React Deployment: MERN Stack

In this chapter, we will continue where we left off in the previous chapter and complete our development cycle by publishing our working app and API to an actual remote live server. This chapter is split into two main sections.

- Setting up the Ubuntu server

- Publishing with the Grunt script

Before we get started, it's a good practice to back up your work. Yes, you can back up your work locally and on an external drive, but when working with a team, you will often need to share your work with others. A common solution is version control, and Git is the most popular version control solution. If you have not set up a version control tool, I highly recommend you set it up in this chapter.

Setting Up a Git Repo for Your Projects

The commands we will be using in this chapter will upload your code to the Git repo that you set up for your project to ensure you don't lose work and also will keep a history of your changes. If you have never set up a Git repo, sign up for GitHub or any other version control you prefer and then create a new repo. On GitHub, go to `https://github.com/new` to create a new repo.

Note You can set up the repo as private (only you will have access) or public (open to the world).

© Elad Elrom 2021
E. Elrom, *React and Libraries*, https://doi.org/10.1007/978-1-4842-6696-0_8

On the project level, set the username and password of your repo in Terminal.

```
$ git config --global user.email YOUR-EMAIL@mail.com
$ git config --global user.name "YOUR NAME"
```

> **Tip**   Learning and setting up Git is highly recommended, as it can help ensure you never lose your work. It will also help you if you ever have to work in a team and track the work history. It also has several other useful features.

Setting Up a Ubuntu Server as a Production Server

As we saw in the previous chapter, the MERN stack makes the development process easier. Not only is that true for the development cycle, it also applies to when it's time to publish your work. If you follow the Agile and Scrum methodologies, you know how important it is to publish quickly and to publish often. In this chapter, I will give you the steps you need to publish your app on a Ubuntu server including setting up SSL for free.

Why Ubuntu Server?

When it comes to publishing your work, there are many servers to use and approaches to take. You can set up a virtual nondedicated server and split up the front end and the back end into two separate servers, Heroku and Windows Server. You can even use Serverless Framework, just to name a few. The options are limitless.

In this section, we will be publishing on a Ubuntu server, but keep in mind that there are many solutions, and you need to do your own research to find the best fit for what you are doing and your exact needs.

Publishing with MERN on a Ubuntu server offers many benefits as we can set up one server and have it store our back end and front end and database as well. Having this resource at our disposal, we can run other scripts in addition to web server such as scripts for automations.

Additionally, the Ubuntu server is the world's most popular Linux server for cloud environments. The Ubuntu server provides a great virtual machine (VM) platform for all workloads, from web applications to NoSQL databases such as MongoDB and Hadoop.

I like this setup because I have full control over one dedicated server in case I want to set cron jobs and modify headers. I used to split the back end from the front end; however, setting up both on the same server is more ideal for small to medium nonenterprise projects.

Ubuntu 16.04, 18.04, or 20.04?

Ubuntu 20.04 LTS, named Focal Fossa, is the latest stable version of Ubuntu. However, it's not always the best to use the latest version as not all server providers will have that option, and a server that has been out for two years may be more "stable." Ubuntu version 20.04 gives some nice features. It reboots quicker and has new features that are worth exploring such as an advanced GUI. It will be supported until April 2025.

Ubuntu 18.04 is more stable than 16.04, and 16.04 is close to the end of its life, so do bother installing 16.04.

If you go with Bionic Beaver (Ubuntu 18.04), which was released on April 26, 2018, you will be able to get security and updates until April 2023. That or 20.04 is my recommendation in regard to the Ubuntu server at the time of writing.

Ubuntu 19.04 is a short-term support release, and it was supported until January 2020, so this release should be skipped altogether.

How to Install the MERN on Ubuntu 18.04/20.04?

I broke down this tutorial into five steps.

- Step 1: Roll out the Ubuntu server.
- Step 2: Set up SSH and set up server software.
- Step 3: Install MongoDB.
- Step 4: Set up the authentication.
- Step 5: Set up SSL.

Setting Up the Ubuntu Server for MERN

In this section, I will give you the steps you need to set up an Ubuntu server for our MERN code. If you follow the steps I describe, you will have an Ubuntu server including MongoDB with authentication as well as a free Secure Sockets Layer (SSL) certificate.

Step 1: Roll Out an Ubuntu Server

The first step is to roll out a server.

Amazon EC2 and Microsoft Azura are the most popular ways to roll out an Ubuntu server. They are both listed on the Ubuntu website (`https://ubuntu.com/public-cloud`). These cloud solutions can be used as your server provided them, but I do recommend you use EC2 or Azura here. These are just suggestions. Each has its benefits and caveats, and you should do your own research (DYOR) before deciding what platform to use.

EC2 and Azura offer a free dedicated server on a Ubuntu server; however, if you don't pay close attention and exceed the allotted usage, you can often find yourself with a hefty invoice.

Amazon and Azura both require that you provide your credit card information, and they will start charging you automatically at the end of the free cycle or usage, whatever comes first. Again, if you forget to cancel, you will be charged.

Azure offers both Ubuntu Server 20.04 LTS and 18.04; see `https://azuremarketplace.microsoft.com/en-us/marketplace/apps/canonical.0001-com-ubuntu-server-focal?tab=Overview`.

On any dedicated server, the steps are similar.

1. Launch Ubuntu Server 18.04/20.04 LTS.

2. Set up the security.

```
HTTP, HTTPS ports sets as: (0.0.0.0/0, ::/0)
Custom TCP: 27017 (for MongoDB) — (0.0.0.0/0, ::/0)
Port 8000 (for express https server)

Important: For HTTP and HTTPS,
8000
```

1. Use SSH to limit access to the server so only your IP address can log in.

2. Download the key pair.

3. Set up the public IP address.

Note   I recommend setting SSH to your current IP address for security. This is a much better setup than leaving your SSH port exposed to any IP address.

Here is an example of how you can Ubuntu on the Amazon EC2 free tier. Follow these steps:

1. Go to `https://us-west-1.console.aws.amazon.com/ec2/v2/home`.

2. Click Instance and then select "Ubuntu Server 18.04 / 20.04 LTS (HVM), SSD Volume Type - ami-06d51e91cea0dac8d (64-bit x86)", as shown in Figure 8-1.

3. Select t2.micro for the instance type, as shown in Figure 8-2.

4. Set up the storage. You can have up to 30GB for free.

Figure 8-1. *EC2, launching Ubuntu Server*

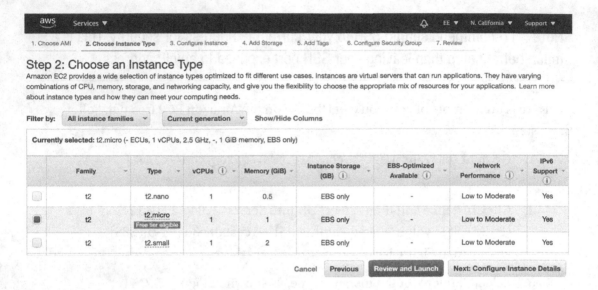

Figure 8-2. *EC2, choosing an instance type*

Next, we need to configure our security group.

1. Configure the security group. Use SSH, HTTP, HTTPS, Custom TCP: 27017 (for MongoDB), 80, 8000, and 443 (for the Express HTTPS server).

    Important: For HTTP and HTTPS, choose "8000 (0.0.0.0/0,::/0)" and set the SSH limit to My IP, as shown in Figure 8-3.

2. Create a new key pair by selecting site-api-amazon-key and then clicking Download Key Pair.

3. Launch!

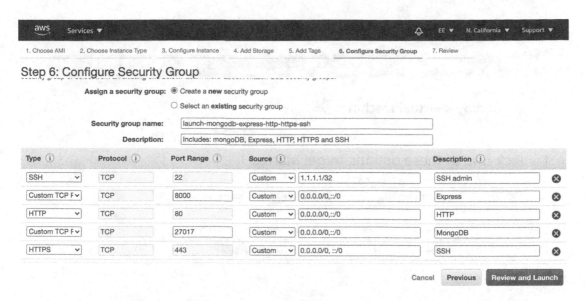

Figure 8-3. *Configuring the security group*

Tip   Intel x86 is almost universally faster than ARM.

On Azure, the process is similar after you create your free account. First, go to `https://portal.azure.com/?quickstart=true`.

In the Quickstart Center, click "Deploy a virtual machine" and click Start (Figure 8-4).

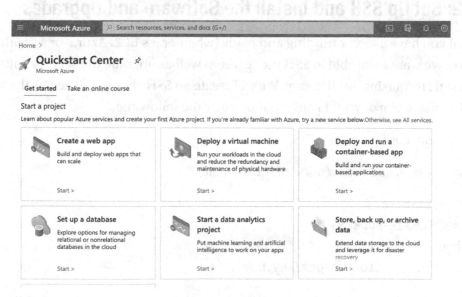

Figure 8-4. *Azure QuickStart Center*

Next, click "Create a Linux virtual machine," as shown in Figure 8-5.

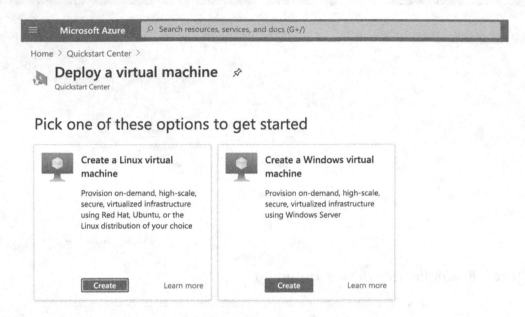

Figure 8-5. *Azure, deploying a virtual machine*

Next, use the options to select the Ubuntu version, select a hard drive, set up the security, and launch.

Step 2: Set Up SSH and Install the Software and Upgrades

Now that you have a server running and ready (whether it's EC2, Azura, or any other solution), we want to be able to SSH the server as well as upgrade the server's software. We will start by making our life easy. We will create an SSH shortcut to access the servers. On a Mac, using vim or your favorite editor, enter the following:

```
$ vim ~/.ssh/config
```

Paste the host and the location of the pem file;

```
Host My-site-name
HostName YOUR-IP-ADDRESS
User ubuntu
IdentityFile location-to-pem/key.pem
```

Note My-site-name that you see in the pem file we created, represents the name you want for your website, pick any name. This is the name you will be using to SSH the server. To find the public instance's IP address, check the EC2 instance details page.

Next, set the permission of the key.

```
$ chmod 600 *.pem
```

Let's give it a try.

```
$ ssh my-site-name
```

Before you can SSH the server, you will need to set EC2 to accept SSH to your IP address. Select EC2, click "security group," click "Edit inbound rules," click SSH, click "Source type," and then click My IP.

Once you've done that, you can log in to the box. I like to set up some aliases so it's easy to manage the server using predefined commands.

```
$ vim ~/.bash_profile
```

Paste the host and the location of the PEM file.

```
alias tailall='sudo lnav /home/ubuntu/www/logs'
alias tailwatchers='tail -f /home/ubuntu/www/logs/watch-log.log'
alias cleanlogs='sudo rm -f /home/ubuntu/www/logs/*.* && sudo touch /home/
ubuntu/www/logs/server.log && sudo touch /home/ubuntu/www/logs/server-
error.log && sudo touch /home/ubuntu/www/logs/watch-error.log && sudo touch
/home/ubuntu/www/logs/watch-log.log'

alias l='ls -ltra'
alias c='clear'
alias cls='clear'
alias ll='ls -ltra'
alias killnode='sudo killall -2 node'

export PORT=8081
sudo iptables -A PREROUTING -t nat -i eth0 -p tcp --dport 80 -j
REDIRECT --to-port 8081
sudo iptables -A PREROUTING -t nat -i eth0 -p tcp --dport 443 -j
REDIRECT --to-port 8000
```

```
parse_git_branch() {
    git branch 2> /dev/null | sed -e '/^[^*]/d' -e 's/* \(.*\)/ (\1)/'
}
export PS1="\u@\h \[\033[32m\]\w\[\033[33m\]\$(parse_git_branch)\
[\033[00m\] $ "
```

These aliases include the port exports for Express, a command to kill all node instances, a nice setup to display the Git directory, and neat commands to access the working directory. Remember to run the file to apply these changes.

```
$ . ~/.bash_profile
```

Next, we want to upgrade and install the software we will need, such as Python, NPM, and Forever (to keep Node.js running). We also need to set our ports for Express and other software.

```
$ sudo apt-get update
$ sudo apt-get -y upgrade
$ sudo apt-get dist-upgrade
$ sudo apt-get install build-essential
$ sudo apt-get install libssl-dev
$ sudo apt-get install git-core
$ sudo apt-get install python2.7
$ type python3 python2.7
```

Next, let's install Node.js on our Ubuntu server.

```
$ sudo apt install nodejs
```

Install NPM and update to the latest version.

```
$ sudo apt install npm
$ sudo npm install -g npm@latest
```

Now, make a web folder where we will be placing our file.

```
$ cd ~
$ mkdir ~/www
$ cd ~/www
```

Install Forever (https://github.com/foreversd/forever) globally.

```
$ cd ~
$ sudo npm install -g forever
```

Forever is a simple CLI tool to ensure that our script will run continuously (i.e., forever).

Next, we want to configure the default website to use port 8080 instead of port 80. You can forward the port from 8081 to 80 using this command:

```
$ export PORT=8081
$ sudo iptables -A PREROUTING -t nat -i eth0 -p tcp --dport 80 -j
EDIRECT --to-port 8081
```

Note   If you need to remove the iptable we set here, just use the -D flag.

sudo iptables -D PREROUTING -t nat -i eth0 -p tcp --dport 80 -j REDIRECT --to-port 8081

Step 3: Install MongoDB

Our MERN server needs a MongoDB server. To install the MongoDB server, use the following command:

Install the MongoDB server.

```
$ sudo apt-key adv --keyserver hkp://keyserver.ubuntu.com:80 --recv
9DA31620334BD75D9DCB49F368818C72E52529D4
```

```
$ echo "deb [ arch=amd64 ] https://repo.mongodb.org/apt/ubuntu bionic/
mongodb-org/4.0 multiverse" | sudo tee /etc/apt/sources.list.d/mongodb.list
```

Now, run the update and install commands.

```
$ sudo apt update
$ sudo apt install mongodb-org
$ sudo systemctl unmask mongod
$ sudo systemctl enable mongod
$ sudo service mongod status
```

You can compare your MogoDB status output with mine, shown here:

```
ubuntu@ip-ip ~/www $ sudo service mongod status
mongod.service - MongoDB Database Server
    Loaded: loaded (/lib/systemd/system/mongod.service; enabled; vendor
            preset: enabled)
    Active: inactive (dead) since
      Docs: https://docs.mongodb.org/manual
   Process: 903 ExecStart=/usr/bin/mongod --config /etc/mongod.conf
            (code=exited, status=
  Main PID: 903 (code=exited, status=0/SUCCESS)

systemd[1]: Started MongoDB Database Server.
systemd[1]: Stopping MongoDB Database Server...
systemd[1]: Stopped MongoDB Database Server.
```

Now that we have MongoDB installed, update MongoDB so all IP addresses are open for incoming calls. To do that, edit the mongod.conf file.

```
$ sudo vim /etc/mongod.conf
```

The change we need to make is to change our port from binding to a specific address.

```
net:
port: 27017
bindIp: 127.0.0.1
```

To bind to all incoming IP addresses, use this:

```
net:
port: 27017
bindIpAll: true
# bindIp: 127.0.0.1
```

Note   Port 27017 should be open already from when we rolled out our server.

Now to stop/start/restart the MongoDB service to run in the background, use the following commands. To start it, use this:

```
$ sudo systemctl start mongod
```

If you want to stop or restart, use this:

```
$ sudo systemctl stop mongod
$ sudo systemctl restart mongod
```

Give it a try to ensure the installation went well. Next, let's create our first database to try MongoDB.

```
$ mongo
```

Compare your Mongo output for running Mongo on the Ubuntu server command line with mine. It may output different results, but it will complete with a command-line input prompt: >. Take a look:

```
ubuntu@ip $ mongo
MongoDB shell version v4.0.21
connecting to: mongodb://ip:27017/?gssapiServiceName=mongodb
Implicit session: session { "id" : UUID("3236f117-2e73-4d78-bd37-
eeffef73fb85") }
MongoDB server version: 4.0.20
>
```

Next, let's use the database and insert the user.

```
> use your-database-name
> db.users.insert({"email":"someemail@gmail.com", password:"123456"})
> db.users.find();
```

Here is the expected output:

```
> use your-database-name
switched to db your-database-name
> db.users.insert({"email":"someemail@gmail.com", password:"123456"})
WriteResult({ "nInerted" : 1})
> db.users.find();
{ "_id" : ObjectId("some-objectId"), "email": "someemail@gmail.com",
"password": "123456"}
>
```

MongoDB Client

I recommend setting a MongoDB GUI client, if you haven't done so in the previous chapter, so it's easier to manage your database. The MongoDB Compass basic version is free, easy to use, and made by the MongoDB team. See `https://www.mongodb.com/products/compass`.

Step 4: Set Up Authentication

Now that we have MongoDB set up on our remote machine, the next step is to create authentication. Authentication is not optional; it's really a must-have on a remote server. Without authentication, any hacker could use your MongoDB database. You don't want unauthorized users just connecting to your database and placing worms on it.

To set up authentication, in Terminal, connect to the remote server via SSH.

```
$ ssh my-site-name
```

We will create a new admin user and set up authentication for that user. Take a look:

```
$ mongo admin
$ db.createUser({ user: 'myuser', pwd: '123456', roles: [ { role: 'root',
db: 'admin' } ]});
```

The output after adding a user to our MongoDB database should be as follows:

```
> db.createUser({ user: 'myuser', pwd: '123456', roles: [ { role: 'root',
db: 'admin' } ]});
Successfully added user: {
    "user": "myuser",
    "roles": [
            {
                "roles": "root",
                "db": "admin"

            }

    ]
}
> db.getUsers()
```

252

That will output the list of users.

```
[
    {
        "_id" : "MyDatabase.myuser",
        "user" : "myuser",
        "db" : "MyDatabase",
        "roles" : [
            {
                "role" : "readWrite",
                "db" : "MyDatabase"
            }
        ],
        "mechanisms" : [
            "SCRAM-SHA-1",
            "SCRAM-SHA-256"
        ]
    }
]
```

Exit the database.

```
$ exit
```

> **Note** In your password, you cannot use the @ sign as part of your password string. You will get "MongoParseError: Unescaped at-sign in authority" when trying to connect to the database from your Express app.

Here I am setting the authentication on the main database and not on the specific database we created, called MyDatabase.

To log into the database, on the remote server, use this:

```
$ mongo -u myuser -p 123456
> use MyDatabase
switched to db MyDatabase
> db.users.find();
{ "_id" : ObjectId("5fb7af6772f31b6884299994"), "email" : "someemail@gmail.
com", "password" : "123456" }
```

For a sanity check, you can run the getUsers command to ensure our user was added correctly.

Next, bind all the IP addresses and set up the security so that we will be able to read and write to the database with security enabled, just as we did locally.

```
$ sudo vim /etc/mongod.conf
net:
  port: 27017
  bindIpAll: true
  bindIp: 0.0.0.0
  security:
    authorization: 'enabled'
```

Note   You could just enable the local ip address if that's what you need: bindIp: 127.0.0.1.

To apply these changes, restart.

```
$ sudo systemctl restart mongod
```

Connecting to the Secure MongoDB

Now we can connect to our remote server and pass the new authentication information.

```
$ mongo -u 'myuser' -p '123456'
> use MyDatabase
switched to db MyDatabase
> db.users.find();
{ "_id" : ObjectId("5fb7af6772f31b6884299994"), "email" : "someemail@gmail.
com", "password" : "123456" }
```

Or from our local machine, via Terminal we can connect without using SSH. Just tell Mongo the remote IP address, port, and user to use.

```
$ mongo -u 'myuser' -p '123456' remote_ip_address:port/admin
```

Now the connection URI will be without the database name, as shown here:

```
mongodb://myuser:123456@ip_address:27017
```

Removing the User

If you ever need to remove the user and set up a new user or if you forgot the password, you would need to first remove the security.

```
$ sudo vim /etc/mongod.conf
```

Then, remove the user with dropUser (note that removeUser was deprecated).

```
$ mongo admin
$ db.dropUser(myuser)
```

You can find information about dropUser here: https://docs.mongodb.com/manual/reference/method/db.removeUser/#db-removeuser.

Changing the Storage Location

Notice that in the mongod.conf file we can change where the actual storage is located via dbPath. Right now it's set to this location:

```
/var/lib/MongoDB
```

Tip   You can change this to any location you like, such as /data/DB. Just ensure you set the path with the right permissions.

If you decide to change the location of the database, here is how you will set the permissions so Mongo can access the file:

```
$ sudo mkdir -p /data/db
$ sudo chown -R $USER:$USER /data/db
```

To see your database on a different path action, you can restart MongoDB or just run mongod with the new location.

```
$ mongod --dbpath /data/db
```

Step 5: Set Up SSL

When building a website today, SSL is not optional. It's required. Browsers will give you an error message if your website is not set up with SSL.

You can set up SSL with all domains and server registrars out there for a yearly fee and reduce the hassel as well as have a reputable SSL certificate shows up on the SSL check, but you can also set it up for free.

To set up SSL for free, you can use Certbot (`https://certbot.eff.org/`). First, install the software.

```
$ sudo apt-get install software-properties-common
$ sudo add-apt-repository universe
$ sudo add-apt-repository ppa:certbot/certbot
Enter to continue

$ sudo apt-get update
For Ubuntu 18.04;
$ sudo apt-get install certbot python-certbot-apache
For Ubuntu 20.04;
$ sudo apt-get install certbot python3-certbot-apache
```

Now set the certificate.

```
$ sudo certbot certonly --manual
```

A command-line wizard starts and asks you questions.

For the site, use your site name, as in `some-site.com`.

If you are OK with your IP address being logged, answer Y. See the "Setting up SSL certbot wizard" information in the Ubuntu output.

```
ubuntu@ip-ip $ sudo certbot certonly --manual Saving debug log to /var/
log/letsencrypt/letsencrypt.log Plugins selected: Authenticator manual,
Installer None Enter email address (used for urgent renewal and security
notices) (Enter 'c' to cancel): your-email@gmail.com
- - - - - - - - - - - - - - - - - - - - - - - - - - - - - - - - - - - - - - - -
Please read the Terms of Service at https://letsencrypt.org/documents/LE-
SA-v1.2-November-15-2017.pdf. You must agree in order to register with the
ACME server at https://acme-v02.api.letsencrypt.org/directory
- - - - - - - - - - - - - - - - - - - - - - - - - - - - - - - - - - - - - - - -
(A)gree/(C)ancel: A

- - - - - - - - - - - - - - - - - - - - - - - - - - - - - - - - - - - - - - - -
Would you be willing to share your email address with the Electronic
Frontier Foundation, a founding partner of the Let's Encrypt project and
```

the non—profit organization that develops Certbot? We'd like to send you
email about our work encrypting the web, EFF news, campaigns, and ways to
support digital freedom.

(Y)es/(N)o: N Please enter in your domain name(s) (comma and/or space
separated) (Enter 'c' to cancel): YourSite.com Obtaining a new certificate
Performing the following challenges: http-01 challenge for YourSite.com

Next, it will ask that you prove that you have access to the domain.

Create a file containing just this data:
[SOME RANDOM GENERATE CODE]

Make it available on your web server at this URL:

http://some-site.com/.well-known/acme-challenge/KEY

Stop and create the file that is asked for.

Change the directory to /home/ubuntu/www/dist/ and create the file as instructed.

```
> cd /home/ubuntu/www/dist/
> mkdir .well-known
> cd .well-known
> mkdir acme-challenge
> cd acme-challenge
> vim "[FILE NAME]"
[CODE]
```

Check http://some-site.com/.well-known/acme-challenge/[string].

Does it work? Great. Now we can continue.

Press Enter to Continue
Waiting for verification...
Cleaning up challenges

IMPORTANT NOTES:
 - Congratulations! Your certificate and chain have been saved at:
   /etc/letsencrypt/live/MY-SITE-NAME.com/fullchain.pem
   Your key file has been saved at:
   /etc/letsencrypt/live/MY-SITE-NAME.com/privkey.pem

Set permissions for the directory.

```
$ sudo chown -R ubuntu:ubuntu /etc/letsencrypt
```

Renewing the Certificate

To renew the certificate, run this command:

```
sudo certbot certonly --manual -d "your-site.com"
```

The process is the same; you just need to set up the challenge.

```
$ mkdir -p public/.well-known/acme-challenge
```

Next, set up the filename with the data.

```
$ vim /home/ubuntu/www/public/.well-known/acme-challenge/[file name]
[some text]
```

443 Security

Add SSH port to the security section. If it wasn't added in the previous step, use this:

```
HTTPS > TCP > 443 > 0.0.0.0/0
Custom > 8000 > 0.0.0.0/0
```

If you recall in `vim ~/.bash_profile`, we are redirecting port 443 to 8000.

```
$ sudo iptables -A PREROUTING -t nat -i eth0 -p tcp --dport 443 -j
REDIRECT --to-port 8000
```

When we create an HTTPS server, we should be pointing to port 8000.

```
let https_server = require('https').createServer({
        key: fs.readFileSync('/etc/letsencrypt/live/some-site.com/
        privkey.pem', 'utf8'),
        cert: fs.readFileSync('/etc/letsencrypt/live/some-site.com/
        cert.pem', 'utf8'),
        ca: fs.readFileSync('/etc/letsencrypt/live/some-site.com/
        chain.pem', 'utf8')
```

```
}, app).listen(8000, function () {
    logger.info('Listening on https://' + os.hostname() + ':8000');
});
```

Bravo!

Publishing with the Grunt Script

When it comes to automation, if using certain tools are selected, setting it up could be a pain point, in other words, a time-consuming task in your development workflow. The MERN stack makes the development process easier. This is true not just for development; it also applies to when it's time to publish your work.

Why Grunt?

When it comes to automation and deployment build tools, there are many to choose from. We already have the Webpack bundle and NPM scripts set up in our CRA project, so why do we need yet another library?

Grunt vs. Gulp vs. Webpack vs. NPM Scripts

This subject really deserves its own chapter, but I will give you a quick rundown here. When we look at popularity of these tools, we will see that Webpack is the most popular, with Gulp in second place.

- *NPM scripts*: 33,600 (https://github.com/npm/cli)

- *Grunt*: 12,000 (https://github.com/gruntjs/grunt)

- *Gulp*: 42,000 (https://github.com/gulpjs/gulp)

- *Webpack*: 55,700 (https://github.com/webpack/webpack)

Although Webpack is the most popular, that doesn't mean it's the winner. Each tool was created to solve a specific problem. It is important to understand what each tool was meant to be used for.

Let's take a step back. What are we trying to achieve here? Our most important task is to publish our files to production. We don't need to do the testing, linting formatting, and so on. We already have scripts for that in CRA.

Webpack is a module bundler. It is for larger projects, and it's harder to set up compared to Grunt and Gulp. It's not meant as a task runner, so although it does have plugins created by the Webpack team as well as the community, it's really not the best tool for the job.

What about the NPM run scripts? CRA already comes with run scripts. In fact, there is a section in our `package.json` file that specifies NPM run scripts and includes calling `react-scripts` for testing and building a deployment build, which we looked at in Chapter 2.

```
"scripts": {
 "start": "react-scripts start",
 "build": "react-scripts build",
 "test": "react-scripts test",
 "eject": "react-scripts eject"
}
```

These `react-scripts` scripts tie well into our development server when we build our project, and you can see them here: `project/node_modules/react-scripts/scripts/start.js`.

That's how CRA turns a mere six libraries into more than 1,000 in our `node_modules` folder when we set up our project. We will use the NPM run scripts through `package.json` to automate tasks, but that is not the right spot to place automotive tasks just to help run them.

NPM run scripts that are set for you, are created to help run automate repetitive tasks, and we will use them to set our deployment automation tasks.

As we are looking to create tasks to publish our code (and not to build our module or do any linting, formatting, testing, or running a repetitive task), Grunt and Gulp are much more suited for the job, and they can be set in the NPM run scripts.

We can eliminate Webpack and NPM run scripts as the best tool for the job of publishing our files to a remote server. See Figure 8-6.

Figure 8-6. *Finding the right tool for the publish automation task*

Grunt and Gulp are meant for automation tasks and are perfect for what we need to do here. Grunt is the oldest. Grunt was created for task configurations. Gulp is more popular and is similar to Grunt, but you can use it to write a JavaScript function in a more intuitive way than setting up a Grunt task. With Gulp your code will be more readable, so Gulp is superior to Grunt in some aspects.

However, when it comes to plugins, Grunt has a large number of plugins and holds the upper hand.

- *Grunt*: 6,250 (`https://gruntjs.com/plugins`)

- *Gulp*: 4,120 (`https://gulpjs.com/plugins/`)

In terms of plugins, we are really at the mercy of the open source community, and if you cannot find the plugin you need, you may need to create your own plugin, or if your plugin fails or is not maintained, you will have to fix it or add functionality on your own.

Additionally, for security, we need to ensure our plugins do what they were intended to do, especially when we rely on what's going to go to our production server. That is a big deal because it can put your entire release at risk or even bring it to a halt.

For instance, in late 2018, a hacker was able to successfully insert malicious code into event stream using an NPM JavaScript library (`https://www.npmjs.com/package/event-stream`). The library is used by millions and targeted a company called Bitpay, which has a Git library called `copay` (`https://github.com/bitpay/copay`).

Like many open source libraries, the developer was not being paid for the work on the event stream and lost interest in the project before giving it away to a new maintainer.

The new maintainer injected malicious code that targeted copay. The code captured account details and private keys from accounts having a balance of more than 100 bitcoin or 1,000 bitcoin cash.

copay then updated its dependency library on version 5.0.2 and included the attacker code, which resulted in a loss of millions.

The code captured the victims' account data and private keys and then, using a service call, sent the data to the attacker server undetected.

The complete detail and analysis of this attack can be found here: https://blog. npmjs.org/post/180565383195/details-about-the-event-stream-incident.

To sum this up, I prefer to use Gulp over Grunt as it goes more hand in hand with the JavaScript paradigm of MERN. However, I often choose Grunt over Gulp because of the larger number of plugins, as well as Grunt's maturity. With that being said, if you use Gulp, you can't go wrong with the simple tasks I am doing here.

How to Publish Your Script with Grunt?

I broke down the process in this section into two steps.

- *Step 1*: Publishing the front end onto a remote server (app/ Gruntfile.js)

- *Step 2*: Publishing the back end onto a remote server (api/ Gruntfile.js)

Publishing Content with Grunt

I want to publish both the back-end and front-end we created on the same Ubuntu server. This is a good setup for relatively small to medium applications. Rolling out multiple servers, load balancer, and other methods used in a more complex application is going to be overkill here and harder to maintain.

To get started, install Grunt globally.

```
$ npm install -g grunt-cli
```

Additionally, install the grunt-shell plugin for running shell commands.

```
$ yarn add -D grunt-shell
```

Step 1: Publishing the Front End

You can download the script from the Apress GitHub location shown here:

https://github.com/Apress/react-and-libraries/08/app/Gruntfile.js

In Grunt, it's all about creating tasks. We will create two main tasks.

- default: This will be my default task to publish the code.

- local-prod-build: This will be a task to simulate the production build for testing.

Our default task will do the following:

1. git_add: Publish our code to the Git repo we set up for our project.

2. format: Format and lint through the Airbnb style guides. As you recall, we set up formatting and linting in Chapter 1.

3. yarn_build: This is the built-in CRA NPM run script that builds the app. Build a production-optimized version of the React app.

4. delete_old_files_api: Delete the old dist folder used to hold our optimized version of our React app.

5. copy_new_files_api: Copy the optimized version of the React app to the dist inside the API app project (this is done so we can run our app using the Express server).

6. server_upload_app: Upload files to the remote Ubuntu server.

7. stop_node: Stop the Node.js script on the production server. This will stop the Express server.

8. start_node: Start the Node.js server.js script on the production server. This starts the Express server.

Similarly, to set local-prod-build, the task needs to do the following tasks:

1. git_add: Publish our code to the Git repo we set for our project.

2. format: Format our code using the Airbnb style guides.

3. yarn_build: Build a production-optimized version of the React app.

4. yarn_serve: This is a CRA built-in NPM script to create a local server to mimic the production server.

5. open_build: Open the localhost with the production build.

To implement these tasks on the code level (app/Gruntfile.js), these tasks and subtasks will look like so:

```
// app/Gruntfile.js

module.exports = function (grunt) {  grunt.loadNpmTasks('grunt-
shell');  grunt.initConfig({    /**
    * We read in our `package.json` file so we can access the package name and
    * version.
    */
  pkg: grunt.file.readJSON('package.json'),shell: {
    git_add: {
      command: [
        'git add .',
        'git add -u',
        "git commit -m '<%= pkg.version %> -> <%= pkg.commit %>'",
        'git push'
      ].join('&&')
    },
    lint: {
      command: 'yarn run lint'
    },
    format: {
      command: 'yarn run format'
    },
    yarn_build: {
      command: 'yarn build'
    },
    yarn_serve: {
      command: 'serve -s build'
    },
```

```
    open_build: {
      command: 'open http://localhost:5000'
    },
    delete_old_files_api: {
      command: 'rm -rf /YOUR-API-LOCATION/app-api/dist'
    },
    copy_new_files_api: {
      command: 'cp -rf /YOUR-APP-LOCATION/app/build/ /YOUR-API-LOCATION/
      app-api/dist/'
    },
    server_upload_app: {
      command: 'scp -r -i /YOUR-PEM-LOCATION/key.pem' +
          ' /YOUR-API-LOCATION/app-api/dist/* ubuntu@YOUR-UBUNTU-PUBLIC-
          IP:/home/ubuntu/www/dist'
    },
    stop_node: {
      command: "ssh -i /YOUR-PEM-LOCATION/key.pem ubuntu@YOUR-UBUNTU-
      PUBLIC-IP 'sudo pkill -f node'"
    },
    start_node: {
      command: "ssh -i /YOUR-PEM-LOCATION/key.pem ubuntu@YOUR-UBUNTU-
      PUBLIC-IP 'sudo forever start /home/ubuntu/www/server.js'"
    },
  }
});
grunt.registerTask('default', ['shell:git_add', 'shell:format',
'shell:yarn_build', 'shell:delete_old_files_api', 'shell:copy_new_files_
api', 'shell:server_upload_app', 'shell:stop_node', 'shell:start_node']);
  grunt.registerTask('local-prod-build', ['shell:git_add', 'shell:format',
'shell:yarn_build', 'shell:yarn_serve', 'shell:open_build']);
};
```

Notice that for the Git task, I am setting the version and commit inside of the package.json file that will be used for the Git comment, so the version and commit message need to be set inside package.json before running the Grunt publishing script.

```
{
  "name": "api",
  "version": "0.0.0872",
  "commit": "add service call",
```

We can now deploy for the production server using a single command.

```
$ grunt
```

You can also run the task to create the production build on our local machine.

```
$ grunt local-prod-build
```

Can we make it easier? You bet! Let's tie Grunt to the NPM scripts. Inside the package.json file's script tag, add a "push" script.

```
"scripts": {
  ...
  "push": "grunt"
}
```

Now that our task automation is tied better to our NPM scripts, we can give it a try.

```
$ yarn push # or npm push
```

Step 2: Publish Back-End Code to the Remote Server

Next, on our back-end side, we want to be able to publish our Node.js Express app with one command, just as we did with our front-end code.

You can download the script from the Apress GitHub location.

```
https://github.com/Apress/react-and-libraries/08/api/Gruntfile.js
```

We will create three tasks.

- default: The default task will upload the code to the remote server.

- upload-app: Upload the React code to the remote server. We are already doing that inside the Grunt task, but it won't hurt to do that here as well.

- node-restart. Restart Node.js, which will restart our Express app.

The Default Task

I am being more selective about what I am uploading as I don't want to upload all the files on every push. Follow these steps:

1. `multiple`: Publish the API code to Git.

2. `server_package`: Upload the `package.json` file to the remote server.

3. `stop_node`: Stop Node.js.

4. `upload_server_file`: Upload the `server.js` file.

5. `server_upload_services`: Upload any get-type services.

6. `server_upload_services_post`: Upload any post-type services.

7. `server_upload_utils`: Upload the utility folder.

8. `start_node`: Start Node.js again, as it was stopped in the previous task.

You may need different folders and files, but you get the idea. Feel free to add them as needed. Let's review these tasks.

The upload-app Task

As you recall, the production files were copied from our CRA to the API server's `dist` folder using the `app/Gruntfile.js` tasks we set. This task we are setting here can use the task we set to upload these files to the remote server.

The node-restart Task

This task is to restart Node.js, in case it's needed. It's neat to have it in one command without the need to SSH the server. We will set two tasks inside `Gruntfile.js` to easily stop and start the node script

1. stop_node

2. start_node

Take a look at the code, shown here:

```
// api/Gruntfile.js

module.exports = function (grunt) {    grunt.loadNpmTasks('grunt-replace');
    grunt.loadNpmTasks('grunt-shell');
```

```
grunt.loadNpmTasks('grunt-open');    grunt.initConfig({          /**
    * We read in our `package.json` file so we can access the package
    name and
    * version.
    */
  pkg: grunt.file.readJSON('package.json'),        shell: {
    multiple: {
      command: [
        'git add .',
        'git add -u',
        "git commit -m '<%= pkg.version %> ->
        <%= pkg.commit %>'",
        'git push'
      ].join('&&')
    },
    upload_server_file: {
      command: 'scp -r -i /YOUR-APP-LOCATION/app/docs/keys/
      ee-amazon-key.pem /YOUR-API-LOCATION/api/server.js
      ubuntu@YOUR-UBUNTU-PUBLIC-IP:/home/ubuntu/www/'
    },
    server_upload_services: {
      command: 'scp -r -i /YOUR-APP-LOCATION/app/docs/keys/
      ee-amazon-key.pem /YOUR-API-LOCATION/api/services/
      * ubuntu@YOUR-UBUNTU-PUBLIC-IP:/home/ubuntu/www/services'
    },
    server_upload_services_post: {
      command: 'scp -r -i /YOUR-APP-LOCATION/app/docs/keys/
      ee-amazon-key.pem /YOUR-API-LOCATION/api/services_post/
      * ubuntu@YOUR-UBUNTU-PUBLIC-IP:/home/ubuntu/www/services_
      post'
    },
    server_package: {
      command: 'scp -i /YOUR-APP-LOCATION/app/docs/keys/
      ee-amazon-key.pem /YOUR-API-LOCATION/api/package.json
      ubuntu@YOUR-UBUNTU-PUBLIC-IP:/home/ubuntu/www/package.json'
    },
```

```
        server_upload_utils: {
            command: 'scp -r -i /YOUR-APP-LOCATION/app/docs/keys/ee-
            amazon-key.pem /YOUR-API-LOCATION/api/utils/* ubuntu@YOUR-
            UBUNTU-PUBLIC-IP:/home/ubuntu/www/utils'
        },
        server_upload_app: {
            command: 'scp -r -i /YOUR-APP-LOCATION/app/docs/keys/ee-
            amazon-key.pem /YOUR-API-LOCATION/api/dist/* ubuntu@YOUR-
            UBUNTU-PUBLIC-IP:/home/ubuntu/www/dist'
        },
        stop_node: {
            command: "ssh -i /YOUR-APP-LOCATION/app/docs/keys/ee-
            amazon-key.pem ubuntu@YOUR-UBUNTU-PUBLIC-IP 'sudo pkill
            -f node'"
        },
        start_node: {
            command: "ssh -i /YOUR-APP-LOCATION/app/docs/keys/ee-
            amazon-key.pem ubuntu@YOUR-UBUNTU-PUBLIC-IP 'sudo forever
            start /home/ubuntu/www/server.js'"
        }
    }
});    grunt.registerTask('default', ['shell:multiple', 'shell:server_
    package', 'shell:stop_node', 'shell:upload_server_file',
    'shell:server_upload_services', 'shell:server_upload_services_
    post', 'shell:server_upload_utils', 'shell:start_node']);
grunt.registerTask('upload-app', ['shell:server_upload_app']);
grunt.registerTask('node-restart', ['shell:stop_node','shell:start_
node']);
};
```

Bravo!

We can run our default script.

```
$ grunt
```

In this section, I broke down the process into two steps.

- Step 1: Publishing the front end to the remote server with Grunt

- Step 2: Publishing the back end to the remote server with Grunt

Now that we have both our React app and our API files uploaded to the remote Ubuntu server. We also have aliases set up. We can use the following commands.

Use SSH to connect to the server.

```
$ ssh my-site-name
```

Navigate to the directory /home/ubuntu/www using the `cdr` alias.

```
$ cdr
```

To start the node instead of `$ sudo forever start`, we can use the `startnode` alias.

```
$ startnode
```

To stop Node.js, instead of using `$ sudo forever stop 0`, we can use the `stopnode` alias.

```
$ stopnode
```

To view all the aliases, type the following:

```
$ vimb
```

If everything was set correctly without errors, you should be able access the app we built in previous chapters using your server's public IP address.

Take a look at some example output of Ubuntu, connect to the server via SSH, stop the Node.js server, and start it again with the help of Forever. Then you can compare your output with mine.

```
ubuntu@ip ~ $ cdr
ubuntu@ip ~/www $ stopnode # stopall # or stopall
ubuntu@ip ~/www $ startnode
warn:     --minUptime not set. Defaulting to: 1000ms
warn:     --spinSleepTime not set. Your script will exit if it does not stay
          up for at least 1000ms
info:     Forever processing file: /home/ubuntu/www/server.js
```

```
ubuntu@ip ~/www $ shownodes
root      23924     1  0 18:38 ?          00:00:01 /usr/bin/node /home/ubuntu/
                                          www/server.js
ubuntu   24052 23003  0 18:41 pts/1      00:00:00 grep node
```

Notice that I am using the commands we set up when we set up the server such as shownodes, which shows all running nodes (ps -ef | grep node). As you recall, you can view the commands with ($ vimb), which is equivalent to vim ~/.bash_profile.

Summary

In this chapter, we started by setting up a Git repo for our projects so we can share our project with other members of our team (if we have any), as well as save a history of our changes. We will also get many other features and advantages of using version control.

We looked into why to use the Ubuntu server and what version to use, and we set up the Ubuntu server as our production server for both our React app and our Node.js Express API scripts.

Next, we installed the MERN stack on an Ubuntu server, and we set up the Ubuntu server for the MERN stack. Once we had the server set up for us, we looked to publish our code. We first looked at the advantages of using Grunt and what our other options are. Then, we looked at how to publish our React and Express scripts with Grunt and created a Grunt file that automates our tasks so we can publish and publish often. In the next chapter, we will look into how we can test our React app.

CHAPTER 9

Testing Part I: Unit Test Your React App

When it comes to testing your React app, there are three areas of testing to consider.

- *Unit testing*: Testing the smallest piece of code that can be isolated.

- *Integration testing*: Combining individual modules and testing them together

- *E2E testing*: Simulating a real end user's experience

In this chapter, you will learn how to unit test a React app like a pro.

When it comes to unit testing, there are many libraries that can be used with React such as Jest, Enzyme, Sinon, Mocha, Chai, Ava, and Tape. These libraries are considered the most used React unit testing libraries.

In this chapter, you will learn how to utilize Jest, Enzyme, and Sinon for unit testing your app.

Setting Up the Project

To learn how to unit test a React TypeScript component, we will create a new project. The final result of our project will be a calculator component. See Figure 9-1.

© Elad Elrom 2021
E. Elrom, *React and Libraries*, https://doi.org/10.1007/978-1-4842-6696-0_9

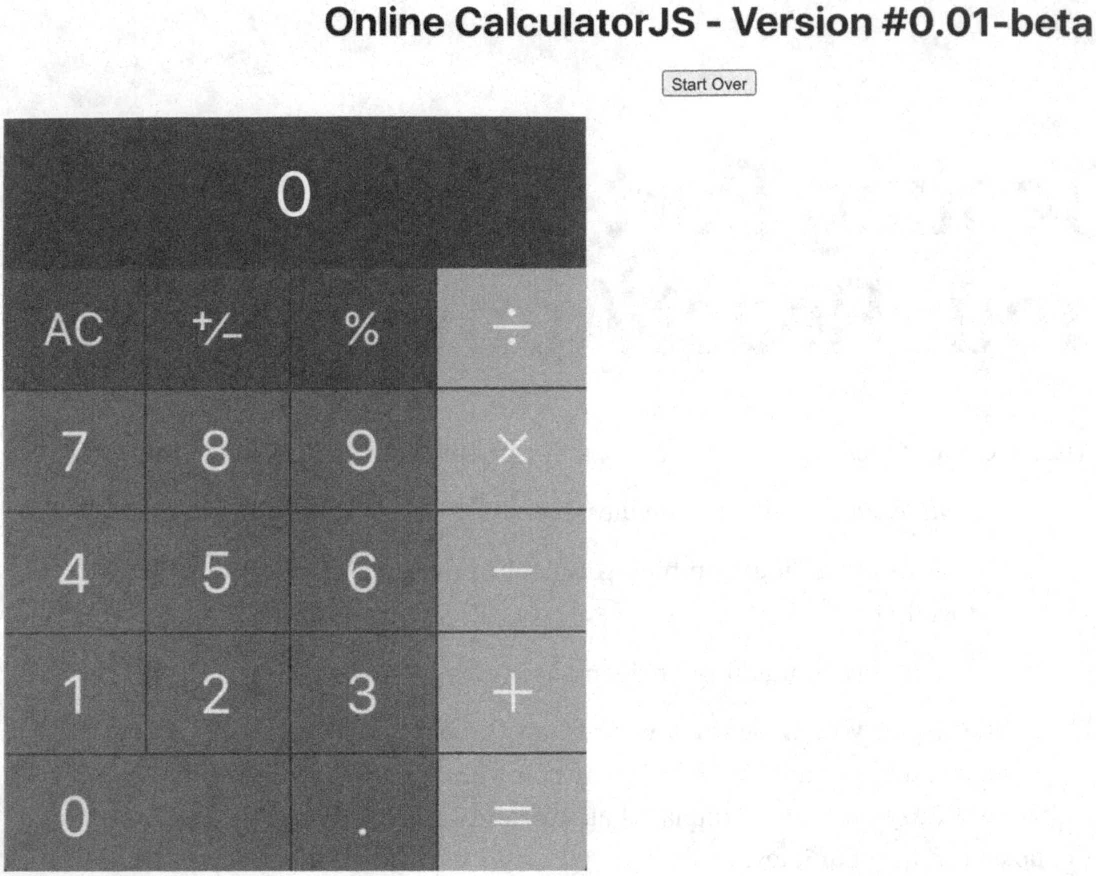

Figure 9-1. *Final results of our Calculator component*

To get started, we will use the CRA project template that we have been using throughout this book. As you recall, to set up that CRA MHL project template, we just need a one-line command. This will set up most of what we need for this project.

For the project name, we will use hello-jest-enzyme-ts.

```
$ yarn create react-app hello-jest-enzyme-ts --template must-have-libraries
```

Once the installation is complete, you will get a "Happy hacking!" message. Next, we will create the Calculator TS component using the generate-react-cli template CLI.

```
$ cd hello-jest-enzyme-ts
$ npx generate-react-cli component Calculator
```

The terminal output will confirm that these three files were created for us:

- *Stylesheet*: `src/components/Calculator/Calculator.scss`

- *Test*: `src/components/Calculator/Calculator.test.tsx`

- *Component*: `src/components/Calculator/Calculator.tsx`

Lastly, make sure you can still run the project and ensure everything works as expected.

```
$ yarn start
```

This is not the first time we have talked about unit testing. In previous chapters, we ran the `format`, `lint`, and `test` commands.

```
$ yarn format & yarn lint & yarn test
```

You learned about formatting and linting in Chapter 2 and installed all the libraries for testing for our project. We also had `generate-react-cli` generate tests for us. We have already also had Jest tests set up for us and `package.json` run scripts set up for us.

Next, let's review the main testing libraries we will be using.

- Jest

- Jest-dom

- Enzyme

- Sinon

What Is the Jest Library?

Jest (`https://github.com/facebook/jest`) is a Facebook JavaScript unit testing framework. It was built to be used with any JavaScript project.

Jest is a test runner, assertion library, and mocking library. It also provides a snapshot if needed. Here are its benefits:

- *Developer ready*: It is a comprehensive JavaScript testing solution. It works out of the box for most JavaScript projects.

- *Instant feedback*: It has a fast, interactive watch mode that only runs test files related to changed files.

- *Snapshot testing*: It captures snapshots of large objects to simplify testing and to analyze how they change over time.

You can find the Jest documentation here: `https://jestjs.io/docs/en/tutorial-react`.

What Is Jest-dom?

Jest-dom (`https://github.com/testing-library/jest-dom`) is a library that extends Jest using custom matchers to make assertions on DOM elements easier.

Jest-dom isn't required to use the react testing library, but it makes writing our tests more convenient.

You can find the Jest-dom documentation here: `https://noriste.github.io/reactjsday-2019-testing-course/book/intro-to-react-testing/jest-dom.html`.

What Is Enzyme?

Enzyme (`https://github.com/enzymejs/enzyme`) is a JavaScript testing utility built for React that makes it easier to test your React components' output.

You can also manipulate, traverse, and in some ways simulate the runtime given the output.

Enzyme's API is meant to be intuitive and flexible by mimicking jQuery's API for DOM manipulation and traversal.

Note   Enzyme can be used without Jest, but it needs to be paired with another unit testing framework. You can find the Enzyme documentation here: `https://airbnb.io/enzyme/docs/api/`.

What Is Sinon?

Sinon (`https://github.com/sinonjs/sinon`) is a stand-alone testing JS framework that includes test spies, stubs, and mocks. It's pronounced "sigh-non."

Why Should You Learn Jest and Enzyme?

Jest + Jest-dom + Enzyme + React = Complete testing abilities on your React project.

Jest and Enzyme integrate well together to provide flexible and creative testing abilities. Sinon adds functionality.

Here are a few interesting facts:

- Jest is created and used by Facebook to test its services and React applications.

- Create-React-App comes bundled with Jest and Jest-dom; it does not need to be installed separately.

- The Enzyme tool was created by Airbnb.

- Sinon can be embedded in the Jest + Enzyme framework and is sponsored by Airbnb.

If you think that testing is expensive and time-consuming, try *not* testing. It will cost you much more in the long term.

Did you know that a survey of more than 1,000 Americans by QA and software testing company QualiTest said that 88 percent of people would abandon an app if they encountered bugs or glitches?

- About 51 percent of those people said they would probably stop using an app completely if they experienced at least one bug every day.

- In addition, 32 percent of all respondents said they were likely to abandon an app the moment they encountered a glitch.

How Can You Learn Jest and Enzyme?

To help you understand Jest and Enzyme, I broke down the process in this tutorial to just three steps.

- *Step 1*: Setting up and configuring our project

- *Step 2*: Writing code for the custom Calculator component

- *Step 3*: Testing the code

We will also look a bit under the hood if you want to better understand the libraries we're using.

Creating and Testing the Calculator Component

In this section, we will create our custom React component, which is a calculator, and set up some tests. Our component is going to be TypeScript, and we will be utilizing Jest and Enzyme to test the component.

Step 1: Setting Up and Configuring Our Project

For Enzyme, we want to install the React 16 adapter (that's the latest version but could change by the time you read this), which works with React 17. We also need to install `react-test-renderer` so we can render React components to pure JavaScript objects, without depending on the DOM. This will be helpful as we will take a snapshot.

Note   Enzyme, the Enzyme adapter, and Enzyme for JSON libraries come out of the box with the CRA MHL template project, so there's no need to install them. Still, here is the command in case you want to start with the vanilla version of CRA:

`$ yarn add enzyme enzyme-adapter-react-16 react-test-renderer`

We will be using Jest's snapshot testing feature to automatically save a copy of the JSON tree to a file and check with our tests that it hasn't changed.

Read more about that feature here: `https://reactjs.org/docs/test-renderer. html`.

We want to make our life easier, so we will install the `enzyme-to-json` library (`https://github.com/adriantoine/enzyme-to-json#readme`) to simplify our code. Check the "Under the Hood" section in this chapter for more details.

`$ yarn add -D enzyme-to-json`

For our calculator, I will be using the macOS built-in calculator for my graphics. I will use image mapping to map each key to turn the image into a clickable buttons.

To do that, we will install a `react-image-mapper` component (https://github.com/coldiary/react-image-mapper), which lets us map areas of an image.

```
$ yarn add react-image-mapper
```

We have set up our project and installed all the libraries needed to get started with our project.

Step 2: Creating Our Custom Component

On the code level, I am creating a custom Calculator component. What I have done is taken a screenshot of the macOS calculator and then used an online tool to map that image (`image-map.net`) to a clickable map area. I am not using the graphic for a production deployment. I'm just using it here to illustrate the testing process. If you build production code, you would need to get permission to use the graphic. Additionally, note that I am using `image-map.net`, but there are many online tools and programs to map an image, and I have no affiliation with that site.

You can download the entire project from the Apress GitHub location.

```
https://github.com/Apress/react-and-libraries/09/hello-jest-enzyme-ts
```

Let's review the code together.

```
// src/components/Calculator/Calculator.tsx

import React from 'react'
import './Calculator.scss'
```

Notice that for the `ImageMapper` component I am placing an `@ts-ignore` comment in front of the `import` statement. That is because the `ImageMapper` component is a JS component and is not set for TS and does not have types. This will cause a Lint compile-time error.

```
// @ts-ignore
import ImageMapper from 'react-image-mapper'
```

Next, I am setting the URL of where I am placing my image as well as mapping the image areas. I am using the `export` constant statement, so I can use the same `const MAP` code in my testing file if needed.

```
export const URL = 'calculator.jpg'
export const MAP = {
  name: 'my-map',
  areas: [
    {
      name: '0',
      shape: 'rect',
      coords: [3, 387, 227, 474],
    },
    {
      name: '1',
      shape: 'rect',
      coords: [2, 291, 112, 382],
    },
    {
      name: '2',
      shape: 'rect',
      coords: [116, 290, 227, 382],
    },
    {
      name: '3',
      shape: 'rect',
      coords: [342, 382, 232, 290],
    },
    {
      name: '4',
      shape: 'rect',
      coords: [3, 194, 111, 290],
    },
    {
      name: '5',
      shape: 'rect',
      coords: [115, 193, 227, 290],
    },
    {
```

```
    name: '6',
    shape: 'rect',
    coords: [231, 194, 343, 290],
  },
  {
    name: '7',
    shape: 'rect',
    coords: [4, 97, 111, 191],
  },
  {
    name: '8',
    shape: 'rect',
    coords: [115, 99, 227, 191],
  },
  {
    name: '9',
    shape: 'rect',
    coords: [231, 98, 343, 191],
  },
  {
    name: '+',
    shape: 'rect',
    coords: [348, 291, 463, 382],
  },
  {
    name: '-',
    shape: 'rect',
    coords: [348, 195, 463, 290],
  },
  {
    name: '*',
    shape: 'rect',
    coords: [348, 98, 463, 191],
  },
```

```
    {
      name: '/',
      shape: 'rect',
      coords: [348, 3, 463, 93],
    },
    {
      name: '=',
      shape: 'rect',
      coords: [348, 387, 463, 474],
    },
  ],
}
```

Next, I am setting the class definition statement with the prop interface (ICalculatorProps) and state interface (ICalculatorState). I am also setting an interface for the class itself (ICalculator). The reason for this is that I can cast an instance of my class that I will be using in my test with this interface.

For ICalculator, it will have the same signature as the React component statement. It needs to include the methods that are part of the class that we will define and use: startOver, calculateTwoNumbers, and clicked. For startOver, I am setting it to ? just to show you how to set a method that doesn't need to be implemented.

```
export interface ICalculator extends React.PureComponent<ICalculatorProps,
ICalculatorState> {
  startOver?(): void
  calculateTwoNumbers(num1: number, num2: number, operator: string): void
  clicked(btnName: string): void
}
```

For ICalculatorProps, I will be passing a title and version.

```
interface ICalculatorProps {
  componentTitle: string
  version: string
}
```

For ICalculatorState, we need to store the output of the calculator, namely, the operator type and the two numbers we are working with.

```
interface ICalculatorState {
  output: number
  operatorType: string
  number1: number
  number2: number
}
```

Now that we have our interfaces ready, we can define our Calculator class.

```
export default class Calculator
  extends React.PureComponent<ICalculatorProps, ICalculatorState>
  implements ICalculator {
  constructor(props: ICalculatorProps) {
    super(props)
```

For the initial state, we set the default values.

```
    this.state = {
      output: 0,
      operatorType: '',
      number1: 0,
      number2: -1,
    }
  }
```

The startOver method just sets the initial default values back to the calculator. We can use that to start over, calculating new numbers.

```
startOver = () => {
  this.setState((prevState) => {
    return {
      ...prevState,
      operatorType: '',
      number1: 0,
      number2: -1,
      output: 0,
    }
  })
}
```

283

The method that does our heavy lifting is `calculateTwoNumbers`. It takes two numbers and an operator and does the math.

```
calculateTwoNumbers = (num1: number, num2: number, operator: string) => {
  let retVal = 0
  switch (operator) {
    case '+':
      retVal = num1 + num2
      break
    case '-':
      retVal = num1 - num2
      break
    case '*':
      retVal = num1 * num2
      break
    case '/':
      retVal = num1 / num2
      break
    default:
      // eslint-disable-next-line no-alert
      alert('Operator not recognized')
  }
  return retVal
}
```

The click handler expects the button name to be passed, and a switch will handle the different use cases. I am only implementing the numbers, plus and equal buttons, but feel free to continue and complete this code.

```
clicked = (btnName: string) => {
  switch (btnName) {
    case '-':
    case '*':
    case '/':
    case '+':
      this.setState((prevState) => {
        const newState = Number(prevState.output)
```

```
      return {
        ...prevState,
        operatorType: btnName,
        number1: newState,
      }
    })
    break
  case '=':
    this.setState((prevState) => {
      const newState = this.calculateTwoNumbers(
        prevState.number1,
        Number(prevState.output),
        prevState.operatorType
      )
      return {
        ...prevState,
        output: newState,
      }
    })
    break
  default:
    this.setState((prevState) => {
      const isFirstDigitNumber2 = prevState.operatorType && prevState.
      number2 === -1
      const newNumberState = isFirstDigitNumber2 ? 0 : prevState.number2
      const newOutput = isFirstDigitNumber2
        ? Number(btnName)
        : Number(prevState.output + btnName)
      return {
        ...prevState,
        number2: newNumberState,
        output: newOutput,
      }
    })
  }
}
```

For the render method, we'll create a button to click to start over and link it to the startOver method. For the calculator, we will use the ImageMapper component with the mapping area MAP we set.

```
render() {
  return (
    <>
        <a href="http://twitter.com/elieladelrom" className="follow">
          @elieladelrom
        </a>
        <h1 className="title">
          {this.props.componentTitle} - Version #{this.props.version}
        </h1>
        <p>
          <button id="btn" onClick={this.startOver}>Start Over</button>
        </p>
        <div className="calculator-output">{this.state.output}</div>
        <ImageMapper src={URL} map={MAP} onClick={(area: { name: string
        }) => { this.clicked(area.name) } } />
      </>
    )
  }
}
```

Note that I have added a div with my Twitter handle. It may look like shameless self-promoting, but I wanted to include it in order to show you how to do some testing.

It's the same with the button that will allow us to start over and the title that we will be setting as a prop. We will be using these both for testing.

For the SCSS, I am creating a style to format my output.

```
// src/components/Calculator.scss

.calculator-output
{
    background:url('/calculator-input.jpg') no-repeat right top;
    color:#fff;
    font-size:50px;
```

```
    width: 464px;
    height: 120px;
    text-align: center;
    display: flex;
    justify-content: center;
    align-items: center;
}
```

Next, we need to update our App.js file to include our custom component so we can see our component when we go to http://localhost:3000.

```
// src/App.ts

import React from 'react';
import './App.scss';
import Calculator from "./components/Calculator";

function App() {
  return (
    <div className="App">
      <Calculator componentTitle="Online Calculator" version="0.01-beta"/>
    </div>
  );
}
export default App;
```

That's it. We can now run the code ($ yarn start) and be able to see and play around with our calculator.

As I mentioned before, I didn't map all the calculator keys and functions, just the basics, but feel free to complete the task. See Figure 9-1 for the final result.

Step 3: Testing the Code

Before we run our tests, we need to do a bit more configuration of our testing environment. I also want to show you what is set up for you out of the box. The good news is that most of what we need is already set up for you with the CRA MHL template project.

Setting Up an Adapter

Open src/setupTests.ts and you will see that it is configured with the Enzyme adapter and Jest-dom. This allows us to add custom Jest matchers for asserting on DOM nodes.

```
// src/setupTests.ts
import '@testing-library/jest-dom/extend-expect'

import { configure } from 'enzyme';
import Adapter from 'enzyme-adapter-react-16'
configure({ adapter: new Adapter() });
```

Setting Up a Snapshot with enzyme-to-json

To get snapshots, we need to create the snapshotSerializers tag inside the package.json file. This will create a snapshot and expediate the Jest testing.

```
// package.json
"jest": {
  "snapshotSerializers": [
    "enzyme-to-json/serializer"
  ]
},
```

Once there is a change in our testing, the snapshot will need to be updated (press U to update) or you will get an error message. See Figure 9-2.

```
› 1 snapshot failed.
 PASS  src/AppRouter.test.tsx

Snapshot Summary
 › 1 snapshot failed from 1 test suite. Inspect your code changes or press `u` to update them.

Test Suites: 1 failed, 2 passed, 3 total
Tests:       1 failed, 10 passed, 11 total
Snapshots:   1 failed, 1 total
Time:        4.968s
```

Figure 9-2. *Snapshot failed from test suite*

This is useful especially if we are running Jest and continually using the Jest watcher feature's --watch flag.

Tip   The --watch flag in Jest will run your tests continually.

You don't need to set up anything. The package.json file already includes an NPM run script that uses react-scripts to run tests with a watcher.

```
// package.json

"scripts": {
  ...
  "test": "react-scripts test"
}
```

For our tests, we have two tests out of the box with CRA MHL for App.test.tsx and for AppRouter.test.tsx. In fact, in previous chapters, we were running the $yarn test command, and these tests were running for us.

Testing App Component: App.test.tsx

Open the src/App.test.js file that was provided through the CRA template project. Our test here is to ensure that our Calculator component is included in our App.tsx component and is not crashing.

```
// src/App.test.tsx

describe('<App />', () => {
  let component

  beforeEach(() => {
    component = shallow(<App />)
  })
  test('It should mount', () => {
    expect(component.length).toBe(1)
  })
})
```

Testing the Router Component: AppRouter.test.tsx

The same goes for AppRouter.test.tsx. We want to ensure that our router gets added without crashing. There are other tests we can run; this is just the basic test, and ideally, we want to cover each function.

```tsx
// src/AppRouter.test.tsx
import React from 'react'
import { shallow } from 'enzyme'
import AppRouter from './AppRouter'

describe('<AppRouter />', () => {
  let component

  beforeEach(() => {
    component = shallow(<AppRouter />)
  })

  test('renders without crashing', () => {
    expect(component.length).toBe(1)
  })
})
```

Now that we have our first test ready, we can run it.

To run our tests on our template, our project is already equipped with a test script to handle everything. We can use the test NPM script that is provided with CRA. Run the test command.

```
$ yarn test # or npm run test
```

The first time we use the test script, we get a message, as shown here:

```
Watch Usage
 › Press a to run all tests.
 › Press f to run only failed tests.
 › Press u to update failing snapshots.
 › Press q to quit watch mode.
 › Press p to filter by a filename regex pattern.
 › Press t to filter by a test name regex pattern.
 › Press Enter to trigger a test run.
```

What's happening is that a snapshot is created, and we can press A to run all the tests. This script will keep running, and it will be updated constantly, so you can ensure you didn't break any functionality while writing your code.

We get the complete test suites, tests, and snapshot results of our test. See Figure 9-3.

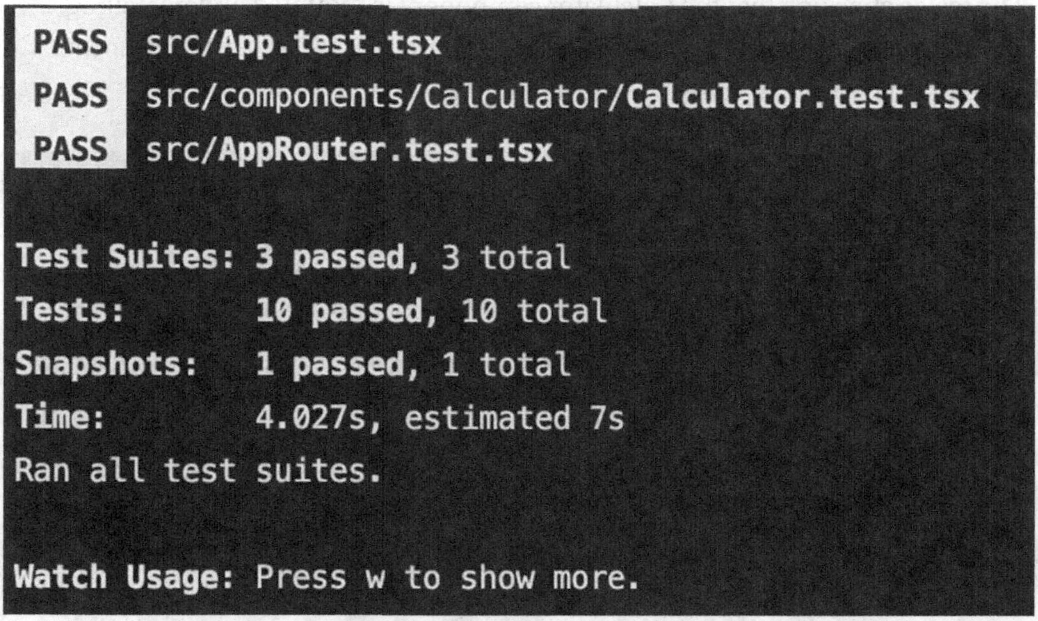

```
PASS   src/App.test.tsx
PASS   src/components/Calculator/Calculator.test.tsx
PASS   src/AppRouter.test.tsx


Test Suites: 3 passed, 3 total
Tests:       10 passed, 10 total
Snapshots:   1 passed, 1 total
Time:        4.027s, estimated 7s
Ran all test suites.


Watch Usage: Press w to show more.
```

Figure 9-3. *Test suites, tests, and snapshot test results*

We created only one test. However, when we were running the generate-react-cli command, tests were created for us by the template file that I included for you in templates/test.js, which is a vanilla-flavor test template. Let's take a look at the code.

```
// src/components/Calculator/Calculator.test.tsx

import React from 'react';
import { shallow } from 'enzyme';
import Calculator from './Calculator';

describe('<Calculator />', () => {
    let component;

    beforeEach(() => {
        component = shallow(<Calculator />);
    });
```

```
test('It should mount', () => {
    expect(component.length).toBe(1);
});
});
```

The test is checking that the Calculator component is mounted and not failing. I want you to notice that inside of our Calculator component folder (`src/components/Calculator`), a new folder called `__snapshots__` was added. See Figure 9-4.

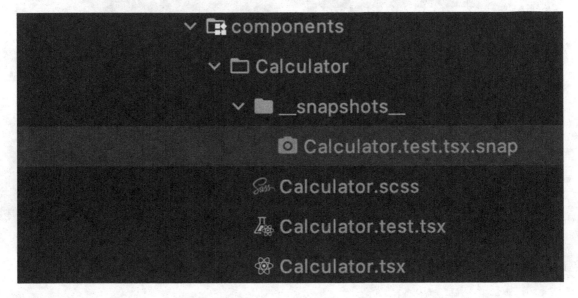

Figure 9-4. *Snapshots folder inside Calculator component*

This folder holds the test file `Calculator.test.tsx.snap`, and it will be updated as long as our Yarn test script is still running. To stop the script, just press Command+C.

When we change our code, the test watch feature will tell us that the test broke. For example, to break the code, empty the contents of the `Calculator.test.tsx` file and save it. See Figure 9-5. As you can see, our test broke due to missing at least one test inside the test file.

```
Watch Usage: Press w to show more.
 PASS  src/App.test.tsx
 FAIL  src/components/Calculator/Calculator.test.tsx
   ● Test suite failed to run

     Your test suite must contain at least one test.

       at node_modules/@jest/core/build/TestScheduler.js:242:24


Test Suites: 1 failed, 1 passed, 2 total
Tests:       1 passed, 1 total
Snapshots:   0 total
Time:        4.646s
```

Figure 9-5. *Test suite failed due to clearing code inside the Calculator.tsx file*

Creating Our Calculator Component Test File

The way Jest works is that it will look for test files in any of the following locations:

- Files with .js and .ts suffixes in __tests__ folders

- Files with .test.js and .test.ts suffixes

- Files with .spec.js and .spec.ts suffixes

generate-react-cli created for us Calculator.test.tsx automatically. I like the test suffix since it's simple, but .spec.js is the norm in other frameworks such as Angular, so whatever you choose is fine.

Let's refactor our code. In our component testing file, we can test a few things. First just import React, the Enzyme APIs we will be using (shallow and mount), and our custom component Calculator.

```
// src/components/Calculator/Calculator.test.tsx

import React from 'react'
import { shallow } from 'enzyme'
import Calculator, { ICalculator } from './Calculator'
```

We need the React library, the `shallow` and `mount` features from the Enzyme project to access methods on the DOM, and lastly the `ICalculator` interface we created so we can cast our object.

A Single Test for Noninteractive Components

To create a single test for noninteractive components, we can test my shameless self-promoting Twitter account.

We can create a wrapper for our custom component and can use the `shallow` feature with the `find` method to access the text field in our link DOM tag.

```
// non-interactive components - using it (single test)
it('should render the link url', () => {
  const wrapper = shallow(<Calculator componentTitle="Online `Calculator"
  version="0.01-beta" />)
  const a = wrapper.find('a')
  const result = a.text()

  expect(result).toBe('@elieladelrom')
})
```

Note   To create a single test, you can use the `test` keyword or `it` keyword. They are the same and are just aliases.

Snapshot Test Suite

So far, we have created a single test. However, what if we want to group a few tests together? To do that, we will be using a test suite. A test suite creates a block that groups together a few tests. We can list all the tests we want to include.

To create a test suite, we can group these single tests together using this format:

```
describe('`Calculator Snapshots', () => {
  it ...
  it ..
})
```

For example, to make sure our wrapper is matching the snapshot and wraps the test as a test suite, use this:

```
describe('`Calculator Snapshots', () => {
  it('should render our Snapshots correctly', () => {
    const wrapper = shallow(<Calculator componentTitle="Online `Calculator"
    version="0.01-beta" />)
    expect(wrapper).toMatchSnapshot()
  })
})
```

Test Component Props

For instance, to set a test to check our props on our title that we are passing from the main entry point, which is App.tsx, using a test suite, the process is similar to our previous test. We set a wrapper and check the h1 text tag against the data we inject.

```
// it(is aliased by test so it does the same thing as it)
test('should render component title', () => {
  const wrapper = shallow(<Calculator componentTitle="Online `Calculator"
  version="0.01-beta" />)
  const title = wrapper.find('h1.title').text()

  expect(title).toBe('Online `Calculator - Version #0.01-beta')
})
```

Testing an Interactive Button

For an interactive component, we can use the simulate method to simulate a user's gesture click of our button. We can then compare the results in the output. We are starting fresh, so the output should clear.

```
test('Testing output indirectly - should clean our result box clicking
clear', () => {
  const wrapper = shallow(<Calculator componentTitle="Online `Calculator"
  version="0.01-beta" />)
  const btn = wrapper.find('#btn')
  btn.simulate('click')
```

```
  const output: string = wrapper.find('.calculator-output').text()
  expect(output).toBe('0')
})
```

Testing a Suite to Test a Function Directly

There are times we need to test functions directly. Take a look. I am creating a test suite here to test my `calculateTwoNumbers`. In the test suite, I can include testing for all the different operators.

```
describe('Testing `Calculator calculateTwoNumbers testsuite directly', ()
=> {
  test('Testing calculateTwoNumbers Directly - add', () => {
    const wrapper = shallow(<Calculator componentTitle="Online `Calculator"
    version="0.01-beta" />)
    const instance = wrapper.instance() as ICalculator
    expect(instance.calculateTwoNumbers(1, 2, '+')).toBe(3)
  })
  test('Testing calculateTwoNumbers Directly - multiple', () => {
    const wrapper = shallow(<Calculator componentTitle="Online `Calculator"
    version="0.01-beta" />)
    const instance = wrapper.instance() as ICalculator
    expect(instance.calculateTwoNumbers(2, 2, '*')).toBe(4)
  })
})
```

Notice that the `instance()` property on the wrapper is powerful, because we can access our methods.

Because we are using TS and not JS, we can cast the `ICalculator` interface we created to have access to our methods (static typing) and ensure our typing is correct. This stuff is big deal because it really make TS shine compared to plain JS.

```
const instance = wrapper.instance() as ICalculator
instance.calculateTwoNumbers(...)
```

Testing an Interactive Button and Our State

Using instance(), we can also test our state. For example, here is a test to check that if we click the 1 button, the output produces 1:

```
test('test clicked calculator button method', () => {
  const wrapper = shallow(<Calculator componentTitle="Online `Calculator"
  version="0.01-beta" />)
  const instance = wrapper.instance() as ICalculator
  instance.clicked('1')
  expect(wrapper.state('output')).toBe(1)
})
```

Testing Using a Spy

Once our app grows, we may need to interact with async data, and Jest has built-in functionality to handle mock data and a function.

Look at more advanced testing topics such as spies and mocks:
https://jestjs.io/docs/en/jest-object.

```
test('spy', () => {
  const wrapper = shallow(<Calculator componentTitle="Online `Calculator"
  version="0.01-beta" />)
  const instance = wrapper.instance() as ICalculator
  jest.spyOn(instance, 'startOver')
  wrapper.find('button').simulate('click')
  expect(wrapper.state('output')).toBe(0)
})
```

Once all of our testing suites and stubs are ready, you should expect the testing output shown in Figure 9-6.

```
PASS    src/App.test.tsx
PASS    src/components/Calculator/Calculator.test.tsx
PASS    src/AppRouter.test.tsx


Test Suites: 3 passed, 3 total
Tests:       11 passed, 11 total
Snapshots:   1 passed, 1 total
Time:        6.102s
Ran all test suites.
```

Figure 9-6. *Snapshot summary with all calculator tests included*

Under the Hood

There is a lot of stuff going on under the hood here. I wanted to point a few things that can help you.

Enzyme includes three rendering methods. We only used Shallow, but there are also Mount and Render. These methods give access to the DOM tree.

- *Mount*: https://enzymejs.github.io/enzyme/docs/api/mount.html

- Shallow: https://enzymejs.github.io/enzyme/docs/api/shallow.html

- Render: https://enzymejs.github.io/enzyme/docs/api/render.html

Mounting

These are the advantages of Mounting:

- Full DOM rendering including child components

- Ideal for use cases where you have components that need to interact with the DOM API or when you have to use React lifecycle methods

- Allows access to both props directly passed into the root component (including the default props) and props passed into child components

Shallow

These are the advantages of `Shallow`:

- Renders only the single component, not children. This is useful to isolate the component for pure unit testing. It protects against changes or bugs in a child component.

- Shallow components have access to lifecycle methods by default.

- It cannot access `props` passed into the root component, but it can access props passed into child components and can test the effects of `props` passed into the root component.

- When we call `shallow(<Calculator />)`, we are testing what Calculator renders, not the element we passed into `Shallow`.

Render

These are the advantages of Render:

- It renders to static HTML, including children.

- It does not have access to React lifecycle methods.

- It uses fewer resources than the other APIs, but has less functionality.

enzyme-to-json

In our code, we used `enzyme-to-json`, but why?

This is done so we have a better component format for our snapshot comparison than the Enzyme's out-of-the-box internal component representation.

The `snapshotSerializers` API allows us to write less code and remove duplication when working with the snapshots. We don't need to serialize each time a component is created with `a.toJson()` before it can be passed to Jest's snapshot matcher.

```
expect(toJson(rawRenderedComponent)).toMatchSnapshot();
```

We did that by adding `snapshotSerializers` in `package.json`.

```
"snapshotSerializers": ["enzyme-to-json/serializer"],
```

Then, we are able to pass a component created by Enzyme to the Jest
`.toMatchSnapshot()` method without the `toJson` syntax.

`expect(wrapper).toMatchSnapshot()`

Jest Matchers

When we were writing our tests, we needed to check that our test values meet certain
conditions. The Expect API gives us access to a number of "matchers" that help us
validate different things.

In terms of Jest, the Expect API provides enough options for most users; see
`https://jestjs.io/docs/en/expect`. However, if you can't find what you are looking
for, check the Jest Community's `jest-extended` for more matches or create your own if
you can't find what you need.

Sinon Library

Another must-have library that we should be aware of and add to our toolbox is Sinon
(`https://github.com/sinonjs/sinon`). You don't need to add it because it's already
included in our CRA template project. (If you did need to add it, you could use `yarn add`
`sinon @types/sinon`.)

Jest and Sinon serve the same purpose. So why add Sinon?

The answer is that there are times that you may find one framework more natural
and easier to work for the specific test you need than the other, so it wouldn't hurt to
have both. You can compare the list of APIs on Jest (`https://jestjs.io/docs/en/api`)
and Sinon (`https://sinonjs.org/releases/v9.2.0/`).

Take, for example, faking timers. Both frameworks have a way to fake times.

- *Jest*: `https://jestjs.io/docs/en/timer-mocks`

- *Sinon*: `https://sinonjs.org/releases/v1.17.6/fake-timers/`

Luckily, we can just add Sinon and use Jest or Sinon for our test. They work together,
so we don't need to choose.

Let's say we want to create a loader for our calculator because we need a service call
or wait for whatever we need.

We can start this time from the test instead of writing the code first. To do that, we can use Test-Driven Development (TDD) by first writing the test and then having our test fail. Lastly, we write the code that will get our test to pass.

TDD is a software development process that relies on a development cycle that requires setting up test cases, and then the code is written so that the tests will pass.

For instance, let's say our requirement is that we need to place a subtitle with a message that will tell the user that the loading phase was completed.

The test with the fake Sinon timer would look like so:

```
import sinon from 'sinon'

describe('Loader component', () => {
  it('should render complete after x seconds', () => {
    const wrapper = shallow(<Calculator componentTitle="Online `Calculator"
    version="0.01-beta" />)
    const clock = sinon.useFakeTimers()
    const instance = wrapper.instance() as ICalculator
    instance.startLoader(3000)
    clock.tick(3000)

    const title = wrapper.find('h1.subTitle').text()
    expect(title).toBe('Loading Complete')
  })
})
```

Our code here uses `sinon.useFakeTimers`, and once we call a method on our class `startLoader`, we can start the clock: `clock.tick(3000)`. Lastly, we ensure that the subtitle changed to "Loading Complete."

Now, in our `Calculator.tsx` code, let's refactor the signature of the `ICalculator` interface and the `ICalculatorState` state.

```
export interface ICalculator extends React.PureComponent <ICalculatorProps,
ICalculatorState> {
  ...
  startLoader(seconds: number): void
}
```

```
interface ICalculatorState {
    ...
  LoaderStatus: string
}
```

Next, we can have a timer start running for three seconds once the component mounts and set a startLoader method to start a timer and update the state.

```
componentDidUpdate() {
  this.startLoader(3000)
}

startLoader = (seconds: number) => {
  setTimeout(() => {
    this.setState((prevState) => {
      const newState = 'Loading Complete'
      return {
        ...prevState,
        LoaderStatus: newState,
      }
    })
  }, seconds)
}
```

Lastly, on the render JSX side, add an h1 tag with the subtitle.

```
render() {
  return (
    <>
        ...
        <h1 className="subTitle">
          {this.state.LoaderStatus}
        </h1>
        ...
    </>
    )
  }
}
```

Run the test to ensure everything is working as expected.

Testing Router Pages

Before we bring this chapter to a close, I want to point out another testing file that comes with the CRA template project.

If you recall, in previous exercises, we built our app using a router. Our router pages are extending RouteComponentProps. This was useful as we were able to use the router APIs and extract the name of the router page. For example, for the article page we set this interface signature, which was the template page created for us via generate-react-cli.

```
interface IArticlesPageProps extends RouteComponentProps<{ name: string }>
{
  // TODO
}
```

This interface used the router history API to extract the name of the page; we then were able to use the name in our render.

generate-react-cli also created for us a companion file called ArticlesPage. test.tsx, which is a Jest test page that includes a way to access the router via routeComponentPropsMock, which is a mock object I created.

Notice that routeComponentPropsMock is implementing just the history API of RouteComponentProps, so if you are using other APIs, you will need to mimic them inside the routeComponentPropsMock object. Take a look:

```
// ArticlesPage.test.tsx

import React from 'react'
import { shallow } from 'enzyme'
import ArticlesPage from './ArticlesPage'

const routeComponentPropsMock = {
  history: {
    location: {
      pathname: '/ArticlesPage',
    },
    // eslint-disable-next-line @typescript-eslint/no-explicit-any
  } as any,
  // eslint-disable-next-line @typescript-eslint/no-explicit-any
  location: {} as any,
```

```
  // eslint-disable-next-line @typescript-eslint/no-explicit-any
  match: {} as any,
}
describe('<ArticlesPage />', () => {
  let component

  beforeEach(() => {
    component = shallow(<ArticlesPage {...routeComponentPropsMock} />)
  })

  test('It should mount', () => {
    expect(component.length).toBe(1)
  })
})
```

We can confirm that the app is passing the format, lint, and test commands.

```
$ yarn format & yarn lint & yarn test
```

I want to point out that the lint and format commands will check the test files as well, so the linting rules we set using the Airbnb styles still apply.

Summary

In this chapter, we focused on unit testing. I broke down the process into three steps: setting up and configuring the project, writing the code, and testing the code.

You learned about Jest, Jest-dom, Enzyme, and enzyme-to-json. You learned how to perform different types of unit testing on your React components, understand better the libraries involved, create snapshots, create single tests, and group tests in a test suite.

We looked at the template's unit testing component and page's test template that I set up for you as well as the App.test.tsx and AppRouter.test.tsx tests.

I also gave you some extra "under the hood" stuff, and lastly, we looked at adding the Sinon library and TDD.

In the next chapter, we will go deep into integrating testing.

CHAPTER 10

Testing Part II: Development and Deployment Cycle

In the previous chapter, we did unit testing with the help of the Jest, Jest-dom, Enzyme, and Sinon libraries. Unit testing is just one type of testing. In addition to unit testing, end-to-end (E2E) testing simulates a real end user's experience, and integration testing combines tests.

This chapter is split into two parts. In the first part, I will cover E2E testing and show you how to implement it using the Jest and Puppeteer libraries. In the second part of this chapter, I will cover how to create a full automated development and deployment integration cycle that includes full code coverage, as well as how to test your code and ensure the quality is maintained.

Performing End-to-End Testing

End-to-end (E2E) integration, Simulating a real end user's experience. The E2E tests do the simulation using a real web environments by using a headless browser.

In this section of this chapter, I will focus on E2E testing for CRA with the help of the Jest and Puppeteer libraries.

Why Should you Care About E2E Testing?

E2E testing is a method that tests our app workflow from beginning to end. What we are doing in E2E is replicating real user scenarios so that our app is validated for integration and data integrity.

E. Elrom, *React and Libraries*, https://doi.org/10.1007/978-1-4842-6696-0_10

You may be surprised to learn that most companies are willing to deploy a full team of quality assurance (QA) manual testers but don't value investing in E2E testing.

E2E is one of these tasks for which I often hear developers say, "We will get there one day; it's on our bucket list." But that day never comes, due to focusing on features and meeting stressful deadlines.

Yes, it does take time to set up an E2E test, but E2E testing reduces human errors and helps deliver quality software. That has been acknowledged by some companies, and in fact, in recent years, I have seen companies start to value E2E testing and keep full-time developers on board just to create and maintain tests.

Did you know, according to a QualiTest survey, that almost 90 percent of people said they would abandon an app if they encountered bugs or glitches maintain tests on a daily basis?

Why TypeScript?

Throughout this book we have used TS. TS shines when it comes to testing. Using TS, it is easier to debug your apps and test them and to prevent potential problems by describing what is the object to expect.

Why Puppeteer?

Here are some of the E2E options and their GitHub popularity:

- *Puppeteer* (`https://github.com/puppeteer/puppeteer`): 66,100 stars

- *Cypress* (`https://github.com/cypress-io/cypress`): 24,200 stars

- *Selenium* (`https://github.com/SeleniumHQ/selenium`): 18,900 stars

- *nighwatch.js* (`https://github.com/nightwatchjs/nightwatch`): 10,000 stars

- *cucumber.js* (`https://github.com/cucumber/cucumber-js`): 4,000 stars

As you can see, based on GitHub stars, Puppeteer is the most popular E2E library. It is Chrome-based and is what we will be using (see Figure 10-1).

Figure 10-1. Puppeteer logo

The Puppeteer library was created by the Google Chrome team. Puppeteer lets us control Chrome (or the Chrome DevTools protocol-based browser) and execute common actions, much like in a real browser—meaning programmatically, through an API.

> *"Puppeteer is a Node library which provides a high-level API to control Chrome or Chromium over the DevTools Protocol. Puppeteer runs headless by default, but can be configured to run full (non-headless) Chrome or Chromium."*
>
> *—https://github.com/puppeteer/puppeteer*

What can we do with Puppeteer and React?

- Generate screenshots and PDFs out of pages

- Crawl pages

- Automate user interaction

- Capture a timeline trace of your site to help diagnose performance issues

- Use them as stand-alone or integrate them with other popular React testing frameworks such as Jest or Mocha

Why Jest and Jest Puppeteer?

We already used Jest (`https://github.com/facebook/jest`) in the previous chapter (see Figure 10-2). In this chapter, we will integrate Jest Puppeteer (`https://github.com/smooth-code/jest-puppeteer`). Jest Puppeteer comes with the functionality to start a server when running a test suite. Additionally, Jest Puppeteer can automatically close the server when the tests are complete.

Figure 10-2. *Jest logo*

How Can I Integrate E2E Testing into My CRA React App?

To help you understand how to use Jest and Puppeteer on the CRA project, I broke down the process in this section into three steps.

- *Step 1*: Setting up and configuring our project

- *Step 2*: Writing code

- *Step 3*: Running E2E testing

Let's get started.

Step 1: Setting Up and Configuring Our Project

Between the Jest's clown shoe icon and the Puppeteer logo, it is starting to feel like a circus around here. But seriously, setting up your project correctly is not a joke and can take more time than you would anticipate, especially since we need to take into account CRA, which has some opinionated libraries that need to be configured, as well as TS that needs extra configurations steps.

The easiest way to get started on a CRA project running TS, Jest, Puppeteer, Jest, Enzyme, and other must-have libraries is to use my CRA template that we have been using in this book. Let's call our test project e2e_testing_with_puppeteer.

```
$ yarn create react-app e2e_testing_with_puppeteer --template must-
have-libraries
```

Tip   Everything is configured, and you don't need to set up anything!

The CRA MHL project already includes the following: puppeteer, jest-puppeteer ts-jest, and the types.

$ yarn add puppeteer jest-puppeteer ts-jest @types/puppeteer @types/expect-puppeteer @types/jest-environment-puppeteer

Besides the type puppeteer, we have @types/expect-puppeteer for the assertion library for jest-puppeteer, and we need to use @types/jest-environment-puppeteer to provide the global browser definition. You can find more information at https://github.com/smooth-code/jest-puppeteer.

To confirm everything is working as expected, run yarn start (see Figure 10-3).

$ cd e2e_testing_with_puppeteer
$ yarn start

Figure 10-3. *Starter project template*

If you look in your project's folder (Figure 10-4), you can see that there is a folder named e2e that includes the test and Jest configuration.

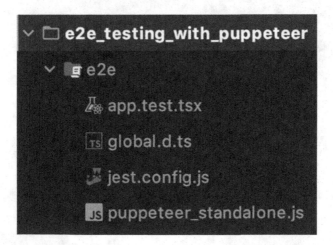

Figure 10-4. *The e2e folder includes the testing and Jest configuration*

In the following section, I will dive into the configurations and the files that are set up for you so you fully understand how to set up E2E. However, you don't need to set these up if you are using the CRA MHL template project.

Configuring Our Project

Before we start configuring our project, here are some housekeeping rules. I am setting up the E2E integration tests inside an E2E folder. The E2E can be integrated with the unit testing of Jest; however, I personally think it's best to separate the task of unit testing and E2E testing. With that being said, if you want or need them together, feel free to change this configuration.

There are a few files that were added and refactored to get our E2E test working.

- `jest-puppeteer.config.js`: This specifies a server.

- `.env`: This sets the environment variables for the Puppeteer server.

- `tsconfig.json`: We use `tsconfig.json` to specify the root-level files and the compiler options that are required to compile a TypeScript project.

- `.eslintignore`: This tells ESLint to ignore specific files and directories.

- `e2e/global.d.ts`: This specifies the global type. We need to add a variable to "magically" have an interface available for us.

- `e2e/jest.config.js`: That's the Jest configuration file.

- `package.json`: We will add to the script tag to run our tests.

Let's review these files and what we need to do.

jest-puppeteer.config.js

The `jest-puppeteer.config.js` file specifies Puppeteer's server config.

The local start is set using `yarn`, but you can change that to `npm start` if you are using NPM to manage your libraries.

```
module.exports = {
  server: {
    command: `yarn start`,
```

```
    port: 3000,
    launchTimeout: 10000,
    debug: true,
  },
}
```

.env

The .env file is used to set the environment variables for the Puppeteer server. Here I am telling the Puppeteer server to do a preflight check and not to use a browser in testing so it will run in the background.

```
SKIP_PREFLIGHT_CHECK=true
BROWSER=none
```

tsconfig.json

We need to refactor this tsconfig.json file to add the folder we're using for testing. This will allow us to compile our TypeScript tests.

```
...
"include": [
  ...
  "e2e"
]
```

.eslintignore

The configuration files need to be ignored as we don't need them to follow our React project's Lint roles. We can ignore these files by adding them at the end of the .eslintignore file.

```
e2e/jest.config.js
e2e/puppeteer_standalone.js
jest-puppeteer.config.js
```

Notice the filename puppeteer_standalone.js, which we will create and talk about shortly to run Puppeteer on its own without Jest.

e2e/jest.config.js

Next, we want to refactor jest.config.js. This file is the Jest configuration file. I am setting it inside the e2e folder because it allows me to define different jest.config.js files (in case I need them). You will see that when we define our package.json script, we can reference the specific one to use.

In testRegex, I am setting up the project that our tests set in this format: [component name].test.tsx. Here's an example: app.test.tsx.

This format aligns well with how we set tests, and this format will allow our e2e to be found.

Notice that I am setting a global variable SERVER_URL, which makes our life easy in case we need to update the server name across the board for all our tests.

```
module.exports = {
  preset: 'jest-puppeteer',
  globals: {
    SERVER_URL: "http://localhost:3000"
  },
  testRegex: './/*\\.test\\.tsx$'
}
console.log('RUNNING E2E INTEGRATION TESTS - MAKE SURE PORT 3000 IS NOT IN
USAGE')
```

Notice that I am using console.log to display a message with a comment to remind you that the localhost needs to run this test.

This config will open a headless Chrome browser to create our test on port 3000, so make sure to use yarn start in the Terminal if you have it running, as we can't have two localhost:3000 instances running at once.

The other alternative is to run this stand-alone test on a different port; you can configure it this way if that's what you need. I wanted to keep it simple.

e2e/global.d.ts

The global.d.ts file lets us add the TS declaration that we need to set. Since we placed SERVER_URL and JEST_TIMEOUT inside jest.config.js, our Lint rules will have a beef with just using these variables without declaring them. TS needs everything defined, so normally I would not recommend just adding declarations, but here we can make an exception since we know what we are doing.

313

```
// globals defined in jest.config.js need to be included in this `d.ts`
// file to avoid TS lint errorsdeclare var SERVER_URL: string
declare var JEST_TIMEOUT: number
```

package.json

Lastly, I am setting up three tests in package.json.

- test:e2e: This runs the E2E tests pointing to the e2e/jest.config. js config file we set inside the e2e folder.

- test:e2e-alone: This runs our stand-alone NodeJs Puppeteer script.

- test:e2e-watch: We use this if we want to have a watcher running.

```
"scripts": {
  ...
  "test:e2e": "jest -c e2e/jest.config.js",
  "test:e2e-alone": "node e2e/puppeteer_standalone.js",
  "test:e2e-watch": "jest -c e2e/jest.config.js --watch"
}
```

Step 2: Writing Code

We will be writing both a stand-alone Nodejs script that can be run on its own and a Jest Puppeteer script to test our App.tsx file.

We will create two files.

- e2e/puppeteer_standalone.js: This stand-alone file is not really needed, but it can come in handy in certain cases, for example if we need to do testing on third-party libraries and scripts or just want to test without Jest.

- e2e/app.test.tsx: This offers E2E integration testing for App.tsx. As I mentioned, although theoretically we could do unit testing and E2E testing together, we will be doing only E2E in this portion of our test.

Let's review these files.

e2e/puppeteer_standalone.js

On the code level, we are creating a headless Chrome browser and testing that the link to http://localhost:3000 will open the URL by actually clicking it using a script. Then we wait two seconds and close the Chromeless browser.

We need to run our app on http://localhost:3000 (with $yarn start), so I left a try-catch message in case you forgot to do so.

```
const puppeteer = require('puppeteer');
const SERVER_URL = 'http://localhost:3000';

(async function main(){
  try {
    const browser = await puppeteer.launch({ headless: false });
    const page = await browser.newPage();
    await page.goto(SERVER_URL, {waitUntil: 'domcontentloaded'});

    const urlLink = await page.$('a[href*="https://github.com"]');
    if (urlLink) {
      await urlLink.click();
    } else {
      console.log('No "urlLink" found on page');
    }
    // wait 2 secs and shut down!
    await new Promise(resolve =>  setTimeout(resolve, 2000));
    await browser.close();
  } catch (error) {
    if (error.message.includes('ERR_CONNECTION_REFUSED'))
      console.log('Make sure you have React running: $ yarn start');
    console.log('Error message', error.message);
  }
})();
```

e2e/app.test.tsx

For our E2E testing of the app.test.tsx component, I will be testing a few things.

First, I placed a sanity check test to open Google.com and check that the word *Google* appears. This is just a demonstration to sharpen our sword. Feel free to discard it.

Our app test suite will include the following three tests:

- Ensure the edit is on the page.

- Check that `<a href>` is correctly placed and linked to the correct URL.

- Check that the React rotating logo image is on the page.

To learn more about the types of E2E tests we can run, visit `https://devdocs.io/puppeteer/`.

Additionally, my file starts with `@ts-ignore`. That's because I have no import statement in this file, and ESLint will have a problem with `isolatedModules` because it will want the file to be part of a module.

```
// @ts-ignore due to isolatedModules flag - no import so this needed
describe('Google', () => {
  beforeAll(async () => {
    await page.goto('https://google.com', {waitUntil: 'domcontentloaded'})
  })

  it('sanity check, test Google server by checking "google" text on page',
  async () => {
    await expect(page).toMatch('google')
  })
})

// @ts-ignore due to isolatedModules flag - no import so this needed
describe('<App />', () => {
  beforeAll(async () => {
    await page.goto(SERVER_URL, {waitUntil: 'domcontentloaded'})
  }, JEST_TIMEOUT)

  it('should include "edit" text on page', async () => {
    await expect(page).toMatch('Edit')
  }, JEST_TIMEOUT)

  it('should include href with correct link', async () => {
    const hrefsArray = await page.evaluate(
        () => Array.from(
```

```
          document.querySelectorAll('a[href]'),
          a => a.getAttribute('href')
      )
  )
  expect(hrefsArray[0]).toMatch('https://github.com/EliEladElrom/react-
  tutorials')
}, JEST_TIMEOUT)

it('should include the React svg correct image', async () => {
  const images = await page.$$eval('img', anchors => [].map.call(anchors,
  img => img['src']));
  expect(images[0]).toMatch(SERVER_URL + '/static/media/logo.5d5d9eef.
  svg')
}, JEST_TIMEOUT)

})
```

JEST_TIMEOUT is needed because Jest is set with a 5000ms timeout, and that may not be enough to run your test, so I am setting the components with a different timeout to ensure I won't get this mean message. Feel free to change the timeout. Here is the Jest timeout error message you will receive:

```
Timeout - Async callback was not invoked within the 5000ms timeout
specified by jest.setTimeout.Error: Timeout - Async callback was not
invoked within the 5000ms timeout specified by jest.setTimeout.
```

I am not doing any user interactions here, because the only interaction is clicking the link on the page, which we already tested on the stand-alone example. If you want to see another example, such as CRA testing a form element and filling in the form, see https://github.com/smooth-code/jest-puppeteer/tree/master/examples/create-react-app.

Step 3: Performing E2E Testing

Now that we have written our stand-alone E2E NodeJS script, as well as the E2E tests for the App.tsx component, we can run these tests and check the results.

As you recall, to run these tests, we created run scripts inside our package.json file to be able to run our tests with one command.

Let's run these.

Start off by running the following command in separate windows:

```
$ yarn start # if not running
$ yarn test:e2e-alone
```

That NPM run script ties into the following package.json command:

```
// package.json
"test:e2e-alone": "node e2e/puppeteer_standalone.js"
```

When you run the command, if everything went well, the script opens the Chrome headless browser using our localhost 3000 build and clicks the link to open a new tab. Then the script closes the browser in two seconds, and you will get the following message. See the stand-alone E2E testing results for localhost:3000.

```
yarn run v1.22.10
$ node e2e/puppeteer_standalone.js
Done in 5.36s.
```

Congrats! We passed the test.

This happens fast because we set Chrome to close in 2 seconds. But as you see, the script opened a browser, clicked the link in our app that opened another window (as we expected), and then closed the test! Pretty impressive, right?

Next, to run our E2E test for the App.tsx component using Jest Puppeteer, stop the local server, and run the NPM script called test:e2e.

```
$ yarn test:e2e
```

This will run the NPM run script command.

```
// package.json
```

```
"test:e2e": "jest -c e2e/jest.config.js --watch"
"test:e2e-watch": "jest -c e2e/jest.config.js --watch"
```

After running that command, you should be getting the following E2E testing Jest and Puppeteer output:

```
Jest dev-server output:
[Jest Dev server] $ react-scripts start
[Jest Dev server] [wds]: Project is running at
```

```
[Jest Dev server] [wds]: webpack output is served from
[Jest Dev server] [wds]: Content not from webpack is served
[Jest Dev server] [wds] : 404s will fallback to /
[Jest Dev server] Starting the development server...
RUNS e2e/app.test.tsx
```

If theE2E test results went well, you will get a sweet success message such as this:

```
PASS
e2e/app.test.tsx (15.264s)
<App />
☑  should include "edit" text on page (189ms)
☑  should include href with correct link (9ms)
☑  should include the React svg correct image (29ms)

Test Suites: 1 passed, 1 total
Tests: 3 passed, 3 total
Snapshots: 0 total
Time: 15.57s, estimated 19s
Ran all test suites.
```

Bravo! We were able to run stand-alone E2E tests as well as cover a specific portion of our app.

Automating Development and Using a Continuous Integration Cycle

When it comes to publishing quality code, there are many ways to configure your project, and there are lots of different opinions about how to do it. What should you use? How should you configure it? The options seem limitless.

In this part of the chapter, my aim is to equip you with some great tools to ensure the quality of your code is high and help you avoid hiccups.

The process starts in our development environment by setting up coding guidelines, sticking to these guidelines, and continuing from there to create unit tests, integrate these tests (integration testing), and then do end-to-end testing and coverage. Once we have done that, we can move to our continuous integration (CI) cycle.

Note   Continuous integration means merging all the development copies into a shared mainline. This is done as often as possible.

On the CI side, our code still needs to be tested and checked for coverage, quality, and dependencies to ensure we really followed the tests and coding guidelines we set, find potential coding errors, and lastly give the green light to show that it's all good to deploy. Rinse and repeat.

In this section of this chapter, I will my ultimate React quality development and deployment cycle, which is Husky ➤ Puppeteer ➤ GitHub workflow ➤ Codecov.io ➤ Coveralls ➤ Travis ➤ DeepScan.

As a bonus, you can get some cool badges to prove your project is up to the standards you set. Figure 10-5 shows the libraries used throughout this cycle.

Figure 10-5. *Ultimate React quality development and deployment cycle*

Motivation

React is just a library and nothing more. It's left to us to ensure our project's quality. Configuring and setting our project's development and deployment cycle are not easy tasks. What tools should you choose, and how can you ensure the quality of the code and that your app is meeting the quality level you set?

Additionally, setting up a good development and deployment process is a crucial part; in my opinion, this process should be set up before you write the first line of code. Ideally, we want to publish fast and publish often and ensure our code does not degrade in quality as our code base grows.

The process in this chapter can ensure you get 100 percent coverage (if that's what you desire) out of the gate and make sure you stay there. The goal is not only to ensure you and your team are achieving the development guidelines and writing bug-free code, ideally, but any new developer coming on board should also adhere to these guidelines without even getting an explanation from the team's lead of what the expected practices are.

Structure

To help you understand, I broke down the process into these steps:

- Step 1: Setup
- Step 2: Husky
- Step 3: GitHub actions
- Step 4: Codecov.io
- Step 5: Travis
- Step 6: Coveralls
- Step 7: DeepScan

Let's get started.

Setting Up the Project

You can start with a new project or implement these changes on any project you like.

```
$ yarn create react-app your_project_name --template must-have-libraries
```

To confirm everything is working as expected, run `yarn start`.

```
$ cd your_project_name
$ yarn start
```

Testing

During the process of writing tests, we may discover new bugs or syntax issues in our source code that are important to resolve before distributing our app. As we save seen, our CRA MHL template project comes with unit testing and E2E opinionated libraries to help you write your tests in a more intuitive way.

Coverage

Once we have our unit tests ready, we can move to check for coverage. To set up the coverage, we can use Jest as well.

Note   Code coverage measures how much our source code is executed when a particular test suite runs.

Jest allows us to create reports in different formats and set where we want to collect these reports from (or not collect them from), as well as ensure the `coverageThreshold` value. Take a look at my `package.json` settings, shown here:

```
// package.json
"jest": {
  "coverageReporters": [
    "json",
    "text",
    "html",
    "lcov"
  ],
  "collectCoverageFrom": [
    "src/**/*.{js,jsx,ts,tsx}",
    "!src/**/*/*.d.ts",
    "!src/**/*/Loadable.{js,jsx,ts,tsx}",
    "!src/**/*/types.ts",
```

```
    "!src/**/store.ts",
    "!src/index.tsx",
    "!src/serviceWorker.ts",
    "!<rootDir>/node_modules/",
    "!**/templates/**",
    "!**/template/**"
  ],
  "coverageThreshold": {
    "global": {
      "branches": 50,
      "functions": 50,
      "lines": 50,
      "statements": 50
    }
  },
```

In this example, I am enforcing 50 percent coverageThreshold. When I set this, it will ensure that I am testing within my threshold or I will get an error. That can come in handy because we can set these values to ensure that every single function, statement, line, and branch gets at least 50 percent test coverage or even 100 percent test coverage.

In package.json, we can set up our run scripts to include tests for coverage by setting watchAll to false so the script will shut down once the test is complete.

```
// package.json

"scripts": {
  ...
  "coverage": "npm test -- --coverage --watchAll=false"
}
```

Once you run the script, like this:

```
$ yarn run coverage
```

you will get a folder created with the report (Figure 10-6).

Figure 10-6. *Jest coverage folder tree and files*

Since my `package.json` file included an HTML report, we can actually open the `coverage/index.html` file created to view our reports with a neat user interface (Figure 10-7).

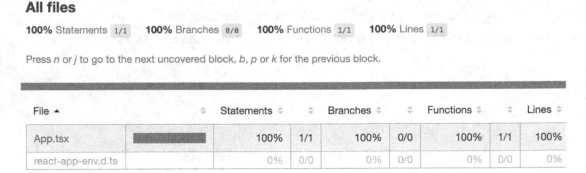

All files

100% Statements `1/1`   **100%** Branches `0/0`   **100%** Functions `1/1`   **100%** Lines `1/1`

Press *n* or *j* to go to the next uncovered block, *b*, *p* or *k* for the previous block.

File ▲		Statements	⇕	⇕	Branches	⇕	⇕	Functions	⇕	⇕	Lines	⇕
App.tsx		100%	1/1		100%	0/0		100%	1/1		100%	
react-app-env.d.ts		0%	0/0		0%	0/0		0%	0/0		0%	

Figure 10-7. *Jest coverage HTML report*

Feel free to configure your project however you need. My recommendation is that you set up your `package.json` file with certain run scripts that ensure the formatting of code and to ensure that style guides are enforced as well as testing coverage is done according to your requirements.

Setting Up Git Hooks with Husky

Next, we will install a library called Husky (`https://github.com/typicode/husky`).

```
$ yarn add husky
```

Husky provides access to Git hooks that we can use to ensure certain tasks are completed successfully before allowing our team members to commit into our repo. Take a look at this example:

```
// package.json
{
  "husky": {
    "hooks": {
      "pre-commit": "npm test",
      "pre-push": "npm test",
      "...": "..."
    }
  }
}
```

If you recall from previous chapters, we were manually running `format`, `lint`, and `test` at the end of each completed exercise. In our case, we can set a precommit hook to run the `format`, `lint`, and unit testing as well as E2E testing as a condition for a precommit.

```
"husky": {
  "hooks": {
    "pre-commit": "yarn format && yarn lint && yarn test:e2e && yarn
    coverage"
  }
},
```

This hook runs once you commit any code. It will not allow committing unless these run scripts are completed without errors. That will ensure our code follows the guidelines, format, and tests we set.

Set your library on a GitHub repo and give a commit a try to see the precommit run.

```
$ git add .
$ git commit -m 'my first commit'
```

Setting Up a Workflow with GitHub Actions

Now that our code made it to our repo in GitHub, we can ensure the quality of the code and then do specific actions. These actions add automation to our repository.

For example, we can ensure the code compiles, passes coverage, and passes other tests and then upload the code to a production server, or we can upload our code to other systems to analyze them.

This can be done using GitHub actions. To learn more about GitHub actions, check out the GitHub documentation at `https://docs.github.com/en/free-pro-team@latest/actions/learn-github-actions`. These actions are written in a language called YAML.

Note   YAML is a recursive acronym for "YAML Ain't Markup Language" and is a human-readable, intuitive data serialization format.

To create these actions, you need to create this folder structure: `.github/workflows`. Then we will create the following GitHub actions:

- *Main*: Run Lint, test Main Action, and upload it to `codecov`.

- *Build*: Ensure Build Action builds.

- *Test*: Test and upload Test Action to `coverall`.

- *Lint*: Ensure our project passes a Lint test.

Main Action: main.yml

Our main task (`main.yml`) is hooked to a push commit. We will be using Node.js version 12.x and running on a Ubuntu server. We will install the project and the dependencies, run Lint, and test as well as upload our code to the Codecov app (we will set up our account shortly).

```
name: CIon: [push]jobs:
  build:
    runs-on: ubuntu-latest    strategy:
      matrix:
        node-version: [12.x]    steps:
```

```yaml
    - uses: actions/checkout@v1
    - name: Use Node.js ${{ matrix.node-version }}
      uses: actions/setup-node@v1
      with:
        node-version: ${{ matrix.node-version }}
    - name: install dependencies
      run: |
        yarn
    - name: run lint
      run: |
        yarn lint
    - name: run tests
      run: |
        yarn test --watchAll=false --coverage --reporters=default
    - name: Upload coverage to Codecov
      uses: codecov/codecov-action@v1.0.14
      with:
        token: ${{ secrets.CODECOV_TOKEN }}
    - name: build
      run: |
        yarn build
```

Build Action: build.yaml

To build our code (build.yaml), I will be using the ubuntu-latest server (at the time of writing, it's at version 20.10). The default is to treat warnings as errors. If you want to disable that default behavior, you can set process.env.CI = false.

You can read more about that at https://github.com/facebook/create-react-app/issues/3657. My hooks will be set to run on push and pull requests. Take a look:

```yaml
name: build

on:
  - push
  - pull_request
```

```
jobs:
  createAndTestTemplateCRA:
    runs-on: ubuntu-latest
    steps:
      - name: Use Node.js 12.x
        uses: actions/setup-node@v1
        with:
          node-version: 12.x
      - name: Settings to fix problem on Ubuntu
        run: echo fs.inotify.max_user_watches=524288 | sudo tee -a /etc/
            sysctl.conf
      - run: sudo sysctl -p
      - name: Create CRA from downloaded template
        run: npx create-react-app --template cra-template-must-have-
            libraries .
      - name: No need to fail due to warnings using CI=false
        run: CI= npm run build
```

Test Action: test.yaml

Our test script (test.yaml) has a hook on push and on pull_request and uses Node
v12. For the testing, we will run the coverage script as well as upload the code to
coverallsapp. We will set up Coveralls later in this chapter.

```
name: test
on:
  - push
  - pull_requestjobs:
  test:
    runs-on: ubuntu-latest
    steps:
      - uses: actions/checkout@v2
      - name: Use Node.js 12.x
        uses: actions/setup-node@v1
        with:
          node-version: 12.x
```

```
- run: npm i
- run: npm run coverage
- name: Upload coverage file to Coveralls using lcov.info
  uses: coverallsapp/github-action@master
  with:
    github-token: ${{ secrets.GITHUB_TOKEN }}
```

The link is for creating a personal access token that can be used for coverallsapp and any other 3rd party tools. Follow the steps here:

https://docs.github.com/en/free-pro-team@latest/github/authenticating-to-github/creating-a-personal-access-token

Lint Action: lint.yml

For Lint, we already were running ESLint during our development cycle, so why do we need this (lint.yml) again on the deployment cycle?

Here we run Lint again to ensure that the developer actually was running Lint and didn't change his local settings and commit the code without Lint.

```
name: lint
on:
  - push
  - pull_request
jobs:
  lint:
    runs-on: ubuntu-latest
    steps:
      - uses: actions/checkout@v2
      - run: npm i
      - run: npm run lint
```

Lastly, you can generate a badge for each GitHub action by clicking Actions, selecting the action name, and then clicking "Create status badge," as shown in Figure 10-8.

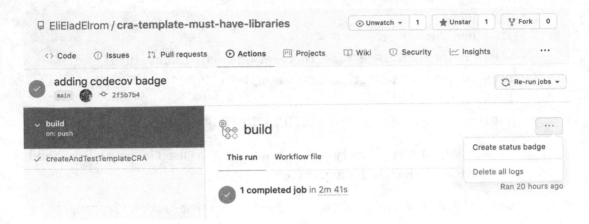

Figure 10-8. *GitHub action build result and badge*

Test Coverage with Codecov.io

Codecov is a tool used to measure the test coverage of your code base. It generally calculates the coverage ratio by examining which lines of code were executed while running your unit tests.

Why Codecov?

Codecov produces coverage reports with features to enhance CI workflow. Using code coverage tools incentivizes developers to write tests and increase coverage.

It allows us to host the coverage reports we generate locally, so we can check the history and enhance our CI workflow and teamwork.

> *"Codecov focuses on integration and promoting healthy pull requests. Codecov delivers or 'injects' coverage metrics directly into the modern workflow to promote more code coverage, especially in pull requests where new features and bug fixes commonly occur."*
>
> —https://docs.codecov.io/docs/about-code-coverage

To set this up, we can create a file called codecov.yml. If you don't set up codecov.yml, the default configuration is set up automatically for you. You can find the Codecov documentation at https://docs.codecov.io/docs/codecov-yaml.

Log in to Codecov with your GitHub account, and you will see your repo since we uploaded it to Codecov during the GitHub action hook (Figure 10-9).

Figure 10-9. Codecov linked repository

CI with Travis

Travis is a hosted CI service used to build and test our code.

Why Travis?

Coverall can be set to connect to Travis by having Travis call the Coveralls run script, `.travis.yml`.

```
language: node_js
sudo: false
node_js:
  - "stable"
branches:
  only:
    - master
cache:
  directories:
    - node_modules
before_install:
  - npm update
  - sudo apt-get update
```

```
  - npm install --global http-server
install:
  - npm install
  - npm build
script:
  - npm run coveralls
```

To enable Travis, log in to your GitHub account, find the repo, and turn it on (Figure 10-10).

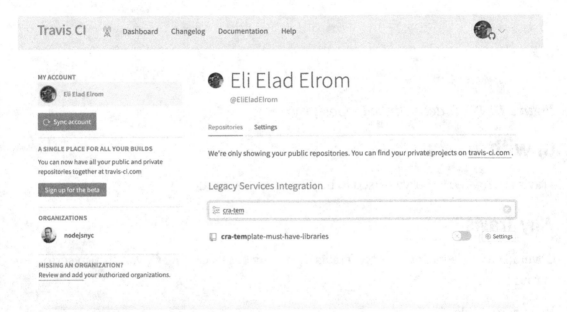

Figure 10-10. *Travis CI integrating a repository*

Make sure the build pushed branches are enabled. You can click the build badge, and Travis will generate a cool badge for you (Figure 10-11).

Travis CI
Dashboard
Changelog
Documentation
Help
Search all repositories
My Repositories
EliEladElrom / cra-template-must-have-libraries
build passing
Current
Branches
Build History
Pull Requests
Settings
More options
EliEladElrom/cra-template- # 1
Duration: 6 min 41 sec
Finished: 6 minutes ago
General
Build pushed branches
Limit concurrent jobs

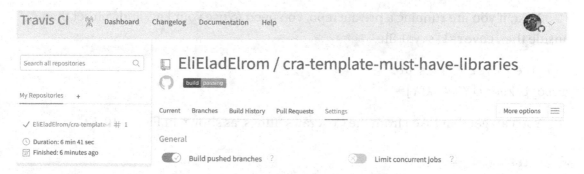

Figure 10-11. *Travis CI integration repository detail page*

Tracking Code Coverage with Coveralls

Coveralls track code coverage over time for GitHub repos and ensure that all new code is fully covered.

Why Coveralls?

We are using Codecov, so why do we also need Coveralls? Isn't that redundant?

Codecov hosts our reports, but Coveralls does more. Coveralls sifts through the coverage data looking for issues we may not find before they become a problem.

Create an account with Coveralls, and turn on the repo, as shown in Figure 10-12.

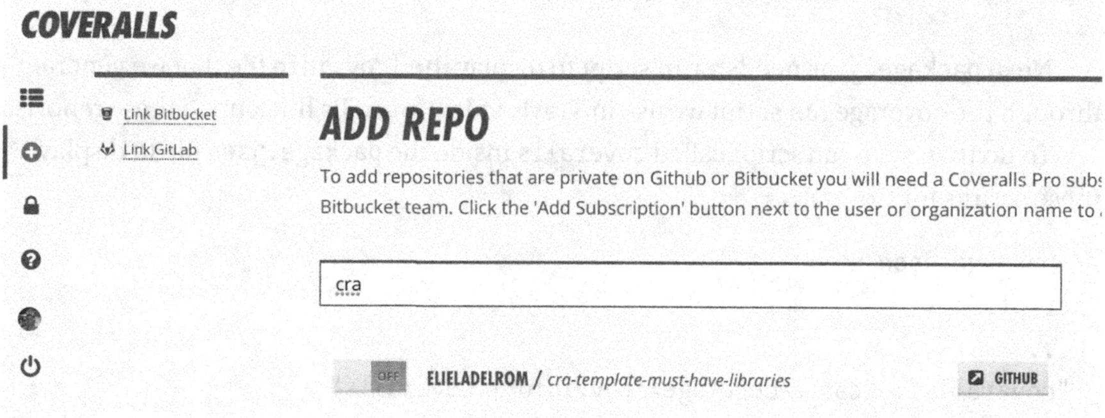

COVERALLS
Link Bitbucket
Link GitLab
ADD REPO
To add repositories that are private on Github or Bitbucket you will need a Coveralls Pro subs
Bitbucket team. Click the 'Add Subscription' button next to the user or organization name to
cra
OFF
ELIELADELROM / cra-template-must-have-libraries
GITHUB

Figure 10-12. *Coveralls integrating a repository page*

Next, if you are running a private repo, you need to use your key, and you set that inside the .coveralls.yml file.

```
service_name: travis-pro
repo_token: [YOUR-KEY]
```

You can get that token from the Coverall settings, as shown in Figure 10-13.

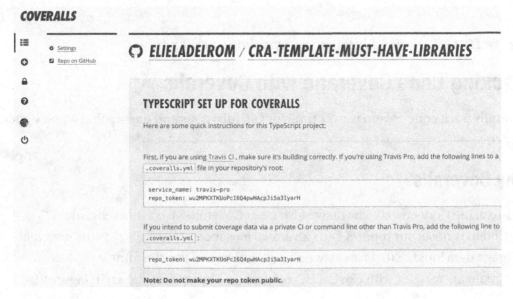

Figure 10-13.   *Coveralls repository key*

Next, package.json needs a run script to display the lcov.info file that we generate through the coverage run script we use in Travis to let Coveralls hook up to these reports.

To do that, set a run script called coveralls inside the package.json file to display these scripts for Coveralls.

```
// pacakge.json
"scripts": {
  ...
  "coveralls": "cat ./coverage/lcov.info | coveralls"
}
```

Checking the Quality of Your Code with DeepScan

DeepScan is a static analysis tool that lets us inspect our code comprehensively.

Why DeepScan?

DeepScan can check the quality of our code beyond just the rules we set in Lint.

Log in with your GitHub account to DeepScan and enable the repo, as shown in Figure 10-14.

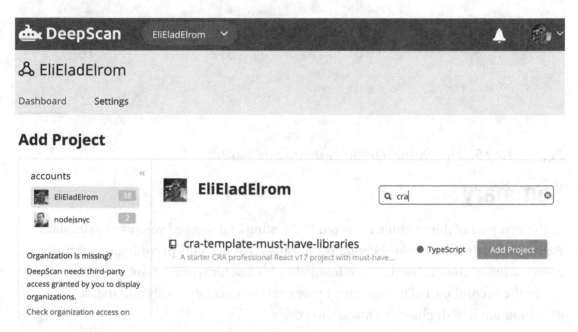

Figure 10-14. *DeepScan integrating a repository*

In DeepScan, you can see the repo and the grade given with any potential issues as well as generate a badge, as shown in Figure 10-15.

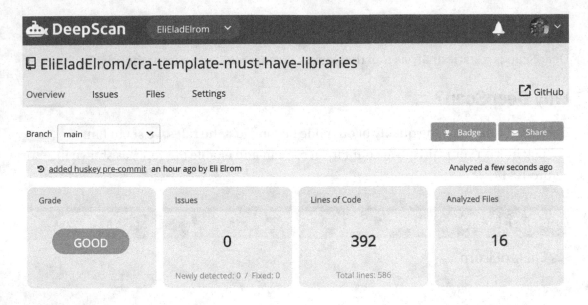

Figure 10-15. *DeepScan repository detail and badge*

Summary

In the first part of this chapter, I covered E2E testing and showed you how to simulate E2E testing using the Jest and Puppeteer libraries. We saw how to configure our project, create stand-alone E2E testing, and integrate with Jest for specific tests.

In the second part of this chapter, I covered how to create a fully automated development and deployment integration cycle.

To help you understand the process from the development side to CI, I broke down the process in this chapter into steps. We used Husky to create a precommit hook to ensure everything was running with no errors. On the CI deployment side, we used the Github actions and YAML files to check our code as well as upload our code to Codecov. io, Travis, Coveralls, and DeepScan to analyze and store our data and reports. Lastly, I showed you how to generate some cool badges for your project.

In the next chapter, you will learn how to debug and profile your React app.

CHAPTER 11

Debug and Profile Your React App

When you are working with a React app, there are some specific tools you can use to debug and profile your React app when you run into problems. Having the right tools for the job and knowing how to use them can remove pain points and expedite the process.

React is based on JavaScript (JS), and all the same tools that work for any JS-based app work for React. Unlike other React-based frameworks such as Next.js or Razzle, CRA is based on a single-page application (SPA) out of the box. To get better insights into what's happening in our app, there are specific tools that can help us debug our app. In this chapter, you will learn about the best tools to help you get the job done.

This chapter is broken down into two sections: debugging your app and profiling your app. In each section, I will give you specific tools that can help you not just debug and profile your app but also help ensure performance is not degraded once your code grows.

You can use any project from the previous chapters to learn how to debug and profile an app.

Debugging Your React App

Debugging is a common practice for detecting and removing errors (also called *bugs*) in your code that can cause undesired behavior. This section covers eight methods for debugging your app. You can use any one or a combination of a few together. The choice boils down to the bug you are trying to crush and the access you have to the code as well as where the code resides. The debugging options I will be covering are as follows:

- Breakpoints
- Console

© Elad Elrom 2021
E. Elrom, *React and Libraries*, https://doi.org/10.1007/978-1-4842-6696-0_11

- Debugger
- Debug Jests tests

Let's get started!

Breakpoints

Setting breakpoints in the code and stopping and examining data is usually used for more than just crushing bugs; it's at the core of any professional development effort.

All major modern IDEs have the option to place breakpoints and inspect data. I will show you how to use breakpoints in VS Code, which we set up in the first chapter, as well as another IDE called WebStorm, which is a popular React IDE; however, you can choose any IDE since most IDEs can be set up to do this task.

Debugging a React App with Visual Studio Code

In Chapter 1, we set up VS Code. VS Code has a feature to debug JavaScript code. In this section, we will install and debug our code.

Step 1: Install additional debuggers tool using the top-level menu in VS Code, see Figure 11-1:

```
https://marketplace.visualstudio.com/items?itemName=msjsdiag.debugger-for-
chrome
```

Figure 11-1. *Debugger extension for Chrome*

Step 2: Configure a launch.json file in the root of the project with port 3000.

```
// .vscode/launch.json
{
    "version": "0.2.0",
    "configurations": [
        {
            "type": "chrome",
            "request": "launch",
            "name": "Launch Chrome against localhost",
            "url": "http://localhost:3000",
            "webRoot": "${workspaceFolder}"
        }
    ]
}
```

Make sure the app is running ($ yarn start). Next, place a breakpoint, for example, in App.tsx.

Step 3: Now select Run from the left menu. Then click Launch Chrome from the top menu. See Figure 11-2.

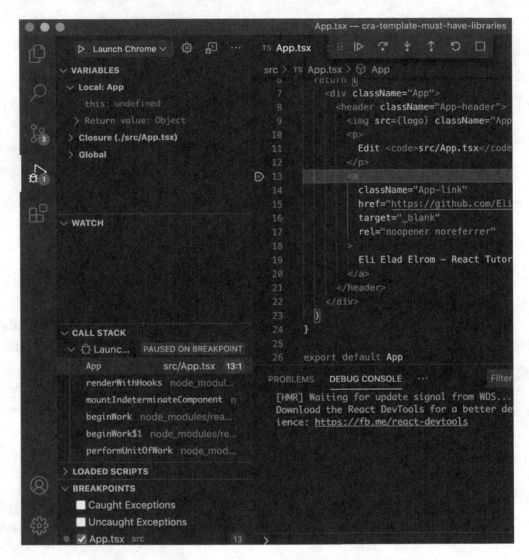

Figure 11-2. *Launching Chrome in debug mode for VS Code*

You can find more about debugging Visual Studio Code here: `https://code.visualstudio.com/docs/editor/debugging`.

Debugging a React App on WebStorm

In Chapter 1, we installed VS Code. I mentioned that there are other IDEs that are popular such as WebStorm. The reason I am showing the WebStorm IDE here as an option is that although it costs money, it includes advanced features that help you debug and profile your apps and is a popular option for writing JavaScript code.

If you're running WebStorm, you can configure your project just like any other project on WebStorm with a configuration wizard.

Click Add Configuration in the top bar, as shown in Figure 11-3.

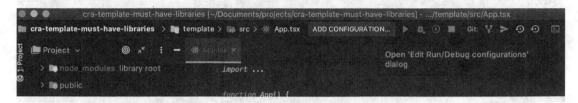

Figure 11-3. *Clicking Add Configuration in WebStorm*

Next, click the + icon to add the new configuration and then select JavaScript Debug, as shown in Figure 11-4.

Figure 11-4. *Add New Configuration window for JavaScript debugging*

Set up the configuration with the name, the URL (`http://localhost:3000/`), and the browser you will be using, as shown in Figure 11-5.

Figure 11-5. *Setting up the configuration to debug our app*

Now, we can set up a breakpoint on the line we want to debug and click the Debug icon to start debugging the app, as shown in Figure 11-6.

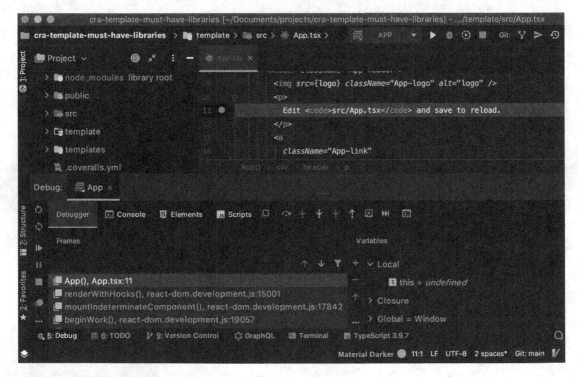

Figure 11-6. *Debugging a React app with WebStorm*

Using the Console

In JavaScript, `console.log()` is the de facto approach for logging messages. You can leave messages and display values. The console is the good, older way to debug web-based applications, and it still applicable today.

Browsers include a console to interact with web platform APIs, and you can use it to leave messages in your code. For example, leave this `console.log` inside `AppRouter.tsx`:

```
// src/AppRouter.tsx
const AppRouter: FunctionComponent = () => {
  console.log('console testing')
  return (...)
}
```

For example, to see this message in Chrome, right-click the page, select Inspect, and then click the Console tab, as shown in Figure 11-7.

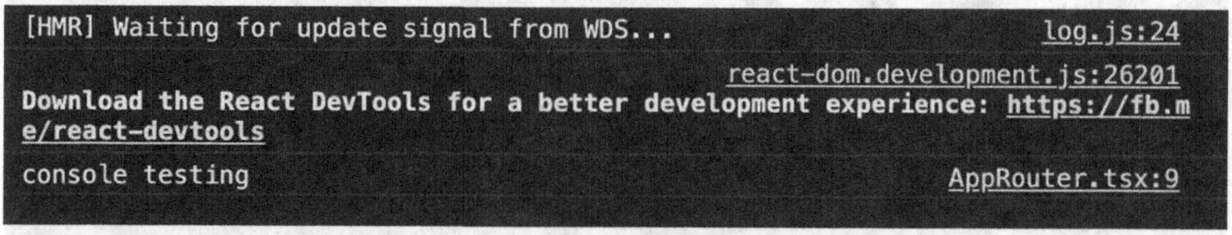

```
[HMR] Waiting for update signal from WDS...                        log.js:24
                                          react-dom.development.js:26201
Download the React DevTools for a better development experience: https://fb.m
e/react-devtools
console testing                                              AppRouter.tsx:9
```

Figure 11-7. console.log messages in the Console tab

Tip   It is advised that you suppress these `console.log()` messages before releasing the code as it's unprofessional to leave them here. It is also considered a side effect. If you recall, we set up ESLint to bark when you leave messages, and we configured Git with a commit hook using Husky to ensure a commit fails if a developer tries to submit code with these messages. Other approaches are to create a debug variable, add a plugin on Grunt or Gulp to remove these messages, or use the Logger API on Webpack.

Using a Debugger Statement

If we want to pause the browser on a certain piece of our code, a good approach is to use a debugger statement. Adding debugger to your component will pause the browser that is rendering the page. See Figure 11-8.

```
// src/index.tsx
debugger
```

Figure 11-8. *Stopping the rendering of the Chrome browser using the debugger statement*

Debugging Jest Tests

What about unit testing and E2E testing? In the previous chapters, we set up unit tests and E2E tests with Jest and the help of other libraries. When the tests fail and you need to debug your tests, there are two main options.

- Debugging using the browser

- Setting up your IDE

Debugging Jest Tests with Chrome DevTools

CRA has a script to help debug tests for unit testing and E2E testing using Jest. We can use a similar way to debug the tests as we did in our development code. To debug the tests, place a debugger statement inside the test.

```
// src/App.test.tsx
import React from 'react'
import { shallow } from 'enzyme'
import App from './App'

describe('<App />', () => {
  let component

  beforeEach(() => {
    component = shallow(<App />)
  })
  debugger
  test('It should mount', () => {
    expect(component.length).toBe(1)
  })
})
```

Next, add a test debug script to the run script in package.json.

```
// package.json
"test:debug": "react-scripts --inspect-brk test --runInBand --no-cache"
```

Open Chrome DevTools by right-clicking the web page and selecting Inspect. In the Chrome DevTools inspector, you'll see a green icon that represent opening a dedicated DevTools for Node.js, as shown in Figure 11-9.

Figure 11-9. *Chrome DevTools inspector*

Now when we run the `yarn` command:

```
$ yarn test:debug
```

DevTools will stop at our debugger point. See Figure 11-10.

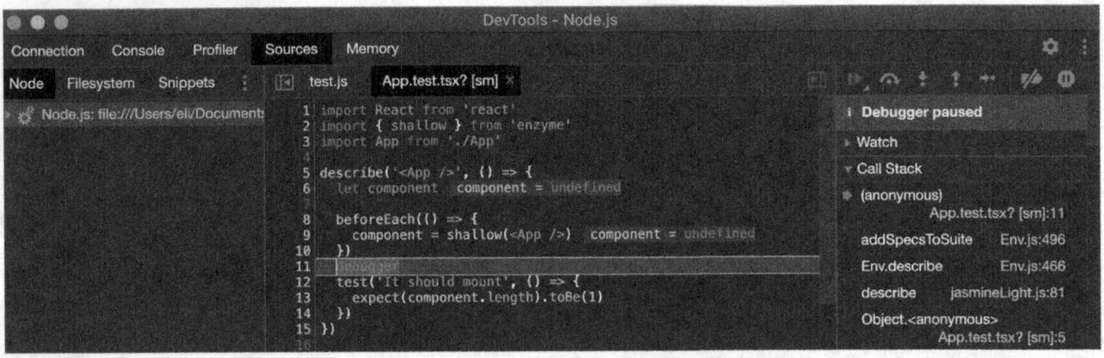

Figure 11-10. *Chrome-dedicated DevTools for Node.js*

Debugging Jest Tests with the VS Code IDE

The second option for debugging Jest tests is to use the debugging tools available in Visual Studio Code.

Step 1: Refactor the `launch.json` configuration file to include the following settings:

```
// .vscode/launch.json
{
    "version": "0.2.0",
    "configurations": [
      {
        "name": "Debug CRA Tests",
        "type": "node",
        "request": "launch",
        "runtimeExecutable": "${workspaceRoot}/node_modules/.bin/react-
        scripts",
        "args": ["test", "--runInBand", "--no-cache", "--watchAll=false"],
        "cwd": "${workspaceRoot}",
        "protocol": "inspector",
        "console": "integratedTerminal",
```

```
    "internalConsoleOptions": "neverOpen",
    "env": { "CI": "true" },
    "disableOptimisticBPs": true
  }
 ]
}
```

Step 2: Place debugger statements anywhere you like.

Step 3: Click the Debug Console button (it looks like the Run icon with a picture of a bug), as shown in Figure 11-11.

Figure 11-11. *Debugging Jest tests with VS Code*

Debugging Jest Tests with WebStorm

In WebStorm, the process is similar.

Step 1: Add a configuration for Jest, similarly to what we did previously. See Figure 11-12.

Figure 11-12. Adding a new configuration for Jest in WebStorm

Step 2: Next in the Run/Debug Configurations dialog, you can set up the configuration file and set the Jest package settings, as shown in Figure 11-13.

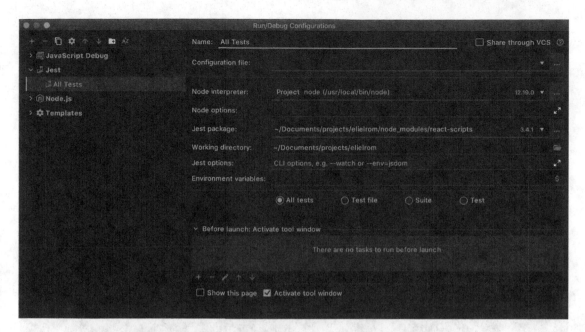

Figure 11-13. *WebStorm Run/Debug Configurations dialog*

Step 3: Next, place debugger statements anywhere you like.

Step 4: Now run the tests in Debug mode (it's the red bug icon, next to the green place icon), as shown in Figure 11-14.

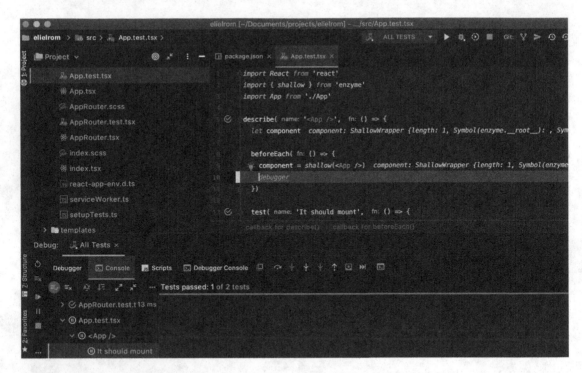

Figure 11-14. *Running in Debug mode on Jests tests*

You can find more here: `https://www.jetbrains.com/help/webstorm/running-unit-tests-on-jest.html#ws_jest_navigation`.

Additionally, visit the CRA page for debugging tests to keep up with any updates: `https://create-react-app.dev/docs/debugging-tests/`.

Using Chrome DevTools

As you recall, in Chapter 1 we covered how React is utilizing the concept of the virtual DOM (VDOM) and keeps a UI version in memory to sync with the "real" DOM.

This is done using the Fiber reconciliation engine in React 16. There are times when you might need some insight into the actual DOM, and Chrome DevTools can help.

To help view, access, and understand the DOM better, I recommend these two resources:

- `https://developer.mozilla.org/en-US/docs/Web/API/Document_Object_Model/Introduction`

- `https://developers.google.com/web/tools/chrome-devtools/dom`

Viewing the DOM Elements

For example, in CRA I can set up index.tsx to render AppRouter into the root element
we have set up in our index.html page (`<div id="root"></div>`).

```
// src/index.tsx
import React from 'react'
import ReactDOM from 'react-dom'
import './index.scss'
import AppRouter from './AppRouter'
import * as serviceWorker from './serviceWorker'

ReactDOM.render(<AppRouter />, document.getElementById('root'))

serviceWorker.unregister()
```

Figure 11-15 shows the DOM structure.

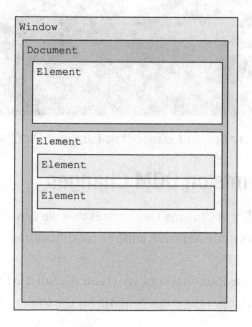

Figure 11-15. DOM structure

We can then open Chrome DevTools and paste into the console.

```
window.document.getElementById('root')
```

That will give us the root element, and we can inspect the DOM subtree elements, as shown in Figure 11-16.

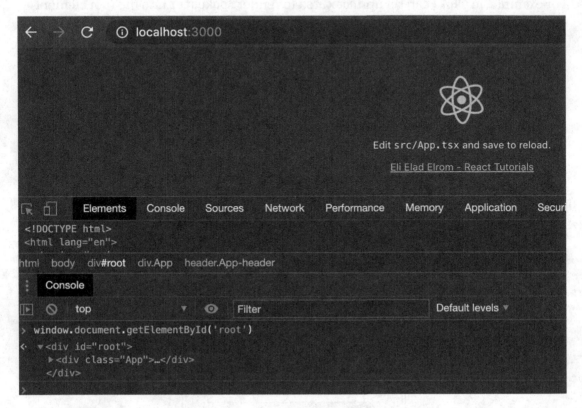

Figure 11-16.   *Inspecting the root element in Chrome DevTools*

Setting Breakpoints on DOM Changes

Another great functionality in Chrome DevTools is that we can set up breakpoints on certain criteria such as node removal, subtree modifications, and attribute modifications.

For example, in the previous chapters, we created a full site that included a theme preference button that changes the color scheme for the footer and header.

Our theme button changed the footer's color from light to dark. I can right-click the element and select "Break on" and then "attribute modifications," as shown in Figure 11-17.

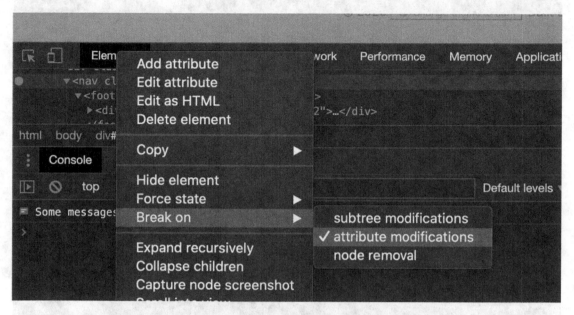

Figure 11-17. *Setting up a break element on attribute modification*

Next, when I click to change the theme to dark, the code will pause in debug mode, and I can see what caused the change. The browser's breakpoint points to react-dom. development.js. You can see a live demonstration in the wild on my site: EliElrom.com. See Figure 11-18.

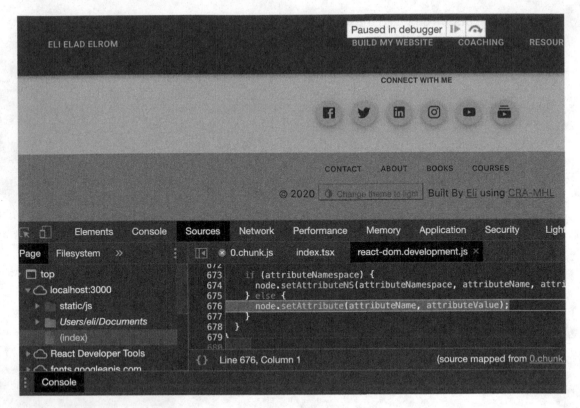

Figure 11-18. *Attribute change caused a pause in the debugger*

Using Chrome DevTools Extensions

As you have seen in the previous examples when we inspected attribute changes, the results we see are not very meaningful in terms of understanding what's happening under the hood in React.

However, there are Chrome DevTools extensions that can help.

What Are Chrome DevTools Extensions?

"A DevTools extension adds functionality to the Chrome DevTools. It can add new UI panels and sidebars, interact with the inspected page, get information about network requests, and more."

—https://developer.chrome.com/extensions/devtools

There are two helpful React development DevTools extensions and two state management tools that you should be aware of. These are the React development DevTools extensions:

- *React Developer Tools*: `https://chrome.google.com/webstore/detail/react-developer-tools/fmkadmapgofadopljbjfkapdkoienihi`

- *Realize for React*: `https://chrome.google.com/webstore/detail/realize-for-react/llondniabnmnappjekpflmgcikaiilmh`

These are the state management tools:

- *Redux*: `https://chrome.google.com/webstore/detail/redux-devtools/lmhkpmbekcpmknklioeibfkpmmfibljd`

- *Recoil*: `https://chrome.google.com/webstore/detail/recoil-dev-tools/dhjcdlmklldodggmleehadpjephfgflc`

Chrome DevTools Extension: React Developer Tools

React Developer Tools lets you inspect React component hierarchies in the Chrome DevTools. You will get two new tabs in your Chrome DevTools interface.

- ⚛ Components

- ⚛ Profiler

To test the tool, use the coding examples from previous chapters such as when we built our app. I am using my site and navigating to a `/books` page.

We can see a lot of information about the component such as the version of React (v17.0.0 at the time of writing), `props` information, router information, and component hierarchies, as shown in Figure 11-19.

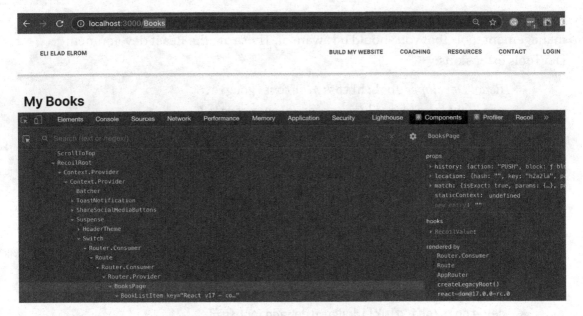

Figure 11-19. *React developer tools, components window*

The second tab is for the Profiler, where we can record a production-profiling build. I will cover more about profiling later in this chapter.

Chrome DevTools Extension: Realize for React

As you have learned in this book, components are at the core of React. Once you have React Dev Tools installed, Realize is a great tool to help you visualize the React components tree.

The tool helps track the state and gives you a holistic overview of the component hierarchy. See Figure 11-20.

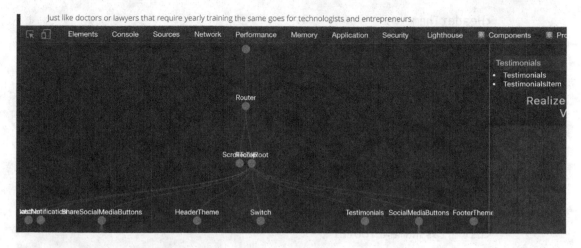

Figure 11-20. Realize for React

The following holistic overview breaks down AppRouter.tsx from our CRA template project that we created in the previous chapters:

```
// src/AppRouter.tsx
const AppRouter: FunctionComponent = () => {
  useEffect(() => {
    // console.log('AppRouter.tsx :: CheckAuthentication')
  }, [])
  return (
    <Router>
      <ScrollToTop />
      <RecoilRoot>
        <ToastNotification />
        <ShareSocialMediaButtons />
        <Suspense
          fallback={
            <div className="home_loading_container">
              <img width="250px" className="loading-home" alt="loading"
              src={myImage} />
            </div>
          }
        >
```

```
        <HeaderTheme />
        <Switch>
          <Route exact path="/" component={App} />
          <Route exact path="/Home" component={Home} />
          ...
          <Route path="/404" component={NotFoundPage} />
          <Redirect to="/404" />
        </Switch>
        <Testimonials />
        <SocialMediaButtons />
        <div className="footer">
          <FooterTheme />
        </div>
      </Suspense>
    </RecoilRoot>
  </Router>
  )
}
export default AppRouter
```

Chrome DevTools Extension: Recoil

When working with state management using Redux or Recoil, as covered earlier in this book, it would be neat to be able to track the internal workings of the state.

There is plenty of information about the Redux Chrome DevTools extension on the Web, but I want to point out how to get insight into Recoil, which we set up earlier in the book. It gives information about atoms, selectors, and subscribers. See Figure 11-21.

Figure 11-21. *Recoil Chrome DevTools extension chart for the book page*

In my case, as shown in Figure 11-21, the atom is based on bookObject, and I can inspect the state value and changes in the browser.

```
export interface bookObject {
  title: string
  author: string
  pubDate: string
  link: string
  thumbnail: string
}
```

Using a Web Proxy

We can use a web proxy server to debug our app. A web proxy is set up as another layer on our computer, which serves as a hub through which all Internet requests will be processed.

Using Charles

Chrome DevTools is great, but sometimes we need more. Charles gives good insight into other resources than just for the Web. For example, you can do throttling (simulating slower Internet), SSL proxying, data formatting, and Ajax debugging, as well as recording and saving different sessions and more. Download Charles from here:

`https://www.charlesproxy.com/latest-release/download.do`

This comes in handy when dealing with an SSL site because the data would normally be hidden. To be able to see the details on an SSL site, you need to set up a Charles root certificate. To set up the Charles root certificate, open Charles.

From the top menu of Charles, select Help, then SSL Proxying, and then "Install Charles root certificate."

The certificate needs to be trusted for each site or all sites. For a Mac, you can double-click the certificate and use the Trust tab to set up the certificate to always be trusted.

Then we can see secure items on SSL sites, as shown in Figure 11-22.

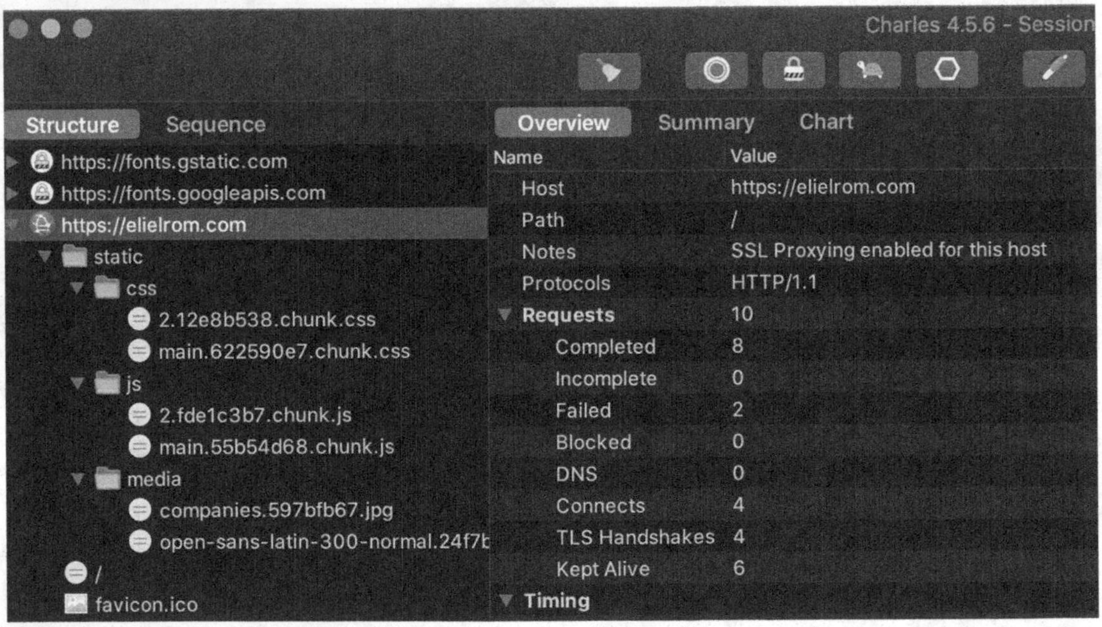

Figure 11-22. Charles configured with SSL proxying

For more information about setting up an SSL certificate, visit `https://www.charlesproxy.com/documentation/using-charles/ssl-certificates/`.

Note   I want to point out that one drawback of Charles is that it is not free. It has a trial version with limited usage. However, there are other similar web proxy tools like Fiddler (`https://www.telerik.com/fiddler`) that are free at the time of writing.

Using a Network Protocol Analyzer

Sometimes we need a deeper look into the network data of our app or the APIs we are connected to and have no direct control of. In those cases, you can use a network protocol analyzer.

Wireshark

When you need a deeper look into the network data—for example, if you need to do a deep analysis of the network protocol—Wireshark is the standard.

It allows you to do a deep inspection of hundreds of protocols and offers a live capture feature.

Download from here: `https://www.wireshark.org/download.html`.

You can filter the results and watch the network requests. Figure 11-23 shows an example.

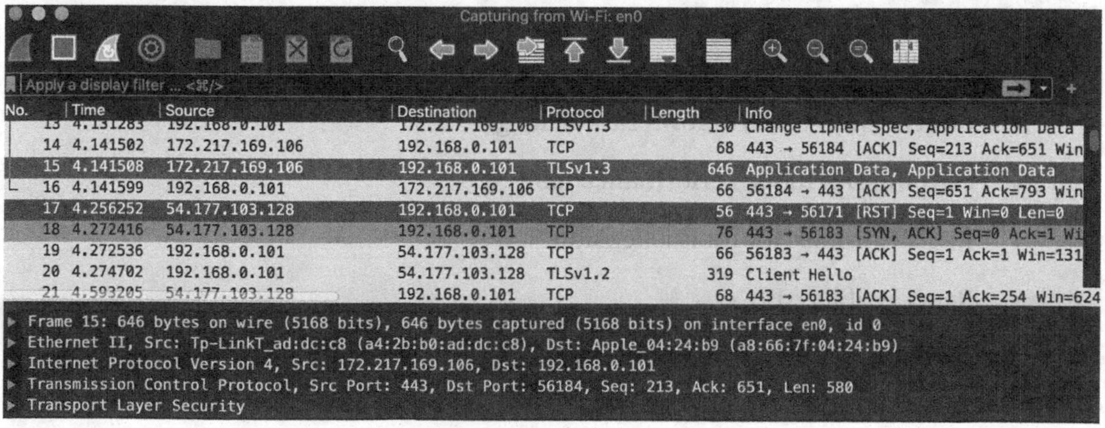

Figure 11-23. Wireshark capture results

Profiling Your React App

React is fast compared to traditional web applications when your code is built right mainly due to the usage of the virtual DOM concept. However, that doesn't mean you cannot write a memory leak or you shouldn't try to improve performance.

In fact, a good development habit is to save a performance profile of your app and reference it every time you add a new feature.

In this section, I will share with you four solid methods to profile your React app.

The memory in JS is managed automatically by the garbage collector. It's easy to cause a memory leak.

Note   The GC is the process of automatic memory management. It's based on collecting memory that is not needed anymore.

But even without memory leaks, a large memory footprint can slow down our app and cause CPU spikes and large memory usage.

Awareness is the key to ensuring your app is performing well. You should continuously measure how a new feature you added is performing and the impact it has on your existing app. In the previous chapter, we automated our development and deployment. Automating performance tests should also be taken into account when publishing your app.

How to Profile My React App?

There are plenty of tools that can help get the job done. Here are my top go-to options to use when handling performance issues:

- Activity Monitor/Windows Task Manager

- Chrome DevTools' Performance tab

- React Chrome DevTools extension

- React Profiler API

Before we start, I want to talk about the build used for profiling.

When profiling the local build, it's preferred to use the production version of the build than the development version as the development is not optimized and is not the same as the production build.

To get the production build to run locally, the CRA MHL template project we were working with already includes the serve library (https://github.com/vercel/serve).

You can install serve globally. To do that, make sure you set up to read-write access to the global node_modules and install it.

```
$ sudo chown -R $USER /usr/local/lib/node_modules
$ npm install -g serve
```

Next, create a profiling build by specifying the --profile flag.

Add these run scripts to your package.json file to build the production build and the profiling build, as well as start a local server for those builds.

```
// package.json
"build:serve": "yarn build && serve -s build && open
http://localhost:5000",
"build:profile": "yarn build --profile && serve -s build && open
http://localhost:5000"
```

Activity Monitor/Windows Task Manager

Personally, I like to start off with the built-in tools on our computer to get a 10,000-foot overview of our memory footprint and the processor usage.

Yes, they are "a poor man's" tools but are a good starting point. Safari, for instance, gives a breakdown of usage by website.

Take a look at the Activity Monitor usage before and after. Figure 11-24 shows the memory usage before and after browser loading website, and Figure 11-25 shows an increase of the CPU usage by 0.6 percent.

Process Name	% CPU	CPU Time	Threads	Idle Wake Ups	% GPU	GPU Time	PID
Safari Web Content	0.1	0.38	4	1	0.0	0.02	84494
SafariBookmarksSyncAgent	0.0	1:52.39	6	1	0.0	0.00	515

Figure 11-24. *Activity Monitor once Safari is opened*

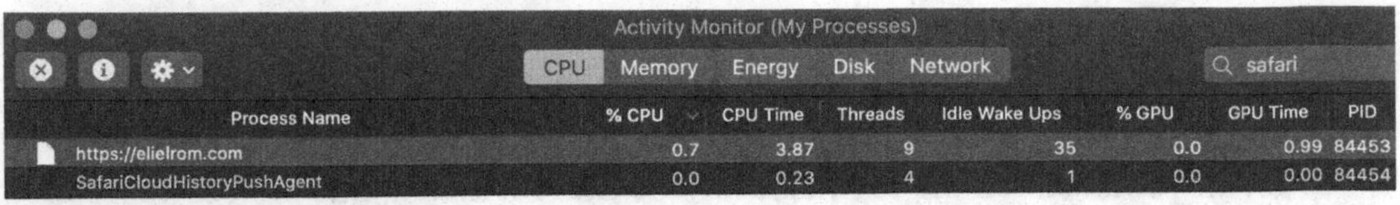

Figure 11-25. *Activity Monitor after navigating with Safari to my site*

Browser's Profiling Tools

The major browsers include tools for developers that can help debug and profile your app. Google is the leading search engine and provides great tools for developers. So here, I will cover Google DevTools, but be aware that other popular browsers such as Safari, Firefox, and Microsoft Edge also include developer tools.

Chrome DevTools' Performance Tab

Chrome DevTools has a Performance tab. To open the Performance tab, right-click the browser and click Inspect.

Next, select the Screenshots and Memory check boxes to see both.

Figures 11-26 and 11-27 show an example of comparing the CRA template against my site.

Figure 11-26. *CRA template in Chrome DevTools' Performance tab*

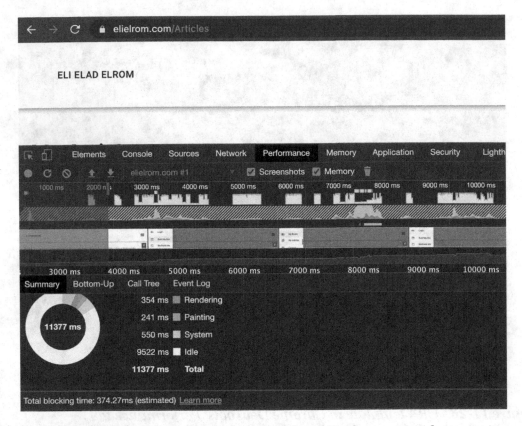

Figure 11-27. EliElrom.com in Chrome DevTools' Performance tab

Chrome DevTools Extension: Profiler in React Developer Tools

Earlier we installed the React Developer Tools extension. The extension has two tabs: Components and Profiler. The Profiler tab gives you insight into what is called a *flamegraph*.

A flamegraph is an ordered chart that shows the total time it took each component to render. The colors indicate the render time (the greener the better) and how long it took to render or rerender these changes from the virtual DOM to the "real" DOM. It includes tabs for different rankings as well as interactions. See Figure 11-28.

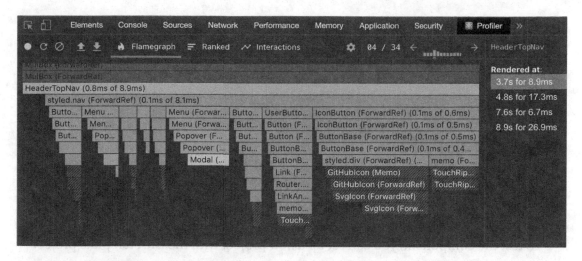

Figure 11-28. *Flamegraph results for my development build*

Remember, we created a run script for profiling a production build. You can compare the different results from the optimized build versus the development build. Figure 11-29 shows the ranked profiling results for a production build ($ `yarn build:profile`).

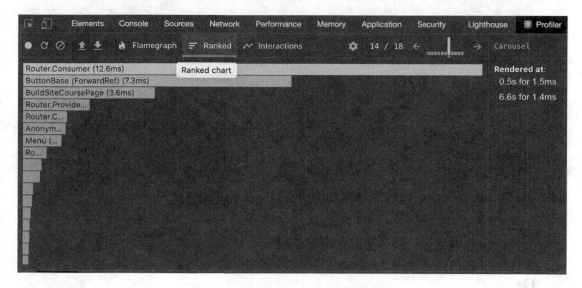

Figure 11-29. *Ranked results for my production build*

You can also opt in to your production build to get profiling working. Keep in mind that setting profiling on a production build does come with a small overhead, so use it only when needed. You can find the instructions here:

https://gist.github.com/bvaughn/25e6233aeb1b4f0cdb8d8366e54a3977

React Profiler API

The React Profiler API (https://reactjs.org/docs/profiler.html) includes a <Profiler/> component that can help us customize the metrics from the source code and measure the component's lifecycle time.

To test the component, you can set up a new project with the CRA template project or use any of the previous projects we created.

```
$ yarn create react-app your-project-name --template must-have-libraries
```

Next, refactor the router sec/AppRouter.tsx and wrap it with the Profiler component, as shown in Figure 11-30.

```
// src/AppRouter.tsx
import { Profiler } from 'react'

const AppRouter: FunctionComponent = () => {
  return (
    <Profiler onRender={(id, phase, actualTime, baseTime, startTime,
    commitTime) => {
      console.log(`${id}'s ${phase} phase:`);
      console.log(`Actual time: ${actualTime}`);
      console.log(`Base time: ${baseTime}`);
      console.log(`Start time: ${startTime}`);
      console.log(`Commit time: ${commitTime}`);
    }}>
    <Router>
      <RecoilRoot>
        <Suspense fallback={<span>Loading...</span>}>
          <Switch>
```

```
        <Route exact path="/" component={App} />
      </Switch>
    </Suspense>
  </RecoilRoot>
</Router>
</Profiler>
)
}
```

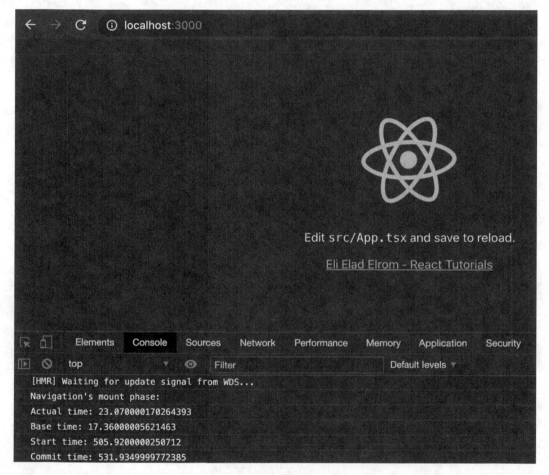

Figure 11-30. *Profiler API results on CRA-MHL template, development build*

As you can see in the Console tab of DevTools, I am getting results. In this example, I am logging everything, but we can create a script that filters the results and handles them in different ways.

Summary

In this chapter, I covered ways to debug and profile your React applications. In the first section of the chapter, I covered eight ways to debug your React app.

- I showed you how to create breakpoints and debug React on the Visual Studio Code IDE as well as WebStorm.

- I showed you how to use the Console tab and interact with web platform APIs.

- You learned about the debugger statement as well as using the debugger statement for Jest tests using Chrome DevTools as well as using the VS Code and WebStorm IDEs.

- We looked at Chrome DevTools by learning how to view DOM elements as well as place breakpoints based on DOM changes.

- We installed these Chrome DevTools extensions: React Developer Tools, Realize, Redux, and Recoil.

- Lastly, we checked the Charles web proxy and the Wireshark network protocol analyzer.

In the second part of this chapter, I covered four methods to profile your React app.

- I showed you how to use the Activity Monitor (Mac)/Task Manager (Windows) to check the memory and CPU footprint.

- I covered the Chrome DevTools' Performance tab as well as the React Chrome DevTools extension's Profiling tab.

- Lastly, you learned how to use the React Profiler API to get the render time of components.

In the next and last chapter, I will show you techniques that you can use to optimize your React app to increase performance and improve the quality of your app.

CHAPTER 12

Optimize Your React App

Optimizing your code is an advanced topic and is needed to ensure we deliver a quality product that lowers resources footprint and loads our app faster. In this chapter, I will highlight some optimizing techniques you should be aware of before you write your first line of code. Topics covered include precaching, lazy loading, code splitting, tree shaking, prefetching, and sprite splitting, to name just a few.

Why Do We Need to Optimize?

As you've seen through this book, CRA is a popular way to create a React app. It is set up to manage your configuration of your app using `react-scripts`. It utilizes Webpack to optimize the production build including minifying, uglifying, and gzipping the code. You don't need to do much because all these techniques come out of the box with CRA.

In addition, in previous chapters, we used automated development and deployment techniques to increase the quality of the code. Specifically, we set up ESLint, Huskey, unit testing, E2E testing, and more to identify poor coding and weak spots.

However, even with all of that, CRA is still a vanilla-flavor, one-size-fits-all tool, and sometimes you will want to fine-tune and configure your app a bit more to your specific needs and to be more aware of what's happening under the hood. Furthermore, if you are not careful, your app can bloat and turn into a "jank."

Note *Jank* is not a typo; it's a low-quality process that leads to poor response times for your app or that blocks user interactions.

One of the main performance challenges with the single-page applications (SPAs) that CRA is based on is that the user needs to wait for the JS bundles that make up the app to complete downloading before being able to see the content.

© Elad Elrom 2021
E. Elrom, *React and Libraries*, https://doi.org/10.1007/978-1-4842-6696-0_12

If the JS bundles get bloated, it can take a lot of time for users on slow Internet connections, making your app sluggish or just not available to some users. This will result in losing visitors and business. Our goal is to build apps that are progressive web apps (PWAs).

> *"Progressive Web Apps (PWA) are built and enhanced with modern APIs to deliver enhanced capabilities, reliability, and installability while reaching anyone, anywhere, on any device with a single codebase."*
>
> —https://web.dev/what-are-pwas/

What Will You Learn?

Following the steps in this chapter, you will learn how to reduce the memory footprint of your app, avoid memory leaks, reduce bundle file sizes, load resources only once in usage, decrease wait time to view content, increase performance, and ensure it works anytime anywhere, even offline.

You will also become more aware of what's happening under the hood in your app so you can configure your app better instead of using the default settings. This subject is a big one, but I aim to give you the most important ways to optimize.

How Can I Optimize My App?

I broke down the top ways to optimize your CRA React TS app into parts.

- Use PureComponent as a class component as much as possible
- Lazy loading
- Pre-render static pages
- Precache—work offline
- Code Splitting
- Tree shaking
- Reduce Media Size

- Prefetching

- Clean unused side effects event handlers

But before we start, let's create a project that we can use to play around with and test. I will be using my CRA starter template project; I'll change its name to optimize-ts.

```
$ yarn create react-app optimize-ts --template must-have-libraries
```

Let's create a page component that we can use to experiment. I am using the generate templates that are already included with the CRA MHL template project. These templates can help us create these pages quickly with one command.

```
$ cd optimize-ts
$ npx generate-react-cli component MyPage --type=page
```

The template generated three files (the SCSS style, a TS component, and the Jest test file) automatically for us, using the template sets inside the templates/page folder. We get a confirmation in Terminal.

```
Stylesheet "MyPage.scss" was created successfully at src/pages/MyPage/
MyPage.scss
```

Test "MyPage.test.tsx" was created successfully at src/pages/MyPage/MyPage.test.tsx
Component "MyPage.tsx" was created successfully at src/pages/MyPage/MyPage.tsx
Next, open AppRouter.tsx. Let's add the page we created to our router.

```tsx
// src/AppRouter.tsx

import MyPage from './pages/MyPage/MyPage'
const AppRouter: FunctionComponent = () => {
  return (
    <Router>
      <RecoilRoot>
        <Suspense fallback={<span>Loading...</span>}>
          <Switch>
            <Route exact path="/" component={App} />
            <Route exact path="/MyPage" component={MyPage} />
          </Switch>
        </Suspense>
```

```
        </RecoilRoot>
      </Router>
  )
}
```

Test that everything is working correctly (you should see just the spinner with the link).

```
$ yarn start
```

At this point, you can navigate to the page http://localhost:3000/MyPage and ensure it is all working correctly.

Next, let's add a link to the page component we created so we can navigate to the page from the main page.

Open src/App.tsx and add the NavLink component so we can link it to our page menu. I am setting it as an array in case we want to add more pages.

```
<List>
  {[
    { name: 'MyPage', url: '/MyPage' }
  ].map((itemObject, index) => (
    <NavLink
      to={itemObject.url}
      key={itemObject.url}
    >
      <ListItem>{itemObject.name}</ListItem>
    </NavLink>
  ))}
</List>
```

You can see the final result in Figure 12-1.

Figure 12-1. *Our CRA template starter project with a page and navigation*

You can download the final and complete project used for this chapter from here:

https://github.com/Apress/react-and-libraries/12/optimize-ts

Analyzer Bundle

Another tool that is good to know about is Analyzer Bundle. It can help you debug and profile your app.

If we want to see what's under the hood when it comes to our JS bundle, we can just eject (https://create-react-app.dev/docs/available-scripts/) from CRA and uglify our code to see the content of our JS bundles.

Another option to tweak the CRA Webpack configuration without ejecting is to use this library: react-app-rewired (https://github.com/timarney/react-app-rewired).

But you don't need to do all of that because ejecting would force you to maintain the configuration files. We can just use `source-map-explorer` to view a map of our bundles.

```
$ npm install -g source-map-explorer
```

Now you can open the libraries and intuitively view the libraries.

```
$ source-map-explorer optimize-ts/build/static/js/[my chunk].chunk.js
```

Alternatively, you can use `bundle-analyzer` (https://github.com/svengau/cra-bundle-analyzer). It's more colorful and includes all the bundles in one page instead of calling them one by one with `source-map-explorer`.

```
$ yarn add -D cra-bundle-analyzer
```

Now we can create the report.

```
$ npx cra-bundle-analyzer
```

This command will generate a `webpack-bundle-analyzer` report in `build/report.html` once you run `yarn build`.

Use PureComponent as a Class Component As Much As Possible

As you recall from previous chapters, React 17 offers two main options when it comes to creating React Component classes.

- `React.Component`
- `React.PureComponent`

Throughout the book, we used `PureComponent` over `React.Component`, but why? When you don't need to access the `shouldComponentUpdate` method, it's better to use `PureComponent` instead.

```
extends React.PureComponent
```

`React.PureComponent` gives a performance boost in some cases in exchange for losing the `shouldComponentUpdate` lifecycle. You can read more about it in the React docs (https://reactjs.org/docs/react-api.html#reactpurecomponent).

In our code, we don't need to access `shouldComponentUpdate`, so we can use `PureComponent`. Here is the code for the initial file that will display the name of the page:

```
import React from 'react'
import './MyPage.scss'
import { RouteComponentProps } from 'react-router-dom'
import Button from '@material-ui/core/Button

// or React.Component
export default class MyPage extends React.PureComponent<IMyPageProps,
IMyPageState> {
  constructor(props: IMyPageProps) {
    super(props)
    this.state = {
      name: this.props.history.location.pathname
        .substring(1, this.props.history.location.pathname.length)
        .replace('/', ''),
      results: 0
    }
  }

  render() {
    return (
      <div className="TemplateName">
        {this.state.name} Component
      </div>)
    )
  }
}

interface IMyPageProps extends RouteComponentProps<{ name: string }> {
  // TODO
}

interface IMyPageState {
  name: string
  results: number
}
```

Re-re-re-re-render

With that being said, there are times where `shouldComponentUpdate` is needed because we can use that method to let React know that the component is not affected by a state change from a parent component and there's no need to rerender. In this case, you need to set up your class as `React.Component`, and then you can access `shouldComponentUpdate`.

```
public shouldComponentUpdate(nextProps: IProps, nextState: IState) {
  return false // prevent rendering
}
```

These are cases where we need to control the component and want to stop the rerender. Using `React.Component` can give better performance as we can stop the rerendering process.

To find misbehaving citizens, you can use a Chrome DevTools extension called React Developer Tools and use its Highlight Updates check box to find components that misbehave. It does this by looking out for over-rendering components.

Lazy Loading

Lazy loading is one of the easiest ways to increase the performance of your app and see significant results quickly. I would say that this effort is the low-hanging fruit of optimization.

The best place to start is on the router. Let's create an optimized production build.

```
$ yarn build
```

If you navigate to the `build/static` folder that was created for us, you can see that we have three JS files and a license file. See Figure 12-2.

Figure 12-2. *CRA production builds before utilizing lazy loading*

Now update the code to include lazy loading. The Suspense component will be shown during the loading phase of the component, and importing the component using the lazy method will ensure the component is loading only once it's used.

The change updates how we import our component, from this:

```
import MyPage from './pages/MyPage/MyPage'
```

to the following:

```
const MyPage = lazy(() => import('./pages/MyPage/MyPage'))
```

The Suspense component includes a fallback while the component is loading. Take a look at the complete code:

```
import React, { FunctionComponent, lazy, Suspense } from 'react'
import { BrowserRouter as Router, Route, Switch } from 'react-router-dom'
import { RecoilRoot } from 'recoil'
import App from './App'

// Normal
// import MyPage from './pages/MyPage/MyPage'

// Lazy loading
const MyPage = lazy(() => import('./pages/MyPage/MyPage'))

const AppRouter: FunctionComponent = () => {
  return (
    <Router>
```

```
      <RecoilRoot>
        <Suspense fallback={<span>Loading...</span>}>
          <Switch>
            <Route exact path="/" component={App} />
            <Route exact path="/MyPage" component={MyPage} />
            <Redirect to="/" />
          </Switch>
        </Suspense>
      </RecoilRoot>
    </Router>
  )
}
```

Run yarn build again. You can see that the build script broke down our bundle chunks from three files to four files due to the lazy loading we put in place. See Figure 12-3.

Figure 12-3. *CRA production build optimized*

When you use yarn start, you don't see the fallback loading message, because it happens too quickly since our page component only includes the name of the page. However, you can see an example in the wild on my site (https://elielrom.com), where I placed lazy loading for the login page and an image spinner for the fallback. Navigate the pages, and you will see the spinner the first time you navigate to the login page. If not, you can reduce the Internet connection DevTools.

If you use Chrome DevTools or Charles (see Chapter 11 for more information about debugging), you can actually measure the results. It depends on the size of your app and what you are doing, but this simple method can gain you as much as a few seconds.

> **Note**   There is a bit of a caveat about lazy loading. There are times that it won't make sense to do lazy loading on all pages, because the pages are light. Splitting and loading multiple bundle files can take longer.

You need to experiment with lazy loading since how well it works is on a case-by-case basis. Also, it may be better to wrap these lazy loading methods on only some components. For instance, a login member area is not used by all users, while other pages can be loaded together. The best approach is to experiment and set up memory profiling and then throttle the network speed to find out what is the best user experience. It's not a one-size-fits-all sort of thing.

You can find more information in the React documentation (`https://reactjs.org/docs/code-splitting.html#route-based-code-splitting`).

Prerendering Static Pages

The CRA (SPA) paradigm is great for certain cases, because you don't get page refreshes and the experience feels like you are inside a mobile app.

The pages are meant to be rendered on the client side. CRA doesn't support server-side rendering (SSR) out of the gate. However, there are ways to configure the routing and get CRA to work as SSR, but that may involve ejecting and maintaining the configuration on your own, so it may not be worth the effort.

> Server Side Rendering (SSR) is the process of rendering a client-side JavaScript site into a static HTML and CSS on the server instead of rendering the site on the client (browser).

If you're building something bigger that needs SSR, it's better to just work with a different React library that is already configured out of the box with SSR such as the Next. js framework, Razzle, or Gatsby (including if you're prerendering a website into HTML at build time).

> **Tip**   If you want to do server rendering with React and Node.js, check out Next.js, Razzle, or Gatsby.

Create-React-App is agnostic on the back end and produces static HTML/JS/CSS bundles. With that being said, with CRA we can do prerendering, which is the closest you can get to SSR at this time. See the CRA documentation: `https://create-react-app.dev/docs/pre-rendering-into-static-html-files/`.

There are many options to generate HTML pages for each route or relative link. Here are a few:

- `react-snap`
- `react-snapshot`
- Webpack Static Site Generator plugin

I recommend `react-snap` (`https://github.com/stereobooster/react-snap`), which is the most popular with 4,000 stars on GitHub, and it works seamlessly with CRA. `react-snap` uses the same Puppeteer we used for our E2E testing in Chapter 10 to create prerendered HTML files of different routes in your application automatically.

The biggest benefit is that once you use `react-snap`, the app doesn't care if the JS bundle is successfully loaded or not because each page you set up will be on its own.

Keep in mind that for each page to load on its own, some bundles may have redundant code, so this does come with a price.

Step 1: To get started, run this:

```
$ yarn add --dev react-snap
```

Step 2: Next, add the `postbuild` run script.

```
// package.json
"scripts": {
  ...
  "postbuild": "react-snap"
},
```

Step 3: The static HTML rendered almost immediately. The HTML is styled by default and can cause an issue that's called showing a "flash of unstyled content" (FOUC). This can be especially noticeable if you are using a CSS-in-JS library to generate selectors since the JavaScript bundle will have to finish executing before any styles can be set.

`react-snap` uses another third-party library under the hood, `minimalcss` (`https://github.com/peterbe/minimalcss`) to extract any critical CSS for different routes.

You can enable this by specifying the following in your `package.json` file:

```
// package.json"scripts": {
  ...
  "postbuild": "react-snap"
},
"reactSnap": {
  "inlineCss": true
},
```

Step 4: `src/index.tsx` is where we will be hydrating, and we can also register for precaching there with `serviceWorker.register()`. You'll learn more about precaching in the next section.

```
// src/index.tsximport React from 'react'

import { hydrate, render } from 'react-dom'
import './index.scss'
import AppRouter from './AppRouter'
import * as serviceWorker from './serviceWorker'

const rootElement = document.getElementById('root')
if (rootElement && rootElement!.hasChildNodes()) {
  hydrate(<AppRouter />, rootElement
  serviceWorker.register()
} else {
  render(<AppRouter />, rootElement)
}
```

Step 5: Now run the Yarn `build` command, and afterward, the build will be called automatically via the NPM script that is configured in CRA. You should see successful results. Compare your results with mine.

```
$ react-snap
☑ crawled 1 out of 3 (/)
☑ crawled 2 out of 3 (/404.html)
☑ crawled 3 out of 3 (/MyPage)
✿ Done in 29.29s.
```

Open the build folder, and you will see the static pages created automatically, as shown in Figure 12-4.

Figure 12-4. *Static pages*

Note   Prerendering and serving static pages is not necessarily always the best approach. It can actually create an undesired experience for your users as each page will load, and the component load will be distributed across pages. For lightweight apps, it may be better to wait half a second so that all the content loads and there is no more wait time versus waiting a bit on each page load. You need to test this and see for yourself, but be aware of this feature.

Step 5: To spin off a local production build locally, run the CRA template run script. It's using the serve library, so you don't even need to install or configure package.json if you are using the CRA MHL template.

Run the serve run script to add a local server and view the production build.

```
$ yarn build:serve
```

I want to point out that another big reason to use prerender is the need for static pages beyond optimizing: search engine optimization (SEO). If you prerendering pages and want to generate a different title, description, metadata, etc., for each page due to SEO reasons, or you need to share individual pages via social media, check react-helmet, which can help you to set up a unique header for each React page component.

How to Get react-helmet to Generate a Title for Each Page?

I'll explain the steps to generate a title for each page in this section.

Step 1: Install `react-helmet` and the types for TS.

```
$ yarn add react-helmet @types/react-helmet
```

Step 2: Now, we can refactor our `MyPage.tsx` and add the `Helmet` component.

```
import Helmet from 'react-helmet'render() {
  return (
    <div className="MyPage">
      <Helmet>
        <title>My Page</title>
      </Helmet>
      {this.state.name} Component
    </div>)
}
```

Notice in our code that the state stores the name of the page, which is extracted from React Router, so we need to use `.replace('/', ')` for `this.state.name`, so if the user refreshes the static page, it will have `about/` at the end.

```
constructor(props: IMyPageProps) {
  super(props);
  this.state = {
    name: this.props.history.location.pathname.substring(
      1,
      this.props.history.location.pathname.length
    ).replace('/', '')
  }
}
```

Now if you view the source, it will have the title once you click the MyPage link.

Precache: Working Offline

Being able to go offline is a core functionality of PWA. We can do that with a serviceWorker.

CRA includes serviceWorker inside the index file.

```
serviceWorker.unregister()
```

What Does It Mean?

CRA includes a Workbox webpack Plugins for the production build (https://developers.google.com/web/tools/workbox/modules/workbox-webpack-plugin).

To enable this feature, just change the serviceWorker state to register.

```
serviceWorker.register()
```

We already added serviceWorker when we did the build for production in the previous section.

```
const rootElement = document.getElementById('root')
if (rootElement && rootElement!.hasChildNodes()) {
  hydrate(<AppRouter />, rootElement)
  serviceWorker.register()
} else {
  render(<AppRouter />, rootElement)
}// serviceWorker.unregister()
```

Now when you build again ($yarn build), the new file appears: build/precache-manifest.[string].js.

See Figure 12-5.

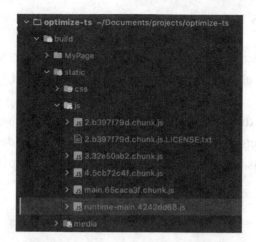

Figure 12-5. *runtime-main bundle file added to our static folder*

To see the worker in action, you need to publish the build again.

$ yarn build:serve.

Take a look at Chrome DevTools' Network tab. In the Size column, you can see it says "(ServiceWorker)," as shown in Figure 12-6.

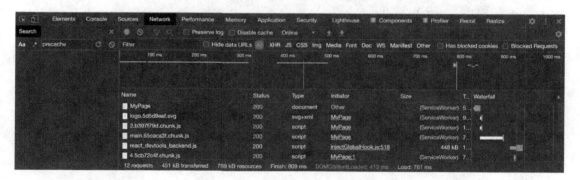

Figure 12-6. *Precache ServiceWorker showing up on Chrome DevTools' Network tab*

You can now simulate the offline experience either by turning off your network and connecting or by selecting the Offline check box on Chrome DevTools' Network tab. Refresh the app and it still works!

How Is Your App Working Offline?

The workbox default precaching strategy for CRA is `CacheFirst`. Static assets are retrieved from the service worker cache mechanism, and on fail, a network request is made.

A workbox supports different strategies such as `CacheOnly`, `NetworkFirst`, etc., but CRA may need to be ejected to use a different strategy than the default.

Read more about this feature at `https://create-react-app.dev/docs/making-a-progressive-web-app/`.

Code Splitting

When we used lazy loading, we were able to break down our JS bundles into multiple chunks and serve them when only they were needed.

Dynamically Import

We can do more. CRA handles the code-splitting task with Webpack. We can tell Webpack to split our JS bundle even more and dynamically import these modules.

Let's take a look. Create the file `src/page/MyPage/math.tsx` and add the following code:

```
// src/page/MyPage/math.tsx

export function square(x: number) {
  return x * x
}export function cube(x: number) {
  return x * x * x
}export function add(x: number, y: number) {
  return x + y
}
```

To use the `add` method, we normally would write our code like so:

```
import { add } from './math'
console.log(add(1, 2))
```

However, if we want to split the code so the JS bundle is retrieved only once it's needed and only bundles what's used, we can do the following:

```
import("./math").then(math => {
  console.log(math.add(1, 2))
})
```

Let's create an actual working example. We can have a state with variable results and a one-click update by using the math add function. Take a look at the MyPage.tsx code, shown here:

```
// src/page/MyPage/MyPage.tsx

render() {
  const onClickHandler = (event: React.MouseEvent) => {
    event.preventDefault()
    import('./math').then((math) => {
      this.setState({
        results: (math.add(1, 2))
      })
    })
  }
  return (
    <div className="MyPage">
      <Helmet>
        <title>My Page</title>
      </Helmet>
      {this.state.name} Component
      <Button type="submit" onClick={onClickHandler}>
        Math.add
      </Button>
      {this.state.results}
    </div>
  )
}
```

Or better yet, let's add the result for every click.

```
import('./math').then((math) => {
  this.setState(prevState => {
    const newState = prevState.results + (math.add(1, 2))
    return ({
      ...prevState,
      results: newState
    })
  })
})
```

Now build the production code and run it on our local machine.

```
$ yarn build:serve
```

Tip Our build is set up to precache, so you need to force cache to clear on a Mac by pressing Shift+Refresh, or you can find a fancy plugin to do this in the Chrome Web Store. Otherwise, you may be serving old pages and pulling out your hair.

See Figure 12-7.

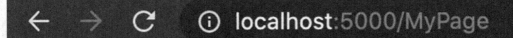

MyPage Component MATH.ADD 3

Figure 12-7. Meth.add code-splitting feature running production build locally

Notice that our bundle increases by one and that the bundle file will be retrieved when we call MyPage and the button instead of having the user wait for the bundle when we first load the page. See Figure 12-8.

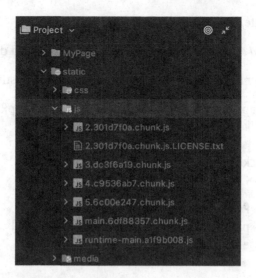

Figure 12-8. JS bundle after code splitting

Module Federation

Can we do even more? The answer is yes and no.

At the time of writing, Webpack is at version 4.42.0 for CRA (see node_modules/
react-scripts/package.json). However, the current version of Webpack is v5.4.0 as
of October 2020, and it includes tons of performance improvements. One major one
involves Module Federation.

Module Federation allows you to import the remote Webpack builds to your
application. With Webpack v5, we can have these chunks imported not just from our
project but different origins (project). You can read more about it at https://webpack.
js.org/guides/build-performance/.

You can eject and upgrade Webpack. Ensure everything builds and include Module
Federation on your own, if that's what you need.

Tree Shaking

Tree shaking (https://webpack.js.org/guides/tree-shaking/) is a term used in a
JavaScript context to mean removing dead code. There is much to do when it comes to
removing dead code.

When I say dead code, it can mean these two things:

- *Never executed code*: Code that can never be executed during runtime

- *The result never used*: Code that is executed, but the result is never used

For example, in the app we built, I defined Recoil in `src/AppRouter.tsx`.

```
<RecoilRoot>
  <Suspense fallback={<span>Loading...</span>}>
    <Switch>
      <Route exact path="/" component={App} />
      <Route exact path="/MyPage" component={MyPage} />
      <Redirect to="/" />
    </Switch>
  </Suspense>
</RecoilRoot>
```

But in this example, I am never using the Recoil feature for anything.

Now, if we dig inside our JS bundles and see what's happening, we can see that Recoil is using almost 38.19KB. See Figure 12-9.

```
$ source-map-explorer optimize-ts/build/static/js/[my chunk].chunk.js
```

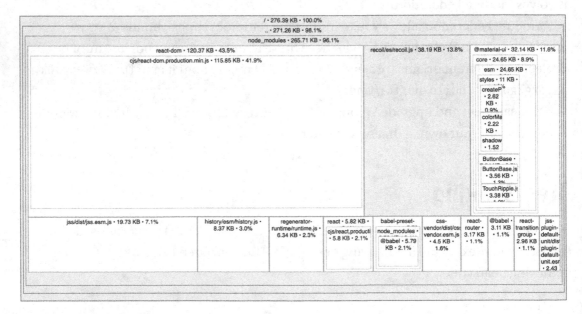

Figure 12-9. *Source map of our bundle with Recoil*

Here we refactor the code and remove Recoil and build again:

```
<Router>
    <Suspense fallback={<span>Loading...</span>}>
        <Switch>
            <Route exact path="/" component={App} />
            <Route exact path="/MyPage" component={MyPage} />
            <Redirect to="/" />
        </Switch>
    </Suspense>
</Router>
```

Now the code went down from 276KB to 224.51KB, and Recoil is not included. See Figure 12-10.

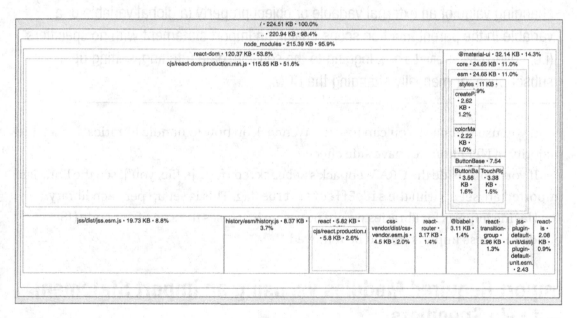

Figure 12-10.   *Source map of our bundle without Recoil*

CRA includes Webpack out of the box to bundle our app with some settings that were already set up for us.

You can see the optimization tag that includes `compression` and `OptimizeCSSAssetsPlugin`.

If you need to make changes, you need to eject and maintain on your own. However, even without ejecting, there are things we can do.

To better understand what's happening under the hood, in CRA open the Webpack config files, which are placed inside react-scripts.

```
$ open node_modules/react-scripts/config/webpack.config.js
```

Or for dev server, use this:

```
$ open node_modules/react-scripts/config/webpackDevServer.config.js
```

Let's talk about side effects.

Note   A side effect is a state change that is observable outside the called function other than its return value. Examples of a side effect include the following: a changing value of an external variable or object property (a global variable or a variable in the parent function scope chain), an import statement with no specifiers (i.e., import 'someLib'), logging to the console, data fetching, setting up a subscription, or manually changing the DOM.

If you use Webpack, you can instruct Webpack on how to handle libraries. In fact, the majority of NPM libraries have side effects.

If you look inside the CRA Webpack's webpack.config.js file, you'll see the libraries imported are set up with the sideEffects: true flag. This is set up per each library.

Having imports for libraries we are not using increases the size of our code (JS bundles). These imports should be removed.

Import Required Modules vs. Using an import Statement with No Specifiers

Let's look at an example. Say I am adding an import statement that I am not using and importing the feature I need such as useRecoilValue.

```
// src/page/MyPage/MyPage.tsx
import { useRecoilValue } from 'recoil'
```

The CRA `react-script` tool allows me to start and build my production build, but I will get a warning message, as shown in Figure 12-11.

```
$ react-scripts start
i [wds]: Project is running at http://192.168.1.31/
i [wds]: webpack output is served from
i [wds]: Content not from webpack is served from /Users/eli/Documents/projects/optimize-ts/public
i [wds]: 404s will fallback to /
Starting the development server...
Compiled with warnings.

./src/pages/MyPage/MyPage.tsx
  Line 13:10:  'useRecoilValue' is defined but never used  @typescript-eslint/no-unused-vars
```

Figure 12-11. Warning for unused code

It is not good to have these warnings, but it is not the end of the world.

In this specific case, Terser (`https://github.com/terser/terser`), which Webpack is using, is trying to figure this out and decided that the code is not needed. So, although it creates a warning, it doesn't include the library inside our build JS bundles.

The code is not included because the bundle is optimized and the library was removed for us (you can verify this by checking the source maps).

But don't rely on Terser to always be able to figure this out. When it can't, it will include the dead code.

However, if I am using an `import` statement with no specifiers (`import 'recoil'`), like this:

```
// src/page/MyPage/MyPage.tsx
import 'recoil'
```

The code will compile, build, and even run ESLint for us, without any warnings, but it will include the *entire* Recoil library.

The reason is that Webpack treated the `import` statement with no specifiers (`import 'recoil'`) as a side effect, and it will include Recoil in our source map as if we intended to do that.

Note   Only include the modules you require, and avoid `import` statements with no specifiers.

You can also fine-tune and add the `sideEffects` property to your project's `package.json` file to tell Webpack how to handle side effects without ejecting. You can read more about this and about tree shaking in the Webpack documentation: `https://webpack.js.org/guides/tree-shaking/`.

Reducing Media Size

We talked about tree shaking and reducing the JS bundle size to the minimum, but besides bundle size, other resources are often used in an app that can take lots of resources. These are media files such as images, videos, audio documents, and syncing with large data.

To optimize resources, there are plenty of tools to use. If you own Adobe products, you have Photoshop with the Save for the Web option, which you can use to ensure the size of your images stays low. Adobe Premiere can encode your videos for different devices and with different settings.

You can use a library that checks the user's network speed and delivers different resources based on the user's connection. That's a common practice for video delivery.

Ideally, we want to upload our resources during runtime instead of compile time, because we don't want the user to wait for a resource.

Another thing is SVG. SVG is vector based, and it's great. It gives the user that crisp graphic look in any resolution screen size; however, it comes with a price. The way React works to increase performance is to reduce the number of requests to the server.

Importing images that are less than 10KB returns a data URI instead of the actual SVG file; see the React documentation (`https://create-react-app.dev/docs/adding-images-fonts-and-files/`). This is by default ignored in CRA development, but you can see this behavior on the production build; see `IMAGE_INLINE_SIZE_LIMIT` (`https://create-react-app.dev/docs/advanced-configuration`).

Having tons of SVG graphics around can easily bloat your app. It's better to gather them into one JPG image file and use an image sprite. Loading a single image is quicker than loading individual images one by one.

Prefetching

You might have seen the higher-order components (HOCs) in React that can enhance a component's capability (`https://reactjs.org/docs/higher-order-components.html`). We can take a similar approach when it comes to our JS bundle.

We want to first load the page and then retrieve the JS bundle so we can display the page as soon as possible.

Let's take a look. If you build a production version with `$ yarn build:serve` and test it in Chrome DevTools, you can take a look at the JS bundle chunks hierarchy; they are at the top. See Figure 12-12.

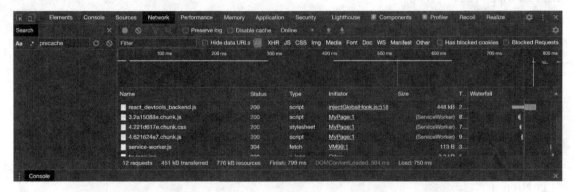

Figure 12-12. *The hierarchy is not set up for the JS bundles to show in a specific order*

We want to move these bundles to the bottom. To do that, we can use Quicklink (`https://github.com/GoogleChromeLabs/quicklink`). Quicklink attempts to make the navigation to subsequent pages load faster by using techniques to decide what to load first. Let's install it.

```
$ yarn add -D quicklink webpack-route-manifest
```

In our case, we will use the React CRA SPA. We will be using the React HOC where we want to add prefetching functionality to the pages that we lazy load. To do that, we just use an empty option object and wrap our component with the Quicklink HOC.

```
<Route exact path="/MyPage" component={withQuicklink(MyPage, options)} />
```

Take a look at the refactored src/AppRouter.tsx shown here:

```tsx
// src/AppRouter.tsx

import React, { FunctionComponent, lazy, Suspense } from 'react'
import { BrowserRouter as Router, Route, Switch, Redirect } from
'react-router-dom'
import { RecoilRoot } from 'recoil'
// @ts-ignore
// eslint-disable-next-line import/extensions
import { withQuicklink } from 'quicklink/dist/react/hoc.js'
import App from './App'
import ScrollToTop from './components/ScrollToTop/ScrollToTop'

// Lazy loading
const MyPage = lazy(() => import('./pages/MyPage/MyPage'))

const options = {
  origins: []
}
const AppRouter: FunctionComponent = () => {
  return (
    <Router>
      <ScrollToTop />
      <RecoilRoot>
        <Suspense fallback={<span>Loading...</span>}>
          <Switch>
            <Route exact path="/" component={App} />
            <Route exact path="/MyPage" component={withQuicklink(MyPage,
            options)} />
            <Redirect to="/" />
          </Switch>
        </Suspense>
      </RecoilRoot>
    </Router>
  )
}

export default AppRouter
```

After implementing the logic, as you can see, the HOC worked, and now our chunks are at the bottom, as shown in Figure 12-13.

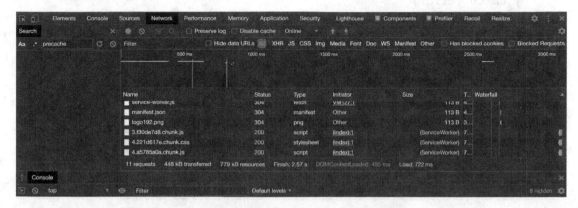

Figure 12-13. Hierarchy set up for About Page component

Cleaning Up Unused Event Handlers

Here's how to clean up any unused event handlers.

Setting Up Side Effects in the useEffect Hook

If we want to scroll to the top of every page update using the browser API, we don't even need to write a class. We can just wrap that code inside the useEffect hook in a React function.

```
// src/components/ScrollToTop/ScrollToTop.tsx

import { useEffect } from 'react'
import { useLocation } from 'react-router-dom'

export default function ScrollToTop() {
  const { pathname, search } = useLocation()  useEffect(
    () => () => {
      try {
        window.scroll({
          top: 0,
          left: 0,
```

```
        behavior: 'smooth',
      })
    } catch (error) {
      // older browsers fallback
      window.scrollTo(0, 0)
    }
  },
  [pathname, search]
  )
  return null
}
```

Note   Side effects need to be wrapped in useEffect. If not done right, side effects can run on every render and turn into a memory leak.

We also need to refactor src/AppRouter.tsx to include the component inside the React Router tag.

```
// src/AppRouter.tsx

import ScrollToTop from './components/ScrollToTop/ScrollToTop'
const AppRouter: FunctionComponent = () => {
  return (
    <Router>
      <ScrollToTop />

      ...

    </Router>
  )
}
```

This specific side effect doesn't need any cleanup because we are not attaching any events.

Cleaning Up Side Effects

Leaving event handlers around after a component has been unmounted can cause memory leaks. Luckily, React components can clean up React-based event handlers once the component is unmounted automatically.

However, if we need to use the browser scroll API event listener, we can, as shown here:

```
window.addEventListener('scroll', scrollHandler)
```

You will have to remove the event manually yourself, as React won't remove it for you.

```
window.removeEventListener('scroll', scrollHandler)
```

You can read more about this in the React documentation (`https://reactjs.org/docs/hooks-effect.html`).

My Final Notes

It's great to know how much can be done to optimize our app. With a little effort on our end, we can increase the performance of our app and improve the user experience. The results are noticeable even on a small app. Additionally, optimizing your app allows you to gain awareness of what's happening and how it all works as well as what needs to be improved.

With that being said, optimizing our app is all about testing and tweaking and testing the results again to fine-tune everything. There will be use cases where it won't make sense to do all or any of these optimization efforts. There is a trade-off for each feature we add.

You need to experiment, and each feature needs to be checked on a case-by-case basis. The best approach is to record memory profiling, throttle the network connection, check bundles, go offline, and try different network speeds to find out what is the best user experience.

Always keep in mind that your development and production builds are different from each other, so don't assume they will just work the same. It's not a one-size-fits-all sort of thing.

Summary

In this chapter, I showed you how you can reduce the amount of memory your app is consuming to the minimum, reduce bundle file sizes, load resources only once, decrease the wait time to view content, increase performance, and ensure your app works anytime anywhere, even when offline.

We also installed Analyzer Bundle, as well as looked at other settings that you can configure to make your app better instead of using the default settings.

We broke down the process into the following areas: using `PureComponent`, lazy loading, prerending, precaching, code splitting, tree shaking, reducing media size, prefetching, and cleaning up side effects.

This subject is big enough to fill a whole book, but my aim was to give you a good starting point and to cover the most important ways you need to be aware of.

For instance, I didn't cover network traffic techniques. Additionally, if you render a large list, you can use `react-window` (`https://github.com/bvaughn/react-window`), which will render only part of a large data set (just enough to fill the viewport); `react-infinite-scroll-component`; or `react-paginate`. The list goes on and on.

This chapter is a good fit as the last chapter in this book, as it is an advanced topic and where you learned how to put the finishing touches on the app you built. I want to thank you again for purchasing this book and say congratulations for completing this chapter! Feel free to drop me a note and let me know how this book helped you. You can also leave a book review online as well as recommend this book to a friend.

As bonus material for purchasing this book, head to `https://elielrom.com/ReactQuestions` to receive a free ebook with the most asked React interview questions including answers.

Index

A

Analyzer Bundle, 24, 51, 375–376
AppBar component, 95

B

brew command, 209
Browser's Profiling Tools
    Chrome DevTools' Performance tab,
      364, 366
    React Developer Tools, 366, 368
Bugs, 84, 130, 277, 306, 332, 337

C

Cascading Style Sheets (CSS), 36–38,
    91–92, 100
Centered.tsx, 72, 73, 187
checkUserInfo operation, 203
Chrome DevTools
    breakpoints, 352, 353
    DOM elements, 351, 352
    extensions, 354, 355
      Realize for React, 356, 357
      React Developer Tools, 355, 356
      Recoil, 358, 359
Codecov, 326, 330–331, 333
Code-splitting task
    dynamically import, 388, 390
    JS bundle, 391
    Module Federation, 391

componentDidUpdate() method, 175
Continuous integration (CI) cycle
    codecov, 330, 331
    Coveralls, 333, 334
    DeepScan, 336
    deployment cycle, 320
    git hooks, Husky, 325
    process, 321
    project, 321–324
    setting up workflow,
      Github actions, 326–330
    structure, 321
    Travis, 331–333
CRA MHL template project, 27, 48, 123,
    311, 322, 373
CRA React TS app, 372
CRA starter template project, 373, 375
CRA Webpack configuration, 375
Create-React-App (CRA), 18, 21–22,
    34, 56, 382
crypto-js library, 221, 230

D

Data transfer objects (DTOs), 153
Debugging, 337
    breakpoints, 338
      Visual Studio Code, 338, 340
      WebStorm, 340–342
    console, 343
    Jest test, 344

403

© Elad Elrom 2021
E. Elrom, *React and Libraries*, https://doi.org/10.1007/978-1-4842-6696-0